The Woman Lawyer's Rainmaking Game:
How to Build a Successful Law Practice
Third Edition

By
Silvia L. Coulter, MPS
and
Catherine Alman MacDonagh, JD

WEST

41490494

© 2013 Thomson Reuters/West

This publication was created to provide you with accurate and authoritative information concerning the subject matter covered; however, this publication was not necessarily prepared by persons licensed to practice law in a particular jurisdiction. The publisher is not engaged in rendering legal or other professional advice and this publication is not a substitute for the advice of an attorney. If you require legal or other expert advice, you should seek the services of a competent attorney or other professional.

ISBN 978-0-314-62051-4

CONTENTS

About the Co-Author x

About the Co-Author xiii

Dedication xvi

Ackowledgments xix

Foreword by Beth I.Z. Boland xxi

Introduction–The World of Law Firms Today xxvii

CHAPTER 1: So, How EXACTLY Do You Sell Legal Services? 1-1
    Highlights 1-1
    What Really Works? 1-1
    Selling: What It Means 1-2
    Marketing Versus Selling 1-3
    You Have the Power—Recognizing Your Hidden Talent for Rainmaking 1-5
    The Successful Woman Rainmaker 1-5
    Qualities of a Strong Rainmaker 1-5
    Relationship Building Is a Strength of Many Women 1-7
    The Unique Aspects of Selling Legal Services 1-10
    Aggressive Is an Okay Style for Representing Your Clients and It Works for Sales Too! 1-12
    Stating Your Case: Selling Is Selling, Whatever Your Field of Law 1-13
    Viewing Opportunities and Pursuits from the Client Perspective 1-13
    Are You Ready?: As Long as You Know the Rules of the Game, You Can Play It 1-14
    Working Tool: Perceived Strengths and Areas for Improvement 1-15

The Woman Lawyer's Rainmaking Game

The Sale Process—An Overview of the Stages 1-16
Discussion Questions 1-17

CHAPTER 2: The Sales Process: Pre-Approach 2-1
Highlights 2-1
Getting Organized: Your Marketing Action Plan 2-2
Form 2A: Sample Practice Description, Health
 and Life Sciences 2-3
Life Sciences and Health Industries 2-3
Form 2B: Marketing and Sales-Oriented
 (Results-Focused) Biography 2-4
Focus Your Efforts: Choose Your Target Markets(s) 2-6
Create an Individual Marketing Action Plan (IMAPsm) 2-7
Working Tool: Form 2C: Individual Marketing
 Action Plan (IMAPsm) 2-12
Working Tool: Form 2C(1): Sample Individual
 Marketing Action Plan (IMAPsm) 2-13
Working Tool: Form 2C(2): Individual Marketing
 Action Plan (IMAPsm) 2-14
Working Tool: Form 2C(3) Individual Marketing
 Action Plan (IMAPsm) 2-14
Stay on Track: Keep a List of Tasks 2-15
Working Tool: Sample Individual Sales and
 Marketing Task List 2-17
Working Tool: Blank Individual Sales and
 Marketing Task List 2-19
Determine Your Investment: What Is Building
 a Successful Practice Worth to You and How Many
 Minutes/Hours Will You Invest Monthly Into Your
 Rainmaking Development Account? 2-20

CHAPTER 3: The Sales Process: Approach 3-1
The Importance of Attitude 3-2
Investing Time Wisely 3-5
Determine Ways to Meet Potential Clients 3-9
Leveraging Firm Seminars and Association Memberships ... 3-10
The Telephone Is a Great Selling Tool. Cold Calling
 Is Not for Everyone, but it Might Work for You 3-12

Table of Contents

Making the Most of Trade Shows and Other
    Approach Opportunities 3-15
Seminars and Sponsored Trade Events Are Not
    Just for Strutting Your Stuff! 3-17
Brochures and Handouts Are Strong Sales Tools
    if Used Correctly 3-18
How and When to Use Sales Tools So They Work for You ... 3-18
Building Business Is About Building Relationships 3-19
Client Development: Approach Opportunity
    Tips Sheet: Trade Shows 3-21
Beginning to Forecast Your Potential "Wins" 3-22
Working Tool: Client Development Monthly Forecast 3-24
Expert Perspective: The Art of Networking 3-26
The Importance of Goal Setting When Networking 3-26
How You Can Create a Professional Presence
    in the Eyes of Others 3-27
When to Arrive and the Hour to Leave to Give
    Yourself "Presence" 3-28
Skills That Make Others Feel Good 3-28
Networking Is Also Listening 3-28
Ways to Empower People 3-29
How to Make Networking Work for You 3-29
How to Network Without Leaving Your Office 3-29
Networking Is a Long-Term Process 3-30
Working Tool: Approach Tip Sheet: The Art
    of Mixing and Mingling 3-30
How to Establish Instant Rapport with Others 3-31
How to Politely Get Rid of a Bore 3-31
The Four Key Ways to Feeling Comfortable
    in a Room Full of Strangers 3-32
Phrases to Use When Interacting with Someone
    You Have Just Met 3-33
How to Begin Enjoying Those Dreaded
    Business Functions 3-33
Making the Most of Your Speaking Opportunities
    and Presentations 3-34
Working Tool: Seminar Follow-Up Strategies Checklist 3-35

CHAPTER 4: The Sales Process:
Qualify and Assess Needs...**4-1**
   Highlights.. 4-1
   Determining Viability of Prospective Clients—
      How They Work with Outside Counsel 4-2
   Needs/Benefits Worksheet 4-3
   Stay In Control of the Next Step, It's Your Game to Win 4-3
   Sales Case Study 4-1: Qualify and Assess Needs...................... 4-3
   Know Your Audience at All Times 4-6
   The 80/20 Rule of Listening and the Art of Asking
      Open-Ended Questions 4-7
   Sample Selling Questions to Ask Corporate
      Decision-Makers (in a Company Setting)......................... 4-8
   Sales Case Study 4-2: Qualify and Assess Needs...................... 4-9
   Sales Case Study 4-3: Qualify and Assess Needs................... 4-11
   Tips on Effective Listening for Building Relationships 4-12
   Understanding the People Part of the Sales Process 4-13
   Personalities Play a Key Role in Building Relationships 4-14
   Selected Personality Characteristics Chart 4-17
   Working Tool: Understanding Personalities 4-18
   Team Selling Can Be Successful — Make Sure
      You Are a Major Member of the Team 4-19
   Tips for Team Selling 4-20
   What You Learn Now Sets the Stage for Closing 4-20
   When You Are on the List of Preferred Outside Counsel ... 4-21

CHAPTER 5: The Sales Process: Strategize **5-1**
   Highlights.. 5-1
   Keeping in Touch With Contacts Is a Key
      to Building Business 5-1
   Using Those Tickets, Dinners, and Golf Games
      to Your Advantage... 5-2
   Sample Schedule for Keeping in Touch.................................... 5-4
   Setting the Stage for Closing the Business 5-7
   Personality Fit: A Sales Case Study.. 5-8
   Strategizing for a Real Opportunity... 5-9
   Practice Makes Perfect 5-10

Table of Contents

CHAPTER 6: The Sales Process:
Address Needs and Present 6-1
    Highlights 6-1
    When You Talk, You Are Presenting 6-1
    A Role-Playing Case Study 6-4
    Checking In So Your Prospect Does Not Check Out 6-6
    The RFP Response and Determining the Response Strategy.. 6-8
    Tips for Mastering the Request for Proposal Process 6-8
    Take the Bull by the Horns 6-10
    Where the Marketing Team Fits In 6-11
    How Much Is Too Much? 6-11
    RFP Logistical Tips 6-12
    Sample Presentation PowerPoint 6-13

CHAPTER 7: The Sales Process: Asking for
the Business and Closing 7-1
    How *Do* I Go About Getting the Business? 7-2
    In Sales, Never Put Anything Off to Tomorrow 7-2
    No Follow-Up Often Means No Business 7-3
    Big Bank Case Study 7-4
    There's No Magic—Don't Beat Around the
        Bush, Take Control 7-5
    Trials and Demos Work for Law too 7-6
    The Prospect's Investment—Making Them Use
        Their Time Wisely, While Investing It in YOU 7-7
    In Person Is Always Stronger than By Mail or Phone 7-8
    Overcoming Objections 7-8
    Addressing the "Price" Objection 7-10
    Working Tool: Objections Worksheet 7-12
    The Myth of Closing 7-12
    Tip Sheet: A Brief Primer on Professional Selling 7-15

CHAPTER 8: Maintaining Client and
Contact Relationships 8-1
    Keep In Touch—It's Critical to Your Long-Term
        Success as a Professional 8-1
    Who, What, and How Often to Connect
        with Contacts 8-2
    CRM—What It Means to Your Client
        Maintenance Program 8-5

As Soon as You Obtain a Client, They Become
    Someone Else's Prospect..8-6
Clients Consider You Their Lawyer Even When
    They Aren't Actively Working with You..........................8-7
Key Tips for Staying in Touch with Inactive Clients.............8-8

**CHAPTER 9: Key Client Strategies for
Retention and Growth..9-1**
What Is a Key Client?...9-1
Why Care About Key Clients?—
    What's the Opportunity?...9-2
Establishing Ten Key Client Sales
    Initiatives at Your Firm..9-3

**CHAPTER 10: Sales Confidence—
Build It and They Will Come... 10-1**
The Good News... 10-2
Why Being Smart Or Working For A Big Firm
    Just Aren't Enough 10-2
Rainmaking Skills 10-3
The Right Attitude 10-4
Women And Relationship Selling 10-5
Superlearning And The Big Switch.................................... 10-6
Feeling Competent Boosts Your Confidence 10-10
The Resilience Factor 10-11
Resiliency... 10-13
Just Say No To Negatives.. 10-13
Building Your Confidence 10-14
Find A Good Mentor 10-16
The Dilemma Of The Strong Woman 10-17
Feelers And Thinkers 10-17
It's Not Selling, It's Helping 10-18

CHAPTER 11: Connecting with Clients................................ 11-1
Your Clients Are Your Most Valuable Asset...
    and Another Lawyer's Prospects................................ 11-1
Contact Your Client for Feedback Before Your
    Client Contacts You... 11-2
Proven Methods for Building Good
    Relationships with Clients 11-3

Table of Contents

Using Market Research to Learn About
What Works for Clients 11-5
The BTI A Team 11-5
Form 11A—Short Client Survey 11-7
The Proof is in the Pudding 11-8
The In-House Counsel and Senior Decision
Makers Speak on Selling, Legal Services,
and Women Lawyers 11-8
Ten Client Development and Service
Strategies for Success 11-15

CHAPTER 12: Coaching 12-1
Highlights 12-1
Coaching 12-2
What Coaches Do 12-3
The Case for Coaching 12-4
Coaches' Approaches 12-5
Training 12-7
Are Women Lawyers REALLY Different? 12-8
Start Early and Often 12-10
Meeting Challenges 12-12
Are You Coachable? 12-13
Planning 12-15
Impact on Firm Relationships 12-16
Clients and the Future 12-17
Coaching tools 12-18
Benefits of Coaching 12-19
Organizational Support 12-20
Coaching Resource Guide 12-24

**Chapter 13: Retaining and Growing
Your Key Clients: SAM-Legal©** 13-1
Highlights 13-1
Background 13-1
Why Are We Writing About SAM In a Sales Book
for Women Lawyers? 13-2
Foundational Principles of Business Development 13-3
Stages of the Sales Cycle 13-4

ix

The Woman Lawyer's Rainmaking Game

Creating Value Propositions That Create Value
    for Clients 13-6
Approaching an Existing Client 13-11
Year-End Review Guide 13-14
Soliciting Client Input; Assessing Goals and Needs............. 13-16
Conducting an Effective Client Meeting 13-18
Components of an Effective Key Client Program 13-20
Three Types of Effective Questions Overview 13-30
Open-Ended or Broad 13-30
Focused 13-30
Closing 13-30

Glossary **GL-1**
Websites **WE-1**
Articles **AR-1**
Index **Index-1**

About the Co-Author

During an exemplary career in professional services sales and marketing, Silvia L. Coulter, co-founding principal at LawVision Group, has provided strategic counsel to hundreds of law firms in the U.S., Canada, and overseas; she is recognized worldwide for her leadership in law firm marketing, sales and sales management strategy. Coulter's experience in strategic market planning and sales was gained in various areas of industry including a Fortune 200 company where she successfully worked with the CEO and Senior Management Team to develop its law firm industry focus. She is a former Chief Marketing Officer at two Global 100 law firms.

In 2003, Silvia co-founded the Legal Sales and Service Organization ("LSSO") (see *www.legalsales.org*). LSSO is devoted to helping law firms develop, grow and retain clients.

Ms. Coulter is on the Editorial Board for Practice Innovations, a Thomson West publication, Marketing For Lawyers, an ALM publication and a column editor for Inside Counsel Magazine. She is a past committee chair of the Massachusetts Women's Bar Association and a member of the ABA's Women's Rainmaking Committee and has written over 200 articles and given over 100 speeches during her career in the legal industry. Ms. Coulter is a past national president of The Legal Marketing Association (*www.legalmarketing.org*) and an adjunct professor at George Washington University where she teaches in the College of Professional Studies, Law Firm Management Masters Program. She lives in Manchester by the Sea, Massachusetts with her husband, Jared W. Stansfield, a practicing attorney and enjoys fly fishing, sailing and other outdoor hobbies.

The Woman Lawyer's Rainmaking Game

About the Co-Author

Catherine Alman MacDonagh, JD is a former corporate counsel and successful law firm executive, having held marketing and business development positions in firms of different sizes. She now provides strategy, business development, process improvement, and project management training and consulting services.

She is a Co-Founder of the Legal Sales and Service Organization (legalsales.org) and directed LSSO's groundbreaking studies on women lawyers and rainmaking; much of what was learned from what was shared by the women lawyers who participated in those studies lies within the pages of this book. For several years, Catherine assisted with the National Association of Women Lawyers (NAWL) National Survey on the Retention and Promotion of Women in Law Firms. Catherine is the co-author of *The Law Firm Associate's Guide to Personal Marketing and Selling Skills*, and accompanying training manual, published by the ABA's Law Practice Management Section in 2007.

Catherine is the Chief Executive Officer and Founder of the Legal Lean Sigma Institute (LegalLeanSigma.com), which offers Process Improvement and Project Management certification courses, programs, and consulting for the legal profession. She is also the Chief Enthusiasm Officer of the Legal Mocktail™ (legalmocktail.com) and The Mocktail which are experiential networking training programs.

She is an adjunct professor at Suffolk University School of Law and at George Washington University (Masters in Law Firm Management program), where she teaches process improvement and project management.

Catherine is a member of the New Jersey and New York bars and the Legal Marketing Association. She is a Fellow of the College of Law Practice Management. She served on Greater Boston Chapter Board of Directors of the American Foundation for Suicide Prevention for more than five years, and is an active volunteer at her children's schools, Mil-

The Woman Lawyer's Rainmaking Game

ton Academy and The Woodward School, where she is Vice-President of the Woodward Parents' Association.

Catherine's family includes two children, Alex and Sarah, husband Colin, their entertaining Havanese, Abbie, assorted fish, and Lil Buddy, the turtle. They live in Massachusetts.

Dedication

To my business friends and colleagues for their ongoing confidence in and support of my work to help others succeed with their business goals. And to my family who never tire of my endless entrepreneurial ideas and dreams. – S.L. Coulter

We stand on the shoulders of those who come before us. This is dedicated to the many women and men in the legal profession who've paved the way and inspired me to help other women succeed. One of those visionary, talented, and passionate women is my dear friend, mentor, and business partner: thank you, Roberta Montafia. Thank you to my sixth grade teacher, Jeff Weisenfreund, for the ways in which you profoundly impacted my life. And, because nothing is more important, this is for my family - with special gratitude to my mother, Sondra Alman Gibbons, and the generations of women who came before me - for making it possible for me to do what I love to do. Alex and Sarah, you are the lights of my life. – C.A. MacDonagh

Acknowledgments

We extend our most special thanks to our all our training and coaching clients for allowing us the privilege of working with each of you. To have earned and kept your confidence as we support you in the pursuit of your dreams and goals is an honor of the highest order.

Catherine Alman MacDonagh, JD and Silvia L. Coulter MPS

October 2013

Foreword

by Beth I. Z. Boland

May 2007

I love hanging with women lawyers. Over the last decade or so I've spent countless hours talking with women attorneys from every corner of the profession. Big firm. Small firm. Solo practice. Government. In-house. Judiciary. Real estate. Corporate. Litigation. Trusts and estates. Although our practices come in all shapes and sizes, one immutable trait we share is a sense that while the rules of the game are not entirely ours, they are changing.

And those changes have been profound, indeed. Over the last twenty years we have moved from about 40 percent of the law-student population to more than 50 percent. That's right—we are now in the majority, at least at the entry level. Women are advancing into government and in-house positions in ever-increasing numbers. Yet progress within law firms, where power and influence are determined by marketing prowess, is achingly slow.

Much ink has been devoted to the need for embracing the different rhythms in the life of our careers. Just when we become profitable for the firm and more confident in our legal skills, many of us arrive at the age where we want to start a family. Those of us in partnership positions dedicate a tremendous amount of time (and appropriately so) worrying about crafting progressive work/life policies, making sure the firm culture embraces them, and attempting to match firm expectations with the realities of parental responsibilities. At the same time, we struggle to ensure that women associates—regardless of parental status—are given appropriate assignments, mentoring, and visibility to position them for partnership in an increasingly competitive economic climate. All the

The Woman Lawyer's Rainmaking Game

while, we continue to lose women associates to a variety of pursuits outside of private firm life.

No wonder we feel that crossing the line into partnership is the holy grail of measuring women's success within private firms. But that's just where the real challenges—and the real opportunities—begin.

To a large extent, the road to partnership is a relatively straight one: We work hard. We polish our briefs. We hone our transactional documents. We develop our presentation skills. And we burnish our professional abilities until they are rock-solid. In other words, it's pretty much all about merit.

After we inch over the partnership threshold, though, the rules change. Legal skill is presumed, and intangible qualities begin to play a much more prominent role in our advancement. Trust. Confidence. Leadership. Presence. And, most importantly, what these qualities spawn: client relationships.

Those of us who continue to develop the same legal skills that made us fantastic associates find ourselves branded mere "service" partners, with little-to-no say in firm management and with less compensation than those who produce significant clients. We begin to cluster at the lower end of the partnership spectrum, and find it difficult to move significantly upward among the ranks. As the saying goes, "there are partners, and then there are *partners*."

So how do we become a "*partner*" rather than a "partner"?

By stepping outside of the worker-bee billing-machine mode and building on our inherent strengths in developing relationships. In other words, we learn to market our legal services in addition to performing them.

I know, I know. Just the thought of marketing conjures up visions of back-slapping, quid-pro-quo-ing, cigar-smoking bluster. Yuck.

It doesn't have to be that way, nor should it. Nothing is worse than trying to bring in a client by trying to be someone or something we aren't. So we crawl back in our cocoons, safe in the knowledge that we

Forward

can craft a brief or structure a deal 10 times better than the guy down the hall.

In doing so, though, we may overlook some of the most important strengths we bring to the table. As a group, we listen to others very well, and we have a deep-seated desire to figure out a way to help them. These natural qualities can be developed and directed in ways that expand our ability to generate business, without having to resort to models that don't jibe with the way we see ourselves. As you'll see in this book, there are as many different styles of legal marketing as there are lawyers.

I, for one, don't think I "market" at all. What I do, however, is spend lots of time figuring out ways I can help people, in whatever way they need help (as opposed to the way *I* want to help them). It's a lot of fun. And it doesn't hurt that, most times, the help revolves around a shared passion between the client and myself.

A few years back, for example, I was asked to speak on a three-women panel on the connection between girls' participation in sports and their development of business skills. Another panelist and I developed a friendship, which grew from our belief in the importance of providing opportunities for girls in sports. During our discussions, I learned that my fellow panelist, who is the CEO of a privately held high-tech company, was not particularly happy with her corporate legal counsel from another large firm in town. As I listened, it became clear that although the lawyer was quite competent, she was not able to have him spend the time necessary to achieve the product she wanted because his rates were higher than what she could afford on a sustained basis.

Rather than suggesting that my friend move her business to my firm (which I'm pretty sure would have produced the same result), I recommended that she consider a part-time in-house lawyer who could handle her day-to-day work and only use outside counsel for specialized work. Through my work with the Women's Bar Association of Massachusetts, I knew a number of very competent women who had the requisite skill set, and my friend quickly hired one of them. Now, my friend's company, through her in-house counsel, hires our firm for its outside legal work—which, incidentally, is performed by some of my women partners.

I don't consider myself to have "marketed" one bit in getting that business. It naturally flowed when I listened closely and decided to help out my CEO friend, my bar association colleague, my women partners, and, incidentally, a number of girls who have received athletic scholarships from the non-profit foundation to which my CEO friend and I contribute.

So, too, do I see similar professional relationships bearing fruit for many other women. Far from leveling off, we've seen exponential growth in the last five years in both the number of women's organizations and the number of women participating in them—a veritable explosion of women reaching out to help other women.

I remember a few years ago thinking that my colleagues and I in the state women's bar association must be doing something incredibly right, since our numbers were growing by leaps and bounds. Just when we were ready to pat ourselves on the back, however, we realized that we weren't the only ones experiencing the same success. All around us were new women's groups popping up, and each one more active and numerous than the next.

And it's not just for social gratification that we get together (although that's why we have so much fun when we do!). Now, we are as likely to sit beside a bank vice president as a bank teller at a charity dinner. When I attend a function with other women, it's not just fun: it's business. And the business consists of helping other women succeed in a myriad of ways. Some need financing. Some need visibility. Some need partners for a special project. And some need legal advice. No matter what the need, the goal is to listen closely and find a way to meet it. *The more you help others get what they want, the more they want to help you get what you want.* Not earth shattering, but true.

I've often heard the refrain that "women don't help other women," and therefore we shouldn't spend so much time trying to get them to do so. I don't believe that for a minute. I think deep inside each of us lies a keen desire to help other women—but that in order to do so we ourselves need to feel we have both the power to help and a realistic expectation of success in doing so.

As a group, I think we truly underestimate the power we hold, perhaps because we measure it against traditional models that don't fit our own styles. In order to capture that potential, *it is up to us to find our own way of creating and passing along power*. We're not going to change (at least for now) the fact that client-generating abilities are the key to our success in law firms, or that in the past the pursuit of those abilities have not followed models we would all emulate. That doesn't mean, though, that we should opt out of the system. Rather, we need to stretch beyond our comfort zones and figure out how do it in ways that make sense for us.

Despite the seemingly endless obstacles we face—both as women in business and as lawyers—there is incredible reason for hope. Slowly but surely, the number of women general counsel grows each year. Slowly, but surely, the number of women partners escalates each year. Slowly but surely, we learn that our success lies in thinking outside the box, and in combining "male" models of success with our own unique styles and sensibilities.

Don't get me wrong: I do not advocate that everybody attempt to build a significant book of business. Some of us can and should concentrate on developing our technical legal skills, if that's what we love to do. But for many others, the time has come for us to break out of our shells. We need to move beyond the familiar—beyond the safe confines of the daily stuff we do as lawyers. Think big. Be bold. Take risks. Support women. And I hope you will find the keys to doing just that within the pages here.

Beth Boland is a partner at Foley & Lardner securities litigation/corporate governance groups. After starting her career as a clerk to the federal district court judge assigned to the Ivan Boesky/Michael Milken insider trading and shareholder cases, Ms. Boland has concentrated her practice on consumer/shareholder class actions, corporate governance, and securities issues. She represents clients in SEC investigations, private and public company shareholder disputes and derivative actions, fraudulent sales practices class actions, and securities arbitrations before the NASD and NYSE.

Ms. Boland has litigated the first judgment of acquittal without submission to a jury involving criminal insider trading charges in the District of Massachusetts, a widely publicized corporate governance enforcement action brought by the Massachusetts Attorney General's office, and the representation of two Democratic fundraisers in their suit against HUD resulting in a $10 million decision in their favor. She currently serves as lead counsel for several of the nation's largest retail chains in multi-party class action litigation over pricing policies.

Active on many fronts in the legal community, Ms. Boland is co-chair of the Boston Bar Association (BBA) Task Force on Corporate Governance and co-chair of the Massachusetts Superior Court Business Litigation Session Resource Committee. As one of the youngest presidents of the Women's Bar Association of Massachusetts, Ms. Boland is considered a pioneer on issues affecting women in the profession. She is a co-author of the WBA's report on part-time work, "More Than Part-Time," which received national attention in 2000, and has served on a variety of nonprofit boards and received numerous awards for her work in this area.

Introduction

The World of Law Firms Today

Competition among law firms is keen. To stay on top means staying at the top of the game.

No, this book isn't about tennis or baseball. It is about practicing law today. Keen business skills and expert sales teams have replaced the neighborhood circle of friends who went to the same lawyer in town for years. Requests for proposals, on-line bidding through forums like E-Law Forum and others; qualification documentation, and corporations requiring competitive selling presentations are common activities for selection of outside counsel. In addition to these changes, firms are aggressively recruiting top talent with portable books of business from their law firm colleagues. The law profession has now become the business of law—and it is indeed, a serious, competitive business.

This climate could mean changing a few things. First, either a bevy of skilled rainmakers reduce their billing hours and increase selling hours to bring in the business. Second, individuals who spent years studying to practice high quality law must now learn how to be high quality salespeople. Last, law firms have begun to recruit sales professionals from the world of corporate sales and are leaving the selling to salespeople and the lawyering to the lawyers.

What occurs now will continue—more lawyers will be required to participate in selling and in bringing new or additional business to the firm, working alongside seasoned sales professionals who will help keep the process on track. Some firms have pioneered and already hired trained professionals with strong sales backgrounds whose titles include sales (chief sales officer, director of sales, sales manager) to assist with business development. Few of the the top 200 firms lack strong focus or dedicated individuals hired specifically for sales.

Whatever direction legal professionals will be required to take, it will always remain critical for lawyers to understand how to bring in business and how to be instrumental in the development of new business initiatives.

This book discusses the process and skills required to develop an individual marketing and sales plan and teaches the steps for building business from initiating contact with the market through closing the business and obtaining new engagements.

Wouldn't it be great to be a significant contributor to your own bottom line and to the firm's increase in revenue? Read on.

What's the Opportunity for Women Rainmakers?

Plenty.

When women enter the ranks of any profession on the sales side, they rise to the top quickly. We've seen this in the technology, banking, real estate, and accounting firms. Like their peers in other industries, women lawyers are and will continue to be extremely successful at selling legal services.

Selling legal services is not really a new idea. Law firms began hiring marketing professionals around 1985. Today, law firms are adding another professional to the administrative team: sales professionals with backgrounds from the technology markets and other competitive industries are beginning to enter law firms. Yet, even from the years when the local law firm in town was the primary service provider to the businesses in town, there was always a rainmaker—someone who sold legal services. Today, women have many opportunities to be the rainmaker. Women, in general, have entered the legal workforce in numbers and thus, women will continue to pursue all avenues of business opportunities that practicing law presents. Building strong books of business and solid relationships with business people is one of those avenues.

Introduction

Practicing law has changed in three significant ways: First, the practice has become extremely specialized. No longer can the local lawyer solve a business person's every legal need. There are employment lawyers, intellectual property lawyers, real estate lawyers, tax lawyers, and on and on.

Second, in 1986, the then General Counsel of Xerox Corporation, Robert S. Banks, co-founded the Association of Corporate Counsel (formerly ACCA, now ACC). I met with Bob shortly after ACCA's founding. He was of the strong belief that we (the corporate counsel) are not backroom citizens who can't make it in a law firm to partnership, but, rather, we've chosen a different route, we are business people and, most important, we write the checks! Since ACCA's founding, the corporate in-house lawyer has taken on a new level of strategic importance to an organization. They are tied to the success of the business and they are ever-increasingly mindful of the rising costs of outside counsel. They are also mindful about the legal service provider's knowledge of the business the in house counsel's company is in, the make up of the in-house law department and its goals, and the attentiveness to value-added services.

Third, the opportunity to provide excellent service is one of the best opportunities to come along in years for legal service providers. Competition is tough, but opportunity is abundant. Few law firms have loyal clients (at least according to the clients!) Two studies (ACCA Serengetti and BTI Consulting, both discussed in Chapter 11) show that most in-house counsel from Fortune 1000 companies don't believe they get the value they should from their outside lawyers. In-house counsel were asked to describe what criteria made firms good service providers. Then they were asked which firms, from their perspectives, met those criteria. The number of firms mentioned through questioning and un-aided awareness, was small (compared to the number of possible firms worth mentioning). What does this mean? Few companies are loyal to their outside law firms. It means there is a tremendous opportunity for women lawyers to pursue new client development opportunities.

As Angela Bradstreet, former president, California Women Lawyers and past president, San Francisco Bar Association points out: "Women are entering the ranks of the law department—this presents

The Woman Lawyer's Rainmaking Game

a lot of opportunity . . . There are still major glass ceiling issues in the legal profession. Less than 5 percent of women nationwide are managing partners and barely 1 percent are partners nationwide. Thus, many women are leaving private practice and entering into the law departments. This trend puts women in the position of decision-making." She continues, "Probably 60 percent of my client base, which is well into seven figures, consists of female in-house counsel. My experience has been that as more and more women get into positions of power in-house and within corporations, those women really try to use and be aware of outside women lawyers who are qualified who meet all their criteria. I have seen a real concerted effort to help qualified women."

Tara Higgins, a noted rainmaker and partner from Bingham McCutchen is of the same thinking. "There are more women purchasers than ever, and the number of women making decisions is the highest ever. . . . This provides great opportunity for women lawyers. I think women are better at building relationships. Women tend to focus on people they like, so relationships can build naturally. Men focus on the business matter at hand, rather than trying to build an ongoing relationship, in my opinion." Kelli Sager, a partner at Seattle's Davis Wright & Tremaine has also focused on the rise of women decision-makers. "This is a significant change—the continued increase of women in-house counsel at major companies, who are interested and willing to look to women at law firms as their primary outside counsel. This development also means that the relationships between inside and outside counsel are not being forged primarily in male-oriented activities and locations."

By building successful relationships that put the client at the center, you have as much a chance at building a successful practice as anyone else. This book looks at sales and the sales process from a solution-providing standpoint. That is, a need exists and the lawyer is providing a solution to that need, be it a complex intellectual property issue or a drunk driving case. Generally speaking, people don't buy from people they don't like. Forging and furthering a relationship and providing solutions to business opportunities, challenges, and problems are what buyers of legal services expect. That is how we define sales. Selling is the focus of this book.

CHAPTER 1

So, How EXACTLY Do You Sell Legal Services?

Highlights
- What Really Works?
- Selling: What It Means
- Marketing Versus Selling
- You Have the Power—Recognizing Your Hidden Talent for Rainmaking

What Really Works?
- Qualities of a Strong Rainmaker
- Relationship Building Is a Strength of Many Women
- The Unique Aspects of Selling Legal Services
- Aggressive Is an Okay Style for Representing Your Clients and It Works for Sales Too!
- Stating Your Case: Selling Is Selling, Whatever Your Field of Law
- Viewing Opportunities and Pursuits from the Client Perspective
- Are You Ready? As Long as You Know the Rules of the Game, You Can Play It
- Working Tool: Perceived Strengths and Areas for Improvement
- The Sales Process—An Overview of the Stages
- Discussion Questions

The Woman Lawyer's Rainmaking Game

Tune in to yourself. Women are so thoroughly unused to setting goals for themselves that in many instances they need to be taught how to do this all-important task.—Carole Hyatt, author

What Really Works?

Have you ever wondered:
- Who are successful women rainmakers?
- How much time is dedicated to business development?
- What business development activities work best?
- What are the barriers to advancement, potential road blocks to success and areas for improvement?
- How are women supported by their firms and others?
- What are best practices for firms and women lawyers?

Throughout this book, we will share our insights from working with women lawyers in different firms, practice areas, and points of career and life. To provide you with compelling evidence of what really works, we will also highlight significant findings from several bodies of research on women lawyers and business development issues. Using this powerful combination, we share answers to these important questions. In turn, you will possess new and supportive ways to help you tune into yourself as you play – and WIN – the women lawyers' rainmaking game.

Selling: What It Means

Selling is often described in a number of ways, including: providing solutions to problems; networking and building relationships; and leveraging contacts to closing business. What does "SALES" make you think?

When we ask lawyers, some of them think the worst of sales; that is, being pushy or manipulative, coercing people into buying things they do not want/need; selling more services than are really necessary just to increase the billing, etc. This perception of sales is not only old-fashioned, it actually is the reason that many people abhor the idea of selling. Given the growth of significant competitive attitude in the legal market, anyone who still thinks selling legal services is "huckster-ish" needs to rethink her understanding of the market and its buyers. A mental shift is required.

Those who think of selling as an opportunity to gain knowledge and provide solutions that enhance a business's goals have the right mindset. Selling is about opening doors to opportunity. As Samuel Johnson, the great English essayist, once said, there is not anyone "who is not in some degree a merchant; who has not something to buy or something to sell." Selling is a means by which buyers educate themselves, create new opportunities for their organizations and businesses, learn about the competition, and improve their network. Buyers of legal services know the value of listening to what lawyers have to say. For lawyers engaged in the sales process, it's an opportunity to learn many new things about prospects, clients, referral sources, companies, products, industries, and competitors. Without selling, lawyers do not get legal work. Likewise, the profession would not move forward as fast.

Anyone can learn how to sell. Will everyone be a multi-million-dollar-a-year contributor? Some will, some will not. By understanding that attitude makes a difference and learning about the process of selling legal services, anyone is able to develop her skills and practice to achieve success and become a valuable contributor to the firm. We've heard some practitioners progress to saying, "I think I like selling legal services better than doing the work" after they explained how they hated the thought of having to sell and would prefer to just practice law.

If you like people, then you will find selling is actually fun, personally and professionally satisfying, and less of a challenge than originally suspected. Selling, like all skills, takes practice. It takes time to become good at it. You also need patience—and lots of follow up—for the relationships to fully develop. Not too much happens over one meeting or from one speaking engagement. In contrast, with time, goals, and a clear focus, the client base will grow.

Marketing Versus Selling

From the Law Firm Associate's Guide to Personal Marketing and Selling Skills by Beth M. Cuzzone and Catherine Alman MacDonagh, JD: *What's the difference between marketing and sales? When clients are considering what lawyers and law firms to hire, there are two primary stages in the process: 1. awareness and 2. rapport and trust. Making potential clients "aware" of you usually happens on a firm level, often*

The Woman Lawyer's Rainmaking Game

called marketing. Developing rapport and gaining trust happens on a personal level, often called selling.

Many lawyers use the word "marketing" to refer to all activities involved in generating new business. But corporate America draws a clear distinction between the sales department, which deals directly with clients and revenue generation, and the marketing department that works behind the scenes, deciding which clients to target and how to reach them.

Marketing and sales are two separate and distinct processes but they are very much intertwined. As we've already implied, marketing exists to support sales.

In other words, marketing describes the practice of activities that support sales, where we obtain new business. The graph below depicts these activities better than describing them. The cycle shows a continuum. Plans and strategies should be updated quarterly to reflect input you receive from the market and your clients.

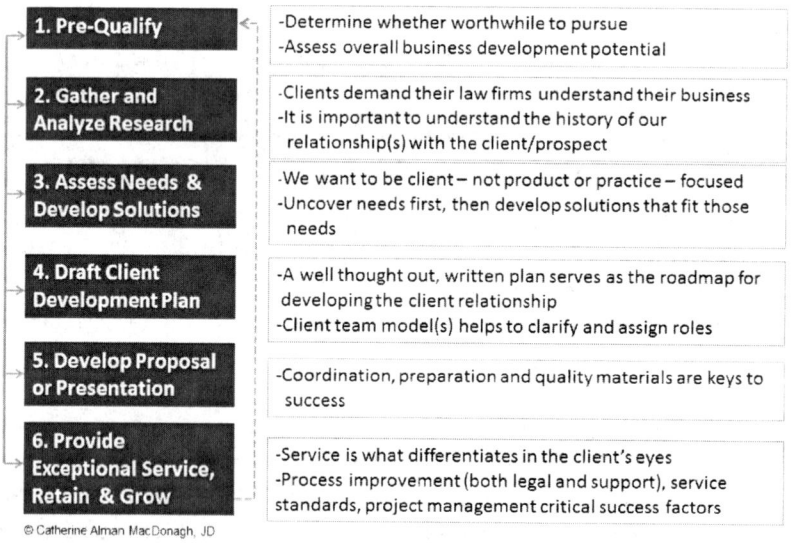

You Have the Power—Recognizing Your Hidden Talent for Rainmaking

As a lawyer, you already possess all of the skills necessary to become quite capable at selling. Those skills include negotiating, listening, overcoming objections, and driving toward anticipated outcomes. Now all that is left is to learn how to apply these skills to your advantage for business development. For example, think of a client development situation where fees may have become an obstacle to obtaining business. The first thing you would do is ask, "If fees were not an issue, would we be able to enter into an agreement to represent you?" By asking this question, you've started the negotiation process. Staying focused on the goal or result helps you implement your legal talent toward a successful business development outcome. Once you know the process, selling legal services is easy.

The Successful Woman Rainmaker

Based on studies conducted by the Legal Sales and Service Organization, we learned that women who spend at least nine hours per week engaged in business development activities stand to generate as much as $145k in annual revenue. Also, when firms set minimums, 75% of our sample reported having met or *exceeded* business development minimums.

What does this mean for you? It means several things. First, it's important to invest the right amount of time doing the right activities. Next, make sure to give yourself credit for all the things you do to forge, maintain, and grow relationships, including delivering excellent service, because those activities are included in the 9 hour count. Finally, it proves that it's important for firms to provide a baseline, a structure, a goal. If the firm does not do that for its women lawyers, find a way to do it for yourself.

Qualities of a Strong Rainmaker

The Legal Sales and Service Organization (LSSO) conducted several goundbreaking studies that looked at women lawyers and business development issues. The LSSO studies found that the successful woman rainmaker:

- Is highly committed and identified with her firm
- Is confident about her ability and personal worth

The Woman Lawyer's Rainmaking Game

- Understands how to use sincerity, sociability, and networks to influence others
- Is extraverted and conscientious
- Takes advantage of mentoring opportunities (with both women and men)
- Feels empowered at work
- Believes she is an above average sales performer
- Works for a firm that recognizes rainmaking accomplishments
- Spends around one hour on rainmaking activities per day, but she engages in a wider variety of activities than less successful women rainmakers

Over the past 20 years we have had the privilege of working with many law firms, conducting sales training sessions, helping lawyers with individual coaching, and developing key client sales strategies. An introductory part of the sales program is to solicit from the attendees their perspective about what makes a good rainmaker. The same qualities come up over and over again. Over 500 lawyers provided input for the following list:

- Personality
- Good listener
- Strong negotiator
- Confidence
- Curiosity
- Personal contacts
- Persistence
- People skills
- Audacity
- Sense of humor
- Good talker
- Reputation
- Creativity
- Initiative
- Knowledge of industry

- Enthusiastic . . . interested
- Appearance
- Expert in field
- Self-motivated
- Some luck . . . being at the right place at the right time

Perhaps you have other attributes you believe are critical to the success of rainmaking? The point here is that the attributes that many people believe are critical to successful rainmaking are all skills that can be developed with some assistance and practice.

Which attributes would you add? Which of these is the most important? It's quite possibly being a good listener! For example, if you tend to talk and listen when meeting with potential clients, then pick up some books on good listening skills and practice the skills at your next meeting with individuals inside or outside of your work environment.

As you review this list, please note that these are the attributes you also need to be a good lawyer. Your law school training, coupled with your client and life experience, has provided you with most of the skills necessary to become a rainmaker. Once you understand the rainmaking process, find a way to practice and sharpen your skills. Try doing for yourself what you do for your clients. In other words, you will be communicating, listening, and negotiating for business. Just like you do not intend to take no for an answer on your client's behalf, do not take no for an answer when it comes to your business development efforts.

The three top skills/qualities are the ability to listen, confidence, and negotiation acumen. The other skills will come into play from time to time, but listening is the most critical skill to learn and learn well. Remember: it is about the client, *not* about you or your firm. Listening shows you care.

Relationship Building Is a Strength of Many Women
Bowman and Brooke's Sandra Ezell is passionate about promoting diversity and believes, "Women do relationships best: 'Women, whether they grow up to be CEO women or PTA women, are encouraged from their very first relationships to work on the quality and not just the fact of the relationships. We ask questions. We don't sit quietly. We remember things. We carry our connectedness into the workplace. We do not have separate approaches to our work and personal connections, we

just connect. Of course, to say that these qualities are exclusive to one gender is not just wrong it is a statement that runs counter to the notion that women look at individuals rather than groups and form individual relationships. But, on average, this is how we are raised, these are our skills, these are strengths and we need to embrace them and not let the fact that these skills and strengths do not currently exist in the power structure in our organization cause us to reject or replace these innate qualities. As more and more women make their way into the power structure, the uniqueness of this quality and skill will fade and it will become part of the tapestry of power, and that will be a good thing.'" As Judge Angela Bradstreet reminds us, "I've seen a lot of women and men go in and sit down and go on and on about themselves. There's got to be some listening time. Questions I always ask: 'What do you like to see in outside counsel?' 'What do you want from outside counsel?' Then I address those needs with my discussion."

As Maura Ann McBreen, chair of Baker & McKenzie's Client Development Committee, points out, "We have more practice and comfort with social skills than men do, which makes us better listeners and better counselors. We are warmer and more personal in the way we communicate and do business. We are less likely to let our egos get in the way of resolving issues or disputes for our clients. A 'woman's touch' packaged with a lawyer's mind makes for an unbeatable combination."

In thinking about the changes over the last 10 years and the opportunity these changes have created for women lawyers, Maura Ann adds, "There are more women on both sides of the relationship—lawyer and client. There are also significantly more women serving as general counsel and in-house counsel. I have found that these women seek out opportunities to work with other well-qualified women attorneys in private practice."

Kirkpatrick & Lockhart's Global Development Partner Janice Hartman agrees, "Women are very good at 'being there,' at being supportive, at being loyal, at not having the need to dominate. For inside counsel with high self-esteem, this is a natural fit."

Susan Paish, the former managing partner of Canada's Fasken Martineau and now on the buyer side, observes, "There are more of us (still not enough and we need to address this), and critical mass is important as we have more credibility (not quite so much tokenism).

So, How EXACTLY Do You Sell Legal Services?

We are starting to be recognized for what we can do and that we can do things very well and, in some situations a woman and her approach will be the best match for a situation. However, the most important change I think is the growth in the number of women in key business and in-house counsel positions. Many women have openly and frankly told me that all other things being equal (NO concessions on quality), they would prefer to deal with women. Tip: what are the values and interests of the person you are prospecting? If they are different from yours, do you really think that you will enjoy working with them and . . . If you are not having fun, what are you doing???"

Jane Potter a practicing lawyer from Seattle reflects, "Women are more natural in looking to build relationships, although that's not true of all women, plus there are many men who see the importance of building and retaining relationships. I rarely hear comments like the one I heard from an older male partner at a firm who, when told he should have a better relationship with his legal assistant, said, 'You mean, I have to make small talk with my secretary?'"

She continues by adding: "Here are two relationship-building examples: one in-house counsel I know collects postcards from all over the world, so when I worked with her, I made a point of finding interesting postcards to send her when I was traveling. Another recently joined a gym I belong to, so we make plans to work out at the same time, then have a quick dinner together. I think the key is moving beyond communications based solely on mutual work, and finding other common ground that will help sustain the relationship if one or both people move to new jobs or new locations. In the end people want to be appreciated as people, and not simply as a function of their job, so to have a good business relationship with someone, you have to make that personal connection."

Potter continues by cautioning, "I think it is easier for women to acknowledge and share with their male colleagues gender-related issues that can be awkward. For example, you mentioned golf; I think it can still be awkward for a woman attorney to engage a male contact or client on a personal level if that activity just involves the two people. To take an example involving the wife of a lawyer I work with: I had loaned him some books unrelated to the work, and she was (jokingly, but still she mentioned it) wondering whom he was getting books from.

So you have to be sensitive to the feelings of women who are not as used to male/female business relationships. Nowadays I feel comfortable raising these issues with male colleagues and getting their input. I sometimes invite a male colleague if I am having dinner with one or more male contacts for the first time and no other women will be present. But I have never run across a blatant example of a potential client preferring to work with a male attorney."

Boston-based Goulston & Storr's rainmaker, Debbie Horwitz, reflects, "Women are more comfortable 'selling' their legal services in ways that are comfortable to them. For some, that may be in more traditional ways, such as golf or corporate board participation. For many of us, it's doing more what comes naturally—building relationships over the long term. Since women have been successful in these efforts, they are being more and more supported and encouraged institutionally. Since there is more opportunity to sell in more comfortable ways, our younger attorneys are not put off and scared by the concept of business development."

Kirkpatrick & Lockhart's Janice Hartmann notes, "Women lawyers, of course, are more of a fixture at the highest levels of the legal scene now, and many 'buyers' grew up in an environment that accepts women lawyers as peers. So there is more of a willingness to be open to having a woman at the point of a relationship, which allows us to 'sell' on a more level playing field. That is not to say that impediments to achieving a high-level 'corporate counselor' role to top companies and their boards no longer exist, because they do."

Davis Wright's rainmaker, Kelli Sager, observes, "Women are viewed as having less of a hard edge than they were previously and some of the 'hits' women took for their intensity are valued more now as 'high energy!'"

As these women have observed, people like to work with people who are like them. This is not a surprising revelation: as humans we are more comfortable with people whom we know and trust, with whom we share values and interests in common with our own.

The Unique Aspects of Selling Legal Services
There is no question that selling legal services, like selling any type of professional services, is not easy. There is no trial period for which a service may be used and then returned; there is no warranty if the rela-

tionship does not work out or if the lawyer turns out to be incompetent. There is little or no tire kicking in this game. Because the product is intangible, it is difficult for the buyer to assess the potential quality of the service. Therefore, once a relationship has been established, it can be tough to break a client away from another firm. However, there is always an opportunity and as long as the goals you create for yourself are kept at the top of your mind, every individual has the same opportunity to close new business. Building loyal clients is critical to selling legal services since a loyal client becomes an advocate on your behalf. While building your levels of expertise and experience is crucial to your long-term career, building a book of business is becoming very important to your ability to maintain your role in a firm as a practicing lawyer.

Bowman and Brooke's Richmond Office Managing Partner Sandra Ezell adds this important note: "As I look back on my career and the many lessons I have learned over my life and think about which one, among all of them, that I wish I had learned sooner, one easily emerges from the rest. I wish that the obvious truth that the bonds between people are as important if not more important as the knowledge and experience you work so hard to obtain. I spent many years focusing on knowledge and experience. What makes it even more ironic is that relationships are easy, they are fulfilling, they are mutual, they flex and adapt, they are dynamic. Knowledge and experience is more linear, more static. When I set out (many) years ago to be the best lawyer I could be, to leave a legacy of excellence in my craft, to be an example not just to women lawyers but to trial lawyers, I grasped for knowledge and I fought for experience and did not approach the building of relationships with the same fervor. It is my single biggest regret, because, as I have become more seasoned, I realize that my relationships are the most fulfilling aspect of my career. The relationships that I now enjoy, the colleagues that I cannot wait to see, the people all over the country who I look so forward to catching up with when I have a chance, even a fleeting one, add to the quality of my knowledge, provide the platform for my experience and as it turns out are the ones who give me the chance to practice the craft of trial law that I have come to love. But more than that, they make the experience more complete and add texture to the tapestry of my career. I plan to spend the second half of my career exploring my opportunities in a way that is more familiar to me, from a place of relationships. I have heard it said that this is something women do more naturally. I don't know if that is true or not, but it feels more natural and it is more authentic and more successful."

Recent studies, like those conducted by the ACC, Serenghetti, Acritas, and the BTI studies discussed in Chapter 11, of Fortune 1000 in-house counsel indicate that very few clients (and this is only magnified, by the way, on regional levels with private companies) believe they are loyal clients. Many are only *satisfied* with their outside counsel and are open to building new relationships with new counsel. The opportunity to introduce yourself, your firm, and to build a new relationship will continue to grow as change in the legal market continues to rise.

Aggressive Is an Okay Style for Representing Your Clients and It Works for Sales Too!

Women professionals have often been criticized for being aggressive and pushy. Well, there is nothing wrong with either. Asserting oneself is a positive attribute and generally few people get anywhere without aggressively pursuing goals. So, ignore anyone who describes you as aggressive. Take it as a compliment, move forward with the sales plan in hand, and focus on achievable goals and outcomes.

As Judge Angela Bradstreet notes, "If women are assertive they are regarded as strident and negative. Where men are regarded highly for the same behaviors. There is still stereotyping that impedes a woman's progress, but it is changing. Noted author Deborah Tannen has written about this. She notes that boys are very comfortable in a competitive environment. When girls play together they want to build a rapport and if a girl wants to lead that play group she is considered bossy." We see this play out all the time when working with partners on their business development goals and objectives. Men will see opportunities to go after a piece of business and go for it. Women, even the most successful, will want to check to see if it's OK to pursue an opportunity so as not to upset their colleague(s). We say it's better to beg for forgiveness than to ask permission. Go for it.

In today's changing and competitive legal environment, it is okay, and in fact, it is crucial to be focused, assertive, and confident. Otherwise, the tremendous opportunity for building business as the legal market shifts may pass you by.

So, How EXACTLY Do You Sell Legal Services?

Stating Your Case: Selling Is Selling, Whatever Your Field of Law
Building contacts is key to building relationships. Once a relationship has been established, position yourself as the conduit for obtaining business for the firm. By focusing on the needs of a particular prospect and, in greater part, a particular market, you may discover that the need for your specific type of practice is not dominant at the time, but opportunity does present itself for an area in which a partner or close contact of yours specializes. Doors will open for opportunities to sell all the areas of practice that a firm may offer. If you are with a small firm or you are a sole practitioner, selling opportunities may provide an occasion for you to refer business to other lawyers in your network or for you to develop new relationships for potential cross-referrals.

This is a key concept to understand about rainmaking: identifying needs and providing information about the services to address those needs will build business, even if it means that the business is sent out to other members of the firm or your peers. The other key concept that goes hand in hand with this is adding value. What are you providing that is adding value to your prospect's business goals? By providing value and keeping in touch long term, an opportunity for your practice will present itself. *Remember, it takes time.* The focus on the market as opposed to the practice provides many great cross-selling opportunities. Think about the great rainmakers in your circle of contacts. They never focus just on selling their practice, but rather the focus is on building contacts, learning about clients' business plans and needs, and selling all the practice areas of the firm. [For more information on market perceptions, visit actritas.com or ACC.com]

Viewing Opportunities and Pursuits from the Client Perspective
Here is another way of looking at sales from a client needs point of view versus a practice point of view. Let us take a business that has been around for a while—the microelectronics industry. As the business goes through various economic shifts, the company may require different types of services. Getting to know the business needs of the president or in-house counsel will be critical to building your legal business. The best way to learn is to listen.

Here is the example. The company is in an expanded growth phase. You may be an intellectual property lawyer. Rather than beginning the conversation with what you can do for the company, think of a few questions you may ask that will get the conversation flowing. With this growth phase of the company comes the need for various services your firm can offer including:

- Executive compensation contracts; non-compete agreements (employment and/or benefits lawyers)
- Acquisition of new business units (corporate M&A lawyers)
- Overseas distribution (licensing lawyers)
- New product development (trademark and intellectual property lawyers)
- New facilities (real estate lawyers)

After five years of strong growth, the economy shifts downward and the company sees the need for new services including:

- Workforce downsizing (labor and employment work)
- Loan restructuring (commercial lawyers; litigation lawyers; corporate lawyers)
- Contract enforcement (litigation lawyers)

The key point here is that effectively targeting an industry or market provides you and the firm with significant leverage once a client relationship is established. Cross-selling the services maintains strong client relationships.

Let us begin the sales journey.

Are You Ready?: As Long as You Know the Rules of the Game, You Can Play It

Take this quick "sales readiness" quiz to determine if your sales priorities are in order.

Circle One

1. I know I need to make time in my schedule to concentrate on client development.   Y   N

2. I am able to spend a half hour per day or 2-1/2 hours per week on sales. (This means contacting clients, existing contacts, and making new contacts.)   Y   N

3. I believe that selling is critical to pursuing a successful practice that will bring revenue to the firm and that selling, today, is part of the responsibility of being a partner in the firm and practicing law.   Y   N

4. I am organized.   Y   N

5. I enjoy meeting people and networking.   Y   N

6. I believe I am able to bring in business, through developing strong relationships with prospects, to support other practice areas of my firm   Y   N

7. I prefer not to sell the business but will work on marketing activities as part of a team to help sell the firm's services.   Y   N

8. My contacts database is up to date.   Y   N

9. I am committed to advancing my professional development in the sales area and will seek out and attend one program a year for personal/professional growth in this area.   Y   N

10. I understand all contacts—personal and business—can lead to new opportunities for building my practice.   Y   N

Hopefully you answered Yes to all 10 questions. If not, review the areas you need to develop to support your selling efforts. Include these on the chart you fill out on page 1-16 to identify your perceived strengths and needs.

Working Tool: Perceived Strengths and Areas for Improvement

Note: creating this list will help you to identify areas for improvement. Choose one need a month and work on developing the skills or framework to help you turn the need into a strength. Like exercising, you will get better if you focus on improving your performance.

The Woman Lawyer's Rainmaking Game

Strengths	**Needs**
Good Networker	Need to create a schedule and focus on follow up

_____
_____
_____
_____
_____
_____

Building relationships and building a book of business—selling—takes time. Even if you set aside 30 minutes a week it is 30 minutes more than you've been doing. Highly successful rainmakers spend about 9-15 hours a week on their relationships. Make sure you create a task list that is achievable each week (one or two items). Stay focused on your goals and follow-up with all your contacts. The next chapter provides information and tools for developing your own marketing action plan.

The Sale Process—An Overview of the Stages

Selling is a process that has distinct stages. By following the process, you will absolutely develop business. Skip an important step and chances are you've hurt your odds for closing new business. If you are familiar with litigation you know that presenting your case before a jury comes after discovery. There is a distinct process and no one but a fool would go to court totally blind and unprepared. Selling is the same way. Presenting your services before hearing about a prospective client's business and legal needs is putting the cart before the horse.

Here is the selling process. (We provide detail in the following chapters about each stage listed below.)

Pre-Approach: Get organized, create an action plan, identify target markets; identify and organize your client and contact lists; create your bio and your service descriptions; identify trade publications and their editors in chief; identify pertinent organizations and executive directors.

Approach: Get in front of the market. Meet potential new clients and referral sources; attend association meetings; write articles; give speeches; follow up on opportunities.

Qualify and Assess Needs: Identify the decision-maker(s); ask questions that provide information and insight (if you are in charge of the questions, you are in control of the sales process); follow the 80/20 rule—talk 20 percent of the time and listen 80 percent of the time to the prospect.

Build the Relationship: Keep in touch; show you care about your contacts' and clients' business needs, strategies, and goals; prepare (and rehearse) presentations. Determine ways in which you can add value to their businesses.

Address Need/State the firm's Solution: Match legal services to specific identified needs; use firm materials to support what you are saying and to showcase services.

Obtain Engagement/Close: Ask for the engagement; "close" the business; obtain a new client.

This process may take an hour over a lunch with a referral or it may take five years. The time it takes is called the selling cycle. The important point is to clearly understand where you are in the process. The other important key is staying in control of the process. Now, let us get started! Read on.

DISCUSSION QUESTIONS

As you review the list of Rainmaker Attributes, please consider: Which of these attributes do *you* think are necessary to be a rainmaker?

CHAPTER 2

The Sales Process: Pre-Approach

Highlights
- Get Organized: Your Marketing Action Plan
- Form 2A: Sample Practice Description, Health and Life Sciences
- Form 2B: Marketing and Sales-Oriented (Results-Focused) Biography
- Focus Your Efforts: Choose Your Target Market(s)
- Create an Individual Marketing Action Plan
- Working Tool: Form 2C: Individual Marketing Action Plan (IMAPsm)
- Working Tool: Form 2C(1): Sample Individual Marketing Action Plan (IMAPsm)
- Working Tool: Form 2C(2): Individual Marketing Action Plan (IMAPsm)
- Working Tool: Form 2C(3): Individual Marketing Action Plan (IMAPsm)
- Stay on Track: Keep a List of Tasks
- Working Tool: Sample Individual Sales and Marketing Task List
- Working Tool: Blank Individual Sales and Marketing Task List
- Determine Your Investment: What Is Building a Successful Practice Worth to You and How Many Minutes/Hours Will You Invest Monthly Into Your Rainmaking Development Account?

The Woman Lawyer's Rainmaking Game

Recognize you are a reputable person with integrity, representing a beneficial product or service—your prospect needs you! —Wendy Weiss, author of Cold Calling for Women

Getting Organized: Your Marketing Action Plan
The first step of the process—pre-approach—is all about getting organized and preparation. To use an analogy, whether taking a road trip, cycling journey, jogging, skiing, or climbing adventure, the first step is to figure out where to go and then how to get there. Among other things, the length of time you have for this activity and your intended destination will dictate the length of the journey. The selling process is no different. The first step is basic: determine what you are selling and to whom you are selling it.

Determining what you are selling can be as challenging as determining the target market, which is your prospective clients. Examples of practice areas and expertise abound on firm websites. As an individual practitioner, either on your own or part of a law firm, it is critical to stay focused on an area of practice and be great at it. The narrower the niche, the easier it will be to plan your approach. So, whether the practice is tax, corporate, estate planning, personal injury, anti-trust, intellectual property, labor and employment, real estate, or one of the other of the myriad of service areas in which lawyers practice, take the time to get as specific as possible. By drafting some text to create a practice description, you will both develop a focus and simultaneously craft a sales tool for use with your in-person meetings.

Part one, then, of the Pre-Approach Stage of the sales process is to identify your practice area and to develop a practice description that communicates your services to the market. See Form 2A for a good example of a practice description that "speaks" to the market and is, in other words, market focused. Use this example from the Health and Life Services practice of this firm as a model to create one for your practice.

While you are at it, since the product is a lawyer, create a sales bio that reflects your expertise in the particular practice area. Form 2B is an example of a sales/market-oriented biography, written by a rainmaker litigator from Wilmer, Cutler, Pickering, Hale and Dorr. Note Karen

The Sales Process: Pre-Approach

Green's focus on clients and results for clients. Karen is an expert at relating to her contacts and markets.

Remain focused on what you do best. Susan Paish urges, "The world is an increasingly specialized place. You had better be able to distinguish yourself from the competition and be the 'best at' something and you can't be the 'best at' everything. Bite the bullet: it's not that painful!!"

Dianna Kempe agrees, "By focusing, I analyzed the market and found areas where there was opportunity to create my own work." Nancy Little, Deputy Managing Partner, McGuire Woods concurs, "I have some particularly focused experience that has certainly led to more target marketing, so on a personal level, there is some evidence that this is quite helpful advice."

Janice Hartmann urges you to focus and to be a team player. "Since I am a corporate lawyer who by nature is not particularly 'specialized,' this ties into my comments about the value of looking for opportunities to offer services in a specific area where I know we can outperform, even though it may not be MY services. Corporate counselor roles grow out of comfort levels with the ability to bring in the right people at the right time, so it really plays into selling a special capability and making inroads on that comfort level at the same time. It also means that the woman partner in question has to develop the self-confidence to collaborate as a member of team, rather than functioning as a lone ranger."

Form 2A: Sample Practice Description, Health and Life Sciences

A Midwest firm has a strong focus on the life sciences and health industries. Notice in its following practice description its focus is on the market and the market's perspective—thereby speaking to the reader as opposed to at the reader.

Life Sciences and Health Industries

The focus of a growing number of the firm's clients is to anticipate and meet the life-sustaining needs of a burgeoning world population in areas such as food and nutrition, agrisciences, disease prevention, and innovations in drug, medical devices, and healthcare services. Research universities, emerging and established biotechnology and pharmaceu-

The Woman Lawyer's Rainmaking Game

tical companies, agricultural businesses, and healthcare providers all share this noble calling. Their approach is simple: foster scientific and business systems innovations; attract capital to exploit those innovations; organize to commercialize their products and systems efficiently and profitably; protect and enforce their rights in their most prized assets; and reinvest revenues into continuing research and discovery, in anticipation of the next wave of innovation.

All along this cycle of innovation, the health and life sciences industries require increasingly sophisticated legal representation from experienced, savvy lawyers. The firm's Life Sciences and Health Care practice group meets that demand by providing integrated legal services to help clients navigate legal and business challenges, particularly:

- venture capital access
- regulatory and contractual issues
- business startup strategies
- research and clinical trials developments
- FDA approvals and regulatory matters
- technology licensing and joint ventures setup
- patent procurement and portfolio management
- corporate compliance issues
- healthcare fraud and abuse
- mergers and acquisitions
- patent litigation
- products liability and commercial litigation
- export controls
- environmental regulatory issues
- tax compliance

Form 2B: Marketing and Sales-Oriented (Results-Focused) Biography

As mentioned earlier in this chapter, writing a bio that describes your practice and provides examples of excellent work and also provides the answer to the question "so why should we hire you?" is important and gives you a selling tool. The following is a portion of the CV of Karen

The Sales Process: Pre-Approach

Green, a well-known litigator and former prosecutor, now at Wilmer, Cutler, Pickering, Hale and Dorr LLP:

> Ms. Green's practice concentrates on complex business litigation, including the defense of white-collar criminal and False Claims Act litigation. She has extensive experience representing companies, particularly within the health care industry, in parallel civil and criminal proceedings alleging: violations of the Anti-Kickback Statute, the Food Drug and Cosmetic Act, and the Export Control Act; health care fraud; securities fraud; government contracting fraud; consumer fraud; conspiracy; and mail and wire fraud. At the request of corporate clients, she also has conducted internal investigations.
>
> As select examples, Ms. Green has represented:
> - a major pharmaceutical company in parallel criminal and civil investigations by the U.S. Attorney's Office in Philadelphia for alleged off-label promotion and improper payments to physicians in connection with the marketing of six drugs and assisted it in globally resolving those investigations, four related qui tam actions brought under federal and state law, and related administrative claims of various federal agencies, including the US Department of Health and Human Services' Office of Inspector General;
> - a medical device manufacturer in a grand jury investigation by the U.S. Attorney for the District of New Jersey and assisted it in globally resolving the government's criminal, civil, and administrative claims;
> - a major medical device manufacturer in a six-year, grand jury investigation by the United States Attorney's Office in Boston into the distribution of an allegedly adulterated and misbranded stent delivery system; the matter was resolved on a civil basis and neither the company nor two officers, who had been designated as targets, were indicted;
> - a third-party billing company in parallel civil and criminal investigations by the U.S. Attorney for the Southern District of New York of alleged Medicare and Medicaid fraud;

- a supplier of durable medical equipment in a grand jury investigation by the U.S. Attorney for the Southern District of Florida of alleged Medicare fraud;
- multiple former employees in parallel civil and criminal investigations in the District of Massachusetts of alleged off-label marketing of a drug;
- an office products supplier in a qui tam False Claims Act suit filed in the District of Columbia allegedly arising from the sale of office supplies to the U.S. government that originated from impermissible countries under the Buy American Act;
- a medical device manufacturer in an investigation by the U.S. Attorney for the District of Massachusetts arising from the sale of allegedly defective blood analyzers to the U.S. Army;
- a medical device manufacturer in an investigation by the U.S. Attorney for the District of Columbia of alleged violations of the Export Control Act;
- a printed circuit board manufacturer in a criminal case charging violations of the Federal Clean Water Act;
- the former president and CEO of a health insurer in a federal grand jury investigation;
- a company's former CEO and director in parallel civil, criminal, and Congressional investigations of alleged improprieties in government contracting;
- a national retailer in parallel civil and criminal proceedings alleging bankruptcy and mail fraud; and
- various companies in corporate internal investigations.

For Karen's full bio, see wilmerhale.com. Once the practice description and bio are complete, you are ready to complete your marketing and business development plan.

Focus Your Efforts: Choose Your Target Markets(s)

Once the practice focus is clear, defining the *target market* is next. A target market is literally how it sounds. It is the external market from which you will generate business. This phase can seem daunting at first. Most practitioners really hate to narrow the target focus. In contrast,

The Sales Process: Pre-Approach

with a bit of understanding as to how much effort one specific target market can take, the task of identifying one key market is easier and makes good sense.

"Being targeted is the best way to ensure that you learn the potential client's business and technology area in depth," advises Jane Potter. "For example, in the patent area, it is not helpful to pitch for work if you can't represent that you, or someone you supervise, will be able to understand the work you are being asked to do, within the context of the prospect's business."

Bingham McCutchen's Tara Higgins, Co-Chair of the Energy and Project Finance Group, remarks on her focused approach, "It's true that the success I have achieved thus far is a result of my experience in investment funds and helping clients with international project finance, which is fairly narrow."

Adds Baker & McKenzie's Maura Ann Breen, "You need to select key targets that you think will increase your visibility and maximize your networking opportunities. There just isn't enough time to manage a successful practice, fulfill your firm commitments, have a personal and family life, and network with the world at large. You need to develop a strategy that identifies targets and techniques that you feel comfortable with and then give yourself a reasonable period of time to develop them and hopefully see some success. If you see no success, then change your targets and techniques. The important thing is to get started."

Create an Individual Marketing Action Plan (IMAPsm)
As discussed by the rainmakers above, developing a plan before beginning the sales process is necessary. This simple form is a good tool to remind you where to focus your efforts. It is worth filling out and keeping close by.

Think about your practice and use the blank form 2C to create an IMAP for your practice. Use the given examples as a basis from which to develop a plan that fits your services and your targeted markets.

Target Market. Identify your target market. Examples of completed IMAP forms that identify sample target markets for sample practice areas follow as Forms 2C(1), 2C(2), and 2C(3).

Referral markets. Once a target market is identified, it is time to think about who else sells to that market. There are often many other practitioners and business people who sell services and products to the same markets. These individuals will become what are often referred to as referral markets. Referral markets are made up of individuals with whom you develop a relationship for referring business to one another.

Your referral sources will always be on your team. Think about your business and how your current clients found your firm. Anyone who is targeting the same markets you are is a potential source of referral business to you as you are to them. Here's a quick list that may apply. Think of your own referral sources to add:

- Firm members
- Firm alumni
- Community members
- Business contacts
- Existing clients
- Accountants
- Bankers
- Lawyers in noncompeting firms

Geographic target market. Once these two markets—the primary target market and the referral market(s)—have been identified the next step is to determine which geographic area the practice will cover. Remember, narrow is better at first until the practice and a solid reputation are built within the market and buyers (the procurers of legal services) are aware of the firm's and your reputation. Keep focused on manageable tasks. For many, the geographic market is limited to the state and courts in which you are licensed and admitted to practice. By narrowing this area further you create an opportunity to build focused relationships. See the sample forms to view the target markets, referral markets, and geographic examples highlighted.

The Sales Process: Pre-Approach

For expansion of the target market, the next step is to now identify all the companies or prospective individuals within the geographic area identified.

Turning to sample IMAP form 2C(1), note that the target market is Emerging Life Sciences Companies. The geographic area is the State of California. The next step is to identify all the life sciences companies that are either located in or do business in California. Perhaps a more manageable first step is to identify companies in a specific zip code area of California. Obtaining this information is quite simple. A librarian (at your firm or at a public business library) can assist with finding this information provided the correct market criteria are given. In this case, ask to have external databases searched for life sciences companies within specific geographic areas of California where technology industries are growing and expanding. You may want to take it a step further and identify the specific zip code areas within the target region, which will make the librarian's job easier.

To assist with your first IMAP task of finding companies listed in your geographic area, a search like this will produce a comprehensive listing of all life sciences companies within the specified zip code. This listing can then be converted to an Excel spreadsheet and the data printed on labels for future mailings. Here is what a librarian will produce for you. Once you have a list like this (a prospect list), you may begin the sales process and future chapters will describe how to approach the market and how to develop the contacts within the market. Here is a sample list as reference:

Sample list of life science companies within an industry and a specific geographic region (data is shown verbatim):

Accelr 8 Technology Corporation
www.acceler8.com
Denver
Accelr 8 Technology Corporation's proprietary surface chemistry and its quantitative instruments support real-time assessment of medical diagnostics, food-borne pathogens, water-borne pathogens and bio-warfare assessments.
Accera, Inc.

The Woman Lawyer's Rainmaking Game

www.accerapharma.com
Broomfield
Accera, Inc., pursues new therapeutic approaches to the treatment and cure of Alzheimer's Disease based upon neuronal cell energy metabolism. The Company's products and services evolve from its proprietary metabolism platform.

    Advanced Nutraceuticats, Inc.
www.advancednutraceuticals.com
Denver
Advanced Nutraceuticals, Inc., manufactures capsule form blended vitamins and nutritional supplements plus liquid and powder pharmaceutical products.

    Affinity Bioreagents, Inc.
www.bioreagents.com
Golden
Affinity BioReagents offers primary and secondary antibodies, proteins, peptides and viral expression kits. The Company also creates custom antibodies to meet specific research needs.

    Agripro Wheat
www.agriprowheat.com
Berthoud
AgriPro Wheat leads the way in the development and delivery of superior wheat seed genetics in North America.

    Altos Therapeutics, Inc.
www.attos.com
Westminster
Altos Therapeutics, Inc. develops small molecule, non-protein drugs for improving cancer treatments. By increasing tumor oxygenation, the Company's products enhance the efficacy of standard radiation therapy and certain chemotherapeutic drugs.

    As you see from the above list, it's quite simple to obtain information about your target markets. A search request like this will yield many more names; we provided this brief list only as a sampling.

The Sales Process: Pre-Approach

So you see, a market can be defined by any criteria. If you have an estate planning practice and would like to obtain a list of wealthy individuals between the ages of 45 and 65 with incomes of over $200,000, you can either buy or obtain such a list. If your focus is in-house counsel, there are great resources such as the Association of Corporate Counsel (acc.com) that can provide you with information about in-house counsel.

Now that we have the information about businesses or target markets, let us complete the IMAP form for this practice. Next, identify the associations that are related to the target market. We have listed three as examples for the life sciences industry on 2C(1) and three for the individuals market targeted for personal injury on 2C(2). On 2C(3) is an example of an estate planning practice targeting private clients as the market.

If the associations for your target market(s) are not apparent, then log onto the Internet and conduct a key word search to determine association names. For those of you with a more individual-based practice such as private clients, or something fairly straightforward like real estate closings, think about the types of businesses in a specific geographical community that also target these areas and develop a list of local chambers of commerce and other businesses for networking opportunities. For specific examples, see the various forms provided in this chapter. Once an association or list of associations has been identified, call each organization to determine if it has a newsletter or runs regular programs. Find out the name of the program chair and newsletter editor. You can do this quite simply by phoning the association and asking for the information or by logging on to its website and checking under programs and by reading the association newsletter or bulletin. Add these names as information to your IMAP. As a next step, phone the individuals to make an appointment with each one of them to learn about what they seek from individual writers or speakers. Prior to leaving the meeting, confirm (from their perspective) the next steps (for follow up) to make sure there is an opportunity for you in the future. Remember to follow up this meeting or phone call with a note that you will be in further contact to pursue what was discussed or recommended.

The Woman Lawyer's Rainmaking Game

Sometimes association involvement may seem like it will never produce anything but a waste of time. Eventually, by being involved, opportunities will arise. Again, all this takes time—sometimes three to five years—set expectations for others and for yourself, accordingly.

Publication lists. The next area of the IMAP to develop is the list of publications related to the target market. One way to accomplish this is to call clients and ask them what they read. The Internet will also produce good information related to specific industry segments. Add this information to your plan. Do not forget to identify the editor-in-chief of the publication. This person will be the one with whom to make contact for writing opportunities or for quotes needed for an article they may be writing. It is always a good idea to add the editor from a city or town's daily newspaper and business journals. Get to know this individual and offer to act as an "expert" on the topic related to your practice if and when he/she writes an article that could use an expert's perspective.

Leadership. When deciding what activities to include in your plan, consider the importance of taking on a leadership role (either inside or outside the firm) in order to meet prospective clients as well as referral sources within your own firm. Such a role provides many opportunities for visibility, making connections, and enhancing leadership skills and experience. There are real connections between leadership activities and rainmaking success.

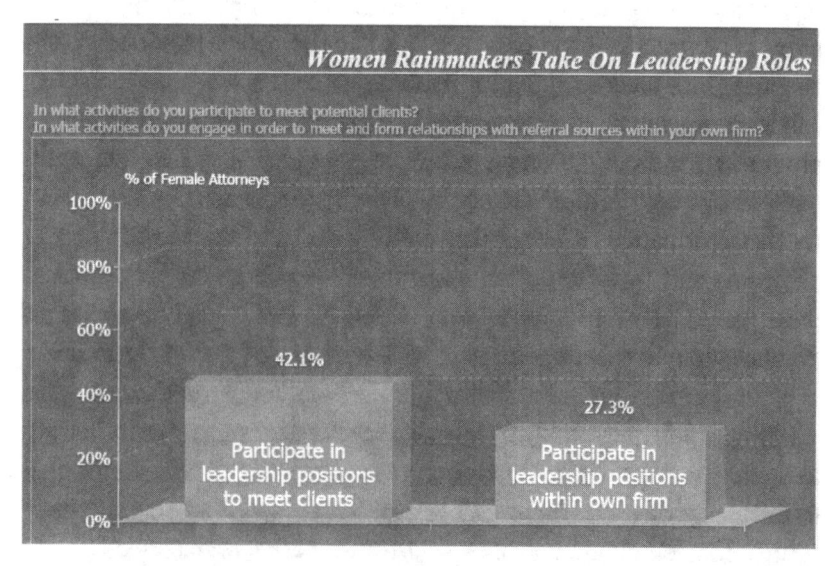

Women Rainmakers Take On Leadership Roles

In what activities do you participate to meet potential clients?
In what activities do you engage in order to meet and form relationships with referral sources within your own firm?

% of Female Attorneys

- Participate in leadership positions to meet clients: 42.1%
- Participate in leadership positions within own firm: 27.3%

The Sales Process: Pre-Approach

Here is a blank form for you to complete. Later in this chapter you will find sample plans filled out to use as references.

Working Tool: Form 2C: Individual Marketing Action Plan (IMAPsm)

Name: _____ Date of Plan: _____
Area of Practice: _____
Target Market: _____
Geographic Area: _____
Referral Markets:
1. _____
2. _____
3. _____
Industry Associations: _____
Industry Publications: _____
Tasks/Next Steps:
1. _____
2. _____
3. _____
4. _____
5. _____

Working Tool: Form 2C(1): Sample Individual Marketing Action Plan (IMAPsm)

Name: Susan Louise Stevens, PhD   Date of Plan: January 2, 20XX
Area of Practice: Target Geographic area:
Intellectual Property   Southeast U.S.
Target Market: Emerging Life Sciences Companies
Referral Markets:
1. Accounting firms' partners who practice in the life sciences area
2. Insurance companies
3. Venture capital firms
4. Existing clients
5. Academic institutions
Industry Associations:
1. Bio Industry Organization (BIO), Washington, DC
2. Advamed, Washington, DC
3. State technology councils

The Woman Lawyer's Rainmaking Game

Industry Publications:
1. BIO IT World
2. MIT Technology Review
3. Red Herring

Next Steps:
1. Identify specific companies within the geographic area.
2. Identify accounting firms and phone main number. Ask who is partner responsible for life sciences area and call him/her.
3. Identify insurance carriers and phone main number. Ask who the broker is for the life sciences area and call him/her.
4. Identify venture capital firms and phone main number. Ask who is partner responsible for life sciences area and call him/her.
5. Create a database using either a handheld database/calendar system, Microsoft Outlook on your individual computer or the firm's database—and begin to input all new contacts' names, addresses, and telephone numbers. By doing so, you will be building your target prospect lists.

Working Tool: Form 2C(2): Individual Marketing Action Plan (IMAPsm)

Name: Camille R. Campbell   Date of Plan: January 2, 20XX
Area of Practice: Target Geographic Area:
Personal Injury—Sports Injuries   Sanborn, MN
Target Market: Junior High, High School, and College athletes

Referral Markets:
1. Ambulance company owners
2. Hairdressers
3. School sports faculty members

Industry Associations: Local chamber of commerce (for networking with other business owners/community leaders which raises your community profile)

Market Media:
1. Local town newspaper
2. Chamber of Commerce Newsletter/website
3. High school newspaper/newsletter

Tasks:
1. Join the local Chamber of Commerce

The Sales Process: Pre-Approach

2. Meet with editor of town newspaper to identify writing opportunities or to propose that you write a column on your subject area once a month

3. Hire a designer in town who will assist with creating a website that allows individuals to check on your information and to learn more about the firm's services.

Working Tool: Form 2C(3) Individual Marketing Action Plan (IMAPsm)

Name: Tamara Friedman   Date of Plan: January 2, 20XX
Area of Practice: Estate Planning
Target Market: Wealthy individuals

Note: This market may be further simplified by identifying specific individual segments for example, musicians, actors, CEOs, etc.

Target Geographic Areas:

Retirement communities along the west coast of Southern Florida

Referral Markets:

1. Private Client bankers
2. Insurance agents
3. Existing clients
4. Law firms that do not have estate-planning practices

Associations: Nonprofit organizations within the specific geographic communities targeted

Industry Publications:

Newsletters published by bankers, wealth management companies, and accounting firms

Target geographic market daily or weekly newspaper

Tasks/Next Steps:

1. Meet with publications' editors for introduction; learn about items/stories of interest; make suggestions about possible story topics; set a plan for regular follow up.
2. Identify the banks in the area and phone them to determine who the contact is for the private banking group.
3. Begin to phone and schedule meetings with referral sources.

Stay on Track: Keep a List of Tasks

To review where we are, we have discussed the steps about identifying the target market, the referral market(s), the industry associations,

The Woman Lawyer's Rainmaking Game

and the publications. All that is left to develop are the tasks to keep you focused. Think of clearly defined next steps to be completed over a year's window of time. Find a system that works for you, whether it is a handwritten list on a legal pad, putting reminders on your calendar, or using the tasks function in Outlook. For most people, relying on memory doesn't work, so it is important to keep a written list of your tasks and hold to the schedule.

Below is a sample task list and a blank task list. Fill it out and stick to it. Work with a coach or ask a mentor, assistant, or friend to help you stay accountable to yourself. It is much like exercising or anything else to which you commit. It is not easy, but before you know it, practicing good rainmaking activities becomes part of your daily routine.

You will probably want to return to this task list to add more items as you read through the book. We have filled one out as an example. Take some time and as you read through the book; fill out the blank one for your own goals to stay focused. Make an appointment with yourself. Write a reminder in your calendar to update your task list at least quarterly. Even focusing on these tasks once in a while is better than not at all.

Remember, the more calls you make, the more tasks you accomplish, the more clients you will develop.

The Sales Process: Pre-Approach

30-day tasks	3-month tasks	6-month tasks	12-month tasks
Develop IMAP*	Continue to schedule meetings with contacts	Continue to call your contacts and schedule face-to-face meetings with them on your way in or out of the office for the day.	Revisit your IMAPsm and make sure you develop it for the next twelve months. If applicable, review it with the managing partner or department chair
Call Referral Sources to schedule meetings. Schedule at least one meeting each week	Meet with two colleagues from business and discuss sales goals		
Clean out existing database/rolodex and identify contacts with whom to connect and begin to call them	Begin to form a networking group to meet quarterly to exchange sales leads and information	Make follow up calls to the association program chairs to keep in touch and remind them you are interested in speaking	Identify college and law school alum whom you will begin to contact over the next three months. Keep them apprised of your practice plans.
Join two associations and begin to calendar meeting dates-attend the meetings!	Phone the editors of the various publications identified and ask about article opportunities	Begin to develop your call log (see sample call log which follows)	
		Begin to develop your sales forecast (see sample forecast) This will help set priorities and focus	Schedule two more follow-up meetings with the marketing department.
Call clients and ask for information about the publications they read.	Phone the association directors and learn about how they select speakers for upcoming meetings. Let them know you are interested. Offer suggestions on topics.		Prepare an article and contact the editors of business publications to have it placed. Keep it to 1500 words.
Subscribe to two industry publications		Create a seminar on a current topic and invite referral sources to co-present and invite their clients. Plan on following up with each attendee.	Update the sales forecast. (See sample in Chapter 3)

*IMAP is a service mark of CKO

The Woman Lawyer's Rainmaking Game

Working Tool: Sample Individual Sales and Marketing Task List

Determine Your Investment: What Is Building a Successful Practice Worth to You and How Many Minutes/Hours Will You Invest Monthly Into Your Rainmaking Development Account?

Managing time with incredible efficiency is required to build a strong client base. Managing time goes hand in hand with being organized. When we ask rainmakers about the obstacles they face to developing new business, we hear "time" over and over again. Meaning, with most firms pushing to have their lawyers billing 1,500 to 2,000 hours a year, time for activities other than client work and billing is sparse. It will be important for you to find time each day to earmark for building your practice. For some, it's first thing in the morning. For others, it's with a headset and cell phone during commuting time. Whatever works for you, find the time and keep it as your sacred time for building your client base and selling your services. Consider it time you are investing in you.

Given that we are all swamped with projects these days, building a practice will require focus and energy that may take extra time or may take away from something else. In any event, determining how much time to devote to building a practice is an individual decision.

Opportunities will find interesting ways of presenting themselves to you, and now that you are becoming sales focused, you will see them jump out at you. For example, a woman litigation partner from a large Chicago-based firm attended her child's day care center potluck dinner one Saturday. While there, she met one of the dads who just happened to be the general counsel of a significant corporation. (Who else but working parents leave their children in day care centers?) They struck up a conversation and kept in touch. Coincidentally it was not long thereafter that he sent her a large piece of litigation business that ended up in over a million dollars in fees. Clearly, this type of opportunity does not occur frequently, but again, by being aware, the partner was open to the possibility.

This scenario highlights a few things. First, you never know where you will meet the next prospect. Always carry business cards and be aware of potential opportunities for meeting decision-makers.

The Sales Process: Pre-Approach

Second, follow-up is key and we discuss this elsewhere in the book. Once you have made a contact, keep in touch until they become a referral source for new business or contacts or, better yet, a client! Selling skills are required for continued, long-term client development; having a sales mindset keeps you on top of opportunities.

As Anne Marie Whittemore from Davis, Wright & Tremaine reminds us, "As in much of life, timing and luck are major factors and sometimes you have to pursue unexpected opportunities—be flexible." Begin by building marketing moments into your schedule. For example, try to make at least one call a day and schedule one breakfast or lunch a week. There will be some weeks even the most sales-oriented lawyer won't be able to achieve anything outside of client work; but, if your goal is there to achieve simple activities such as one call and one lunch, you will begin to make an investment in your future, one step at a time, and it will pay off!

Bingham McCutchen's Tara Higgins has figured out a way to make this work, "I focus on people I genuinely like and want to spend time with. I often go out to lunch and dinner with clients and often do things with them and their families. For example, I will take my family and their family to the circus." In short, sometimes finding the time to develop your practice means marrying personal and professional activities. Women often find this easier to do than men, given that they build relationships with their contacts and clients, based on a number of common interests outside of just business interests. Determining whom to connect and stay in touch with begins to pave the way for the rest of the sales journey.

Before turning the page to read the next stage of the process, take the time to review or create your bio, your practice description, and to build your marketing plan and task list. Go through your contact management system and update your contacts by deleting outdated information and keeping the names as well as updating the contact information of people with whom you'll want to connect. Remember to include former, inactive clients. These individuals will be critical to your business development initiatives. They are already contacts

The Woman Lawyer's Rainmaking Game

of yours and assume you are still interested in their business—get in touch with them first before your competition does.

The next step of the process is approaching the market—meeting contacts and clients.

CHAPTER 3

The Sales Process: Approach

Highlights
- The Importance of Attitude
- Investing Time Wisely
- Determine Ways to Meet Potential Clients
- Leveraging Firm Seminars and Association Memberships
- The Telephone Is a Great Selling Tool. Cold Calling Is Not for Everyone, but it Might Work for You
- Making the Most of Trade Shows and Other Approach Opportunities
- Seminars and Sponsored Trade Events Are Not Just for Strutting Your Stuff!
- Brochures and Handouts Are Strong Sales Tools if Used Correctly
- How and When to Use Sales Tools So They Work for You
- Building Business Is About Building Relationships
- Client Development: Approach Opportunity Tips Sheet: Trade Shows
- Beginning to Forecast Your Potential "Wins"
- Working Tool: Client Development Monthly Forecast
- Expert Perspective: The Art of Networking
- The Importance of Goal Setting When Networking
- How You Can Create a Professional Presence in the Eyes of Others

The Woman Lawyer's Rainmaking Game

- When to Arrive and the Hour to Leave to Give Yourself "Presence"
- Skills That Make Others Feel Good
- Networking Is Also Listening
- Ways to Empower People
- How to Make Networking Work for You
- How to Network Without Leaving Your Office
- Networking Is a Long-Term Process
- Working Tool: Approach Tip Sheet: The Art of Mixing and Mingling
- How to Establish Instant Rapport with Others
- How to Politely Get Rid of a Bore
- The Four Key Ways to Feeling Comfortable in a Room Full of Strangers
- Phrases to Use When Interacting with Someone You Have Just Met.
- How to Begin Enjoying Those Dreaded Business Functions
- Making the Most of Your Speaking Opportunities and Presentations
- Working Tool: Seminar Follow-Up Strategies Checklist

The answer to any problem "pre-exists." We need to ask the right question to reveal the answer.—Jonas Salk

The Importance of Attitude

A key to success, based on LSSO's bodies of research on women lawyers and their business development success, is attitude. It may not be everything, but it surely counts for a lot. We know this intuitively and the research supports what we thought to be true: Successful women leverage their successes. They also learn from their failures.

When respondents in LSSO's studies were asked how they responded when a business development effort was successful, the most successful women lawyers answered that they were supportive of them-

The Sales Process: Approach

selves. In other words, they acknowledged their successes and celebrated them.

Examples of supportive reflections
- Yes! Way to go!
- Woohoo!
- Exceptional team!
- Finally, I have a huge sense of relief.
- Yippee!!
- I'm on a roll.
- This is exciting; I want more.
- It's based on hard work – efforts have paid off.
- I am proud of the results and encouraged to keep trying.
- Well done.
- Another step on the way to creating the practice I want for myself.

When things did not go well, the distinguishing approach taken by the same group of successful women was to reflect and evaluate:

Examples of Evaluative Reflections
- I try to figure out what I did not do well - and how NOT to repeat it.
- Where did things go wrong …and what can I do better next time?
- "Why were we chosen?" (asked to new client)
- I should do more of [insert specific activity].
- I need to spend more time on this and narrow the focus, because I can actually do it when I try.
- I need to try harder or change my approach.
- What happened here? Review steps and try to evaluate…
- Talk to the client to figure out why we weren't chosen.

Supportive
- Change your strategy.
- Better luck next time.

The Woman Lawyer's Rainmaking Game

- Try again and be patient.
- It's not me, it's them.
- #^$@! Oh well next time, maybe…
- That was yesterday, now move forward.

Not surprisingly, the women who struggled had a negative attitude:

Negative
- I'm never to be able to make this happen. It is too hard.
- My head is hitting the glass ceiling…and it hurts.
- I'm not a good lawyer.

This book may help you with an attitude adjustment if you need it (and we hope it does). In contrast, just like a repeat trip to the chiropractor is needed, you must be on guard to ensure that you are supportive of yourself, that you learn from your successes and failures, and be aware that being negative about yourself really can hurt you.

LSSO's rainmaking studies on women lawyers concluded that:

Successful rainmakers tended to:
- Be committed to their firm
- Think and feel positively most of the time
- Be confident and empowered at work
- Possess high self-esteem
- Be Politically skilled

Getting the right attitude is more likely when women lawyers:
- Have access to mentorship experiences
- Engage in positive mentorship
- Meet their billable hours

The Sales Process: Approach

Copyright LSSO reprinted with permission:

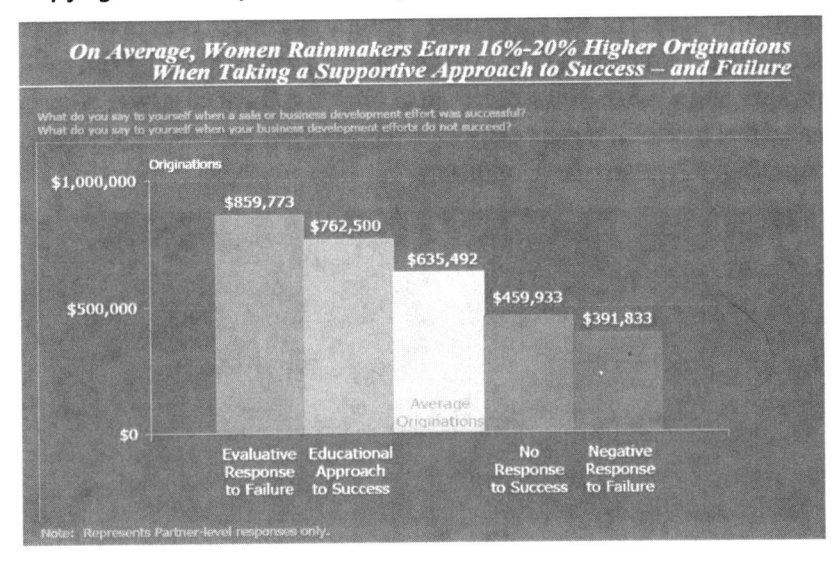

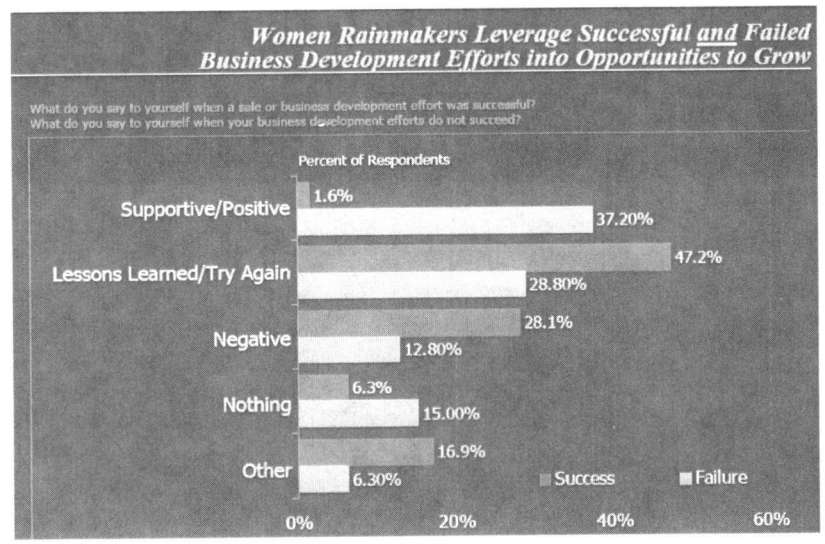

On Average, Women Rainmakers Earn 16%-20% Higher Originations When Taking a Supportive Approach to Success – and Failure

What do you say to yourself when a sale or business development effort was successful?
What do you say to yourself when your business development efforts do not succeed?

Category	Originations
Evaluative Response to Failure	$859,773
Educational Approach to Success	$762,500
Average Originations	$635,492
No Response to Success	$459,933
Negative Response to Failure	$391,833

Note: Represents Partner-level responses only.

Women Rainmakers Leverage Successful and Failed Business Development Efforts into Opportunities to Grow

What do you say to yourself when a sale or business development effort was successful?
What do you say to yourself when your business development efforts do not succeed?

Percent of Respondents

Category	Success	Failure
Supportive/Positive	1.6%	37.20%
Lessons Learned/Try Again	47.2%	28.80%
Negative	28.1%	12.80%
Nothing	6.3%	15.00%
Other	16.9%	6.30%

Investing Time Wisely

It's a simple equation: spending more time + doing the right things = more success.

In parallel, we know it is important to ask: how do you make the time? Likewise, what are the right things for you?

3-5

The Woman Lawyer's Rainmaking Game

LSSO's 2003 study indicated women rainmakers who devoted a range of 10-15+ hours per week to business development activities were more successful. At the same time, two-thirds of an audience of women rainmakers at an ABA Mid-Career Workshop for Women Lawyers indicated that lack of time and skill were their biggest personal obstacles to excelling at business development

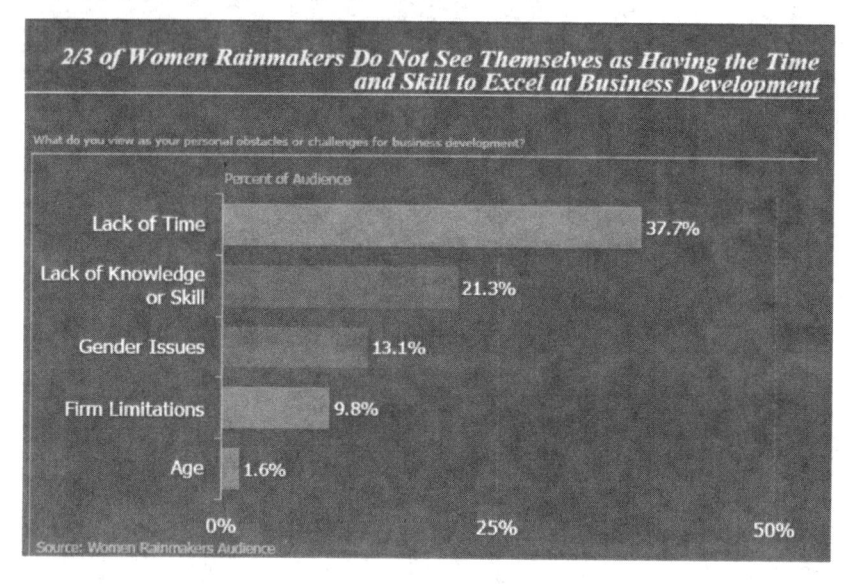

2/3 of Women Rainmakers Do Not See Themselves as Having the Time and Skill to Excel at Business Development

What do you view as your personal obstacles or challenges for business development?

Obstacle	Percent of Audience
Lack of Time	37.7%
Lack of Knowledge or Skill	21.3%
Gender Issues	13.1%
Firm Limitations	9.8%
Age	1.6%

Source: Women Rainmakers Audience

The Sales Process: Approach

We can't tell you how to add more to the 24 hours in a day that we all get, but we can give you a very good reason to figure out how to spend your time wisely. In LSSO's 2003 survey, we found significant correlations between the amount of time invested and revenue generation:

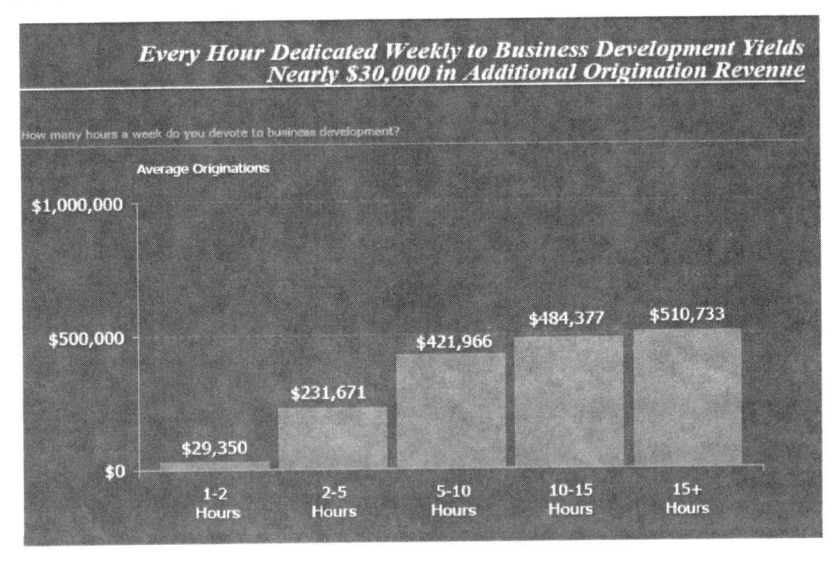

Every Hour Dedicated Weekly to Business Development Yields Nearly $30,000 in Additional Origination Revenue

How many hours a week do you devote to business development?

Average Originations:
- 1-2 Hours: $29,350
- 2-5 Hours: $231,671
- 5-10 Hours: $421,966
- 10-15 Hours: $484,377
- 15+ Hours: $510,733

We also looked at how this affects women lawyers at different career points. LSSO's women rainmakers realized an exponential increase in originations for each additional hour spent each week on business development activities. Every hour dedicated weekly to developing existing clients and attracting new business yields female attorneys nearly $30,000 in additional origination revenue, regardless of category (equity partner, non-equity partner, counsel, or senior associate).

Female partners develop more business, in part, because they simply spend more time selling. They invest an average of 9.5 hours in business development activities per week, while non-equity partners and counsel spend 8.4 hours and senior associates 6.1 hours, on average.

- It's about persistence: it could take six-eight communications/ touch points before a sale is made

This finding is particularly interesting in light of the revelation that nearly 70% of respondents report that they do not devote adequate time to business development activities.

The Woman Lawyer's Rainmaking Game

Every Hour Dedicated Weekly to Business Development Yields Nearly $30,000 in Additional Origination Revenue

How many hours a week do you devote to business development?

	Equity Partner	Non-Equity Partner or Counsel	Senior Associate
Average number of hours devoted weekly to business development	9.5	8.4	6.1
Average originations	$635,492	$330,275	$125,276

By 2008, survey results show that women lawyers should spend at least eight hours per week engaged in various business development activities to generate as much as $145k in annual revenue

Every additional hour spent developing business = over $56k (compared to $30k in the first study)

Spend the right amount of time

- These hours could be any types of activity you choose

Which Activities Produce the Best Results?

	Activity Used	Most Effective Activity
▸ Associations/Legal	87%*	39%
▸ Seminars/Events	70%	10%
▸ Networking	64%	43%*
▸ Associations/business	56%	23%
▸ Speaking	51%	21%
▸ Leadership positions	48%	23%

*Highest response percentage

© Legal Sales and Service Organization

LSSO
Legal Sales and Service Organization
Women Lawyers Study 2008

3-8

The Sales Process: Approach

Focus
What Successful Female Rainmakers Do

The activities they use	The activities that work
• 31% join legal associations • 25.1% attend social events • 22.3% network • 20.1% join business associations • 17.9% participate in speaking engagements *Note: most of these are networking activities...*	• 15.1% say networking works • 14% report that legal associations work • 8.4% indicate that leadership positions are useful • 7.8% believe that business associations and speaking engagements are useful practices • 6.7% report that client referrals are effective rainmaking tools

Determine Ways to Meet Potential Clients

"Approach" in the sales process means meeting clients, prospective clients, and new contacts. Clients and prospective clients are also known in sales as the target market. There are indirect and direct ways to approach potential clients. Indirect ways include advertising, direct mail, email, sponsorships, speaking engagements, public relations, and telephone calls. Direct ways of meeting the market include seminars and in-person meetings.

Advertising, direct mail, email communications, event sponsorships, and public relations are methods of approaching the market that are indirect and grouped under a term called marketing communications. Marketing communications is a specialty area within general marketing. There are many good books and on-line tools about effective marketing communications (also often referred to as public relations) and I will not attempt to provide detailed awareness about the subject. Instead, I will focus on the most direct ways to reach a market, which include direct sales and in-person meetings. That said, remember to put together a savvy marketing plan using sound marketing communications methods that support the direct sales efforts. All combined, these approaches to the market support one another and build continuous market awareness. If you are in a firm that has a marketing department, give them a call and make an appointment to obtain some assistance for building your practice. The staff will be more than happy to assist.

Some professionals are limited by other ethics rules as to how they may approach prospective clients and customers. With respect to those limitations, this book leaves the ethics up to the individuals as to how to deal with them.

The objective of the Approach Stage of selling is to meet new contacts who will either become referral sources, colleagues with whom to network, or prospective clients. The overall objective once you have met a prospect is to continue the sales process and get to the next step. The Approach Stage of the sales process is key in that either you "connect" with someone or you do not. Use every opportunity for meeting someone to learn more about him or her or his or her business. Rather than meet someone and begin to discuss the firm or your practice area, it is imperative to understand that meeting face to face is the first opportunity to develop the relationship. Good selling means letting the prospective client speak 80 percent of the time. Remember to make the most of each approach opportunity. For example, use the seminar at which a speech is given to follow up with new contacts and to renew old acquaintances. Let us look at the most common direct opportunities that take place for meeting people.

Leveraging Firm Seminars and Association Memberships
Most firms produce seminars on a regular basis. The real objective of a seminar is to meet new prospects or to provide opportunities to inform clients about new practice areas or issues in the law. These are often ideal opportunities for creating additional business from existing clients.

Attend firm seminars. Many firms run seminars and yet the only lawyers who attend are those who are speaking or are from the practice area represented by the panel. By attending firm seminars (or at least the breakfast or lunch or networking portion) you have a great opportunity to meet existing clients and to develop cross-selling opportunities.

Take it upon yourself to be aware of all the firm-run programs and try to attend as many seminars as your schedule permits. The best time

The Sales Process: Approach

to attend is during the networking portion either prior to the program or immediately after the program. By attending some of the programs, you will have an opportunity to educate yourself about the practice of others. Knowing this information will allow you to potentially sell a broader range of your firm's services to prospects.

Debbie Horwitz, a senior litigation partner at Boston-based Goulston & Storrs, agrees that seminars are a key way in which to get prospects in the door and network on your turf: "One of the most successful (and comfortable) ways I've found to approach sales in the law firm context is actively planning and attending the events our women attorneys hold annually for our women clients, prospects, and contacts. We use the occasions to facilitate our women clients networking with each other and giving them opportunities to expand their businesses— all under the umbrella of our firm. These types of events play to the strengths of women in building relationships for others and ourselves and create an enormous amount of goodwill toward the firm and its women. They also help increase awareness internally of the business development skills and efforts of our women lawyers."

Other rainmakers, like Davis Wright's Kelli Sager, use association membership and participation as a way of building contacts. "I participate in a number of different committees, including the Forum on Communications Law of the ABA, Center for State Courts lawyers committee, I am a delegate to the 9th Circuit Court of Appeals conference from the Central District and on the Advisory Boards for the Southwestern University Law School Entertainment Law Center, among others. I couple the committee and board activities with speaking and article writing. I do a great deal of speaking at conferences around the country, where clients and prospective clients will be in attendance and write or co-write articles on media law topics."

Bowman and Brooke's Sandy Ezell add this advice: "I seek out people who I would like to know, because they are fascinating, because they are similar or because they are different. I reach out with confidence and I accept a lack of interest in me as a natural, expected cost of being willing to reach out. Once I make a connection, I like to add depth. I really like to know people and I like them to know me. I believe it is much easier to do business with someone who you have had dinner with. I think that sharing stories about your children is a great way to build the bonds that will take you through the business crises we all face. I look forward to making business and personal relationships interrelated to make both more rich and more interesting and more productive. And, as it turns out, I am a huge sports fan. This has allowed me to take the skill of relationship building and bring it into my business world. At the end of the day, I think if you are authentic and seek connection, you will meet the people you need to know. Once you do that, then you have to be diligent in keeping in touch and staying in front of mind with the people you have met. There are various methods to this, but organization and methodology (other women skills) are key."

Once you've either run a seminar or attended one, do not let that be the "final destination" of the sales journey. Instead, leverage the seminar and view it as a starting point from which to follow up with attendees. Seminars are the beginning of the sales process, not the end of another process. A seminar is the best way to identify qualified prospects—they attend because the topic is of interest to them. Many lawyers drop the ball here. Instead, meet with the panel or group of lawyers who will present the program and determine how a follow-up should be conducted. Again, if the firm has a marketing team, ask some of the people on the marketing or business development team to assist. They will be happy to work with you to identify ways to follow up and even forecast potential revenue. Just to show how aggressive selling has become, many individuals create prospect lists and review their prospect logs monthly to determine next steps toward closing new business. This is key to running a seminar. Otherwise, it can be a colossal waste of time just to show you know the topic. Follow up!

The Telephone Is a Great Selling Tool. Cold Calling Is Not for Everyone, but it Might Work for You

One of the two most direct and effective approaches by phone is cold calling. Although not widely used by most legal practitioners, cold calling is effective, direct, and provides immediate feedback. Cold calling takes skill and sales confidence to achieve successful results. When time is a key factor, cold calling provides the most effective means of approaching the market—it can be done anywhere. Remember, every-

The Sales Process: Approach

one is key in the relationship. The in-house counsel's secretary is just as important as the in-house counsel. Treat everyone as a client and you will continue to have success.

Here is a typical scenario. Let us say the general counsel of ABC Manufacturing, Steven Solkoff, recently appeared in a legal publication. ABC is on the prospect list as a company in the target market you identified. A cold call might initially produce one of the two following scenarios: One, his secretary will answer the phone or; two, you will get voicemail. If you get voicemail, you might leave the following message: "Hi Steven [always use a person's full name unless he has indicated a shortened version is okay] this is Sandra Colburn from Kimball, Frederick & Cannon. I saw your interview in *American Lawyer* and wanted to say congratulations. I am dropping some information in the mail about our firm and will follow up in a week or so. If you would like to return my call, I may be reached at 884-439-0001."

That is all there is to it. Remember to send information that is both relevant and interesting to your target in the mail immediately or chances are he will not remember the call or he will not be impressed if there was no follow up.

If his secretary answers the phone, here's a scenario that may work for you:
"I'm Sandra Colburn from Kimball, Frederick & Cannon. I saw Steven's recent article in the law journal this morning and I wanted to congratulate him on the great exposure." Chances are, if he is available his secretary will try to get him to take the call. If not, leave a voicemail as above. Let's say he is available. The call could go something like this:
S. Solkoff: This is Steven Solkoff.
You: Steven, I'm Sandra Colburn from Kimball, Frederick & Cannon. I saw your interview/article/quote in the *National Law Journal* and wanted to say congratulations.
S. Solkoff: Thank you. Was there something specific I may help with?
You: Very briefly, I wanted to know if you would be available in the next few weeks to meet with me. I'd like to hear more about your busi-

The Woman Lawyer's Rainmaking Game

ness and how you run the law department and also take the opportunity to give you an overview of Kimball, Frederick & Cannon.

S. Solkoff: I'm very busy right now, is there something you could send me?

You: Certainly. To make sure I send you the appropriate information, for which areas of the company do you work with outside counsel?

S. Solkoff: Primarily tax and labor and employment.

You: I'd be happy to send along the appropriate information, along with some highlights from a few other areas. Why don't I follow up in about a month or so and perhaps we can meet at that time.

S. Solkoff: Very good. Thank you.

There are three important aspects to note about this conversation. First, stay focused on the goal, which is to meet with the decision-maker in person at some point and begin to develop the relationship; second, to lay the groundwork for identifying potential needs and thus, opportunities for selling legal services; and third, make absolutely sure you enter a date in your calendar a month away for the follow-up call. He will remember it and even if the answer is still no (sometimes it is no five or six times!) it is impressive you followed up. Most people do not. By doing so, you begin to differentiate yourself from the competition and it shows you are organized and responsive. It also sends the message that your firm gets things done in a timely manner.

For most practitioners, the second most effective way to initiate contact using a direct approach is what is known in corporate sales as warm calling. Warm calling means someone else who has contact with the recipient of the call has given you the referral to make the call. The approach is totally acceptable for lawyers and is often preferred. It is direct, within the ethical framework of most jurisdictions, and it saves time. Social networks have made this even easier. Here is an example that would work if you were calling the general counsel at a major company:

> Hi Steven, my name is Sandra Colburn. I am a partner with the firm of Kimball, Frederick & Cannon. I'm calling at the suggestion of Tim Winters from the accounting firm of TKM Worldwide. I also practice in the area of life sciences and would welcome the opportunity to meet with you within the next few

The Sales Process: Approach

weeks. What looks good on your schedule in terms of availability either the week of March 10 or March 17?

Notice a couple of things. Use a question that will not allow the recipient to answer yes or no, but rather, that encourages a response in your favor. Let the recipient know right up front that you were referred by a contact of his or hers. Get right to the point—no one has time to waste.

Be clear about your message once you have a decision-maker on the phone. Successful salespeople often find it helpful to write their message down—this may work for you as well.

Another effective approach to the market, and one we have seen work many times over now, is email. Simply introduce yourself via email and ask for an appointment. Its beauty is that you can write the email at any time and it is nonintrusive to your target. Besides that, it works and is highly effective in building relationships. Once a response has been given, send your bio and an overview of your firm. Remember not to send a lot of other information since that comes later in the presentation stage of selling. Keep it simple until you meet the potential client. If you do not receive a response send a follow-up email in about one week's time. Try to maintain confidence and do not speculate about whether or not the recipient cares to hear from you.

Making the Most of Trade Shows and Other Approach Opportunities

Most firms spend significant marketing dollars on sponsoring trade show events and industry programs. While these events are certainly worth the investment, often only the very sales savvy understand how to leverage them. The first rule is to bring more business cards than you believe you need. Exchange cards with everyone. If you meet someone who does not have a card, have him or her write his or her information on the back of one of yours.

One of the most difficult challenges for anyone in the sales game is to meet qualified prospects. A qualified prospect is an individual who is in a position to make a decision in his or her organization or an individual who is able to refer you to the decision-maker in his or her organization. Trade shows and industry programs are fabulous opportunities to meet potential qualified decision-makers or "prospects," as they are called in sales.

Let us first examine the trade show. Chances are your firm will have a booth at the show, or you will have a speaking opportunity, or both. Most attendees have an interest in the particular topics covered by the conference or they would not be there. Try to be at the booth as much as possible during large breaks in the programming and during other times when the exhibit hall is full. As people come up to you at the booth, introduce yourself, ask who they are, and what they do at their company. If it sounds like they are not a referral source or potential buyer, keep the conversation short and continue to meet other attendees/prospects.

You may however want to get this person's business card and add them to your database of contacts if they are in the targeted field of business. You never know where they might end up or whom they may know. It is amazing to see from where business actually generates. You will learn after a few years at the rainmaking game that business comes from many sources. Some people appreciate the fact that you keep in touch with them and will provide your name to their friends who may be in a position to obtain your services. Ask any rainmaker and you will hear that she has people she has tried to obtain business from for years to no avail and yet these very same people have referred her to others! Senior partner, Jane Potter, takes advantage of investments in trade shows or sponsored events: "In the context of firm activities, I think the most important issue is the personal contact. In the past, I have helped 'man' my former firm's booth at a conference, and I try to engage as many attendees as possible in conversation. Some of them may start out by not thinking they have anything to talk about in my area (patents) but then they get to talking, and often remember an issue they had, or a question that their current attorney or in-house counsel hadn't answered. If the person doesn't have a business card I offer them one of mine and get their contact information on the back. Basically, I don't let them leave without having a record of whom I spoke to, then I follow up as appropriate by sending information about the firm, or an article or website link they might be interested in. I attend many business-related breakfast, lunch, and dinner meetings, and when possible I take the opportunity to introduce the speakers and say a few words about the firm. On a more personal level, I try to become friends with in-house counsel at local companies, or at least arrange non-work activities with them, such as hiking."

Kirkpatrick & Lockhart's Janice Hartmann's approach to the market and, therefore, meeting potential clients is as follows: "In line with K&L's positioning campaign, I spend much of the time I have available for marketing and business development on events and venues that create visibility in the client community, not with other outside lawyers. I have co-chaired national sponsored events and seminars with industry-leading general counsels, for a business audience, and have spoken to a high-level national general counsel group on developing issues of import. At the local level, I am a member of, and regularly attend meetings of, an organization consisting almost exclusively of in-house corporate counsel."

Seminars and Sponsored Trade Events Are Not Just for Strutting Your Stuff!
As I previously mentioned seminars also provide a great way to meet in-person contacts who may be strong referral sources or decision-makers. Aside from the seminars your firm creates, industry association groups run quite a few seminars each year. If you are a speaker, you have the unique opportunity of connecting with some strong referral sources and perhaps even a prospect who might be a speaker on the panel or in the program. Again, make sure you have business cards handy along with the marketing materials you've created and perhaps other firm-related information.

Remember why you are attending this program in the first place—to develop contacts for future business. With that goal in mind, it is a good idea to take advantage of the situation and try to meet at least three new contacts at the program. Let the individuals know that you would like to meet with them again and ask if it is okay for you to contact them for a meeting. People will be blunt if they are not interested. They may say, "I'm already working with a law firm." If that is the case, ask them which firm and make a note of it on their business card so you are aware of whom the competition's clients are. Otherwise, let the individual know that you will be adding them to your email or mailing lists to keep them informed about future firm seminars and about updates in the law related to their business.

Always assume that everyone wants to do business with you or with your firm. Keeping a positive attitude is critical to achieving sales success. If you believe you are the best or your firm is the best, then that energy will be conveyed to your contacts. It is difficult to argue with a positive attitude.

Brochures and Handouts Are Strong Sales Tools if Used Correctly
One thing that salespeople have learned is how to use their marketing materials as selling tools. Marketing materials are basically product descriptions. They are written representations about the services a firm offers. To make sure the tools will work for you as a practitioner, make sure the brochures or practice descriptions are documents people will want to read. Keep it simple: very little text and lots of pictures (but please, no clip art—this is not the cartoon or less sophisticated image you want to convey). No one reads all this stuff. Do you? Like a PowerPoint presentation, marketing materials should contain useful nuggets of information from which to speak or to initiate a prospect's interest.

Rather than attend a meeting and say such a statement, "Here's some of our firm propaganda," which is a phrase we've heard, why not think about how to use the materials as sales tools?

How and When to Use Sales Tools So They Work for You
Your firm's brochures and other written materials are marketing tools that are developed for one primary purpose—to support lawyer selling. Taken a step further, these materials provide an additional way for you to connect with the prospect. Think of it this way: you have a meeting with an important client or prospect for new business. Determine the purpose of that particular meeting. Is it to initiate contact? Is it to begin to develop a relationship for expanding existing or obtaining new business? The meeting is the opportunity to ask a lot of questions and listen to the answers. The marketing materials are the perfect sales tools to use for a follow-up *after* the in-person meeting or telephone call.

The Sales Process: Approach

After leaving the meeting, it is important to send a quick note off saying you enjoyed the time they spent with you and that you *appreciated* their taking the time (in sales believe it or not, it is not generally appropriate to thank them for their time because this subordinates you). The marketing materials provide a focused follow-up to your meeting.

When using marketing materials, remember to put a sticky note, paperclip or otherwise mark the page on which you want specific attention focused. It is doubtful that anyone today has the time to read an entire marketing piece and especially an entire firm brochure. So, make it easy and show that you listened by highlighting specific information you know will be of interest to them. People appreciate it. Marketing materials are sales support and sales closing tools. The less you send or hand over at this stage of the process just as you are beginning the relationship the better. People just do not have the time to read endless pieces of marketing information you know will be of interest to them. It can also make you appear arrogant - that you presume to know what is important to a prospect before you have confirmed her needs. Too much information slows the sales process down—the prospect may feel obligated to read it all and this stalls the momentum. "I did not have a chance to go through all the material you sent to me," are the last words you want to hear. So keep it simple and focused.

Building Business Is About Building Relationships

Baker & McKenzie's Maura Ann McBreen focuses her initial emphasis on building strong relationships. "Personal relationships are vital to establishing trust and credibility among professionals. Clients are seeking not only superior legal skills but also a sense of character and trust. I find that one-on-one activities are superior to other more remote marketing activities like writing and giving speeches. Accordingly, I look for networking opportunities both internal and external to the firm that can help me make business contacts. I am at present on the boards and actively involved in several high-profile charitable and philanthropic organizations. I am also actively involved in business associations (e.g., The Economic Club of Chicago, The Chicago Council on Foreign Relations) whose members are culled from senior management of Fortune 500 companies."

The Woman Lawyer's Rainmaking Game

Susan Paish, managing partner of Canada's Fasken Martineau, offers some sage advice on building relationships: "This may sound trite and it is not meant to, but 'marketing' for lawyers (quite different from marketing for law firms), is, in my view all about building relationships. There is no one right method for a lawyer to market, other than that whatever you do must feel right and comfortable. Clients are humans and can easily tell when something is forced or not sincere: if you don't like hockey games: don't go. If you like the opera and your client does, then do that."

Paish adds, "I have always believed that building a relationship and a friendship with a prospective client that is founded on credibility is the best source of marketing. Personally, I first built the credibility side by relentlessly pursuing speaking and writing opportunities. I made it a goal about ten years ago to engage in at least three speaking or writing opportunities each month. I constantly volunteered for articles (the easiest place to get accepted as few people volunteer for these projects) and then after one or two opportunities to speak came along, I made sure that I was over-prepared for the presentation, tried to make the presentation entertaining and practical as well as informative. I never, ever, ever read a paper (clients are pretty good at reading!!). Rather I try to turn legalese and potentially boring verbiage into practical tips, i.e., 'if you do nothing else after this presentation...do these three things regarding' (whatever the topic is that I am speaking about). In addition to the speaking and writing I volunteered on committees, every one that I could get on and once there, rolled up my sleeves and volunteered for the drudge jobs. Through the committees (charitable, professional, conference organizing etc. etc.), I made friends and built credibility (I think) as someone who will get a job done, no matter what that job may be. Finally, I look for things that are meaningful for the client, i.e., if I know someone has kids and there is a good kids' show in town, I have suggested that we go out as families, if someone likes hockey as much as I do, I invite them, if they don't then I don't put them in the unpleasant spot of receiving an invitation that they wished they never got."

Dianne Kempe, past president of the International Bar Association and former managing partner of Bermuda's Appleby, Spurling &

The Sales Process: Approach

Kempe, leverages her referral source contacts. "Becoming the darling of the big four accounting firms is fundamental to my success. I act for liquidators, not for creditors. By focusing, I analyzed the market and found areas where there was opportunity to make my own mark." Kempe also takes advantage of major speaking opportunities. "If you take the Marketing Partner Forum, sponsored by Glasser LegalWorks as an example, after major plenary sessions, I always find opportunity to meet people. If you want to, as someone new, offer yourself to seminar organizers, you can show your interest. I develop a lot of business simply by being in conversation at this and other types of events. You need to be prepared to be an extrovert and understand how to talk about your product when the opportunity arises."

Whether you attend firm-sponsored seminars or trade shows, speak at seminars, on panels at firm seminars or industry events, these are ways to begin to meet prospective clients and existing clients. When you attend an event, keep in mind why you are there. In some cases it is to showcase your skills and provide expertise, but a close second to these reasons is to meet new clients and prospects. So a good rule is to attend these events with the goal of meeting at least three new people with whom you have something in common and with whom you will follow up. *Meeting this goal will be critical to the future success of your sales efforts.*

Last, be organized and give your secretary (or add them in yourself) the cards you have obtained and have him or her enter them into your contacts file immediately. Note on the cards where you met the person; it's easy to forget if you don't do it right away. The following trade show tips sheet offers some more ideas.

Client Development: Approach Opportunity Tips Sheet: Trade Shows

Name Badges: Always wear on your right—when you shake someone's hand, they may then easily glance at your nametag.
Business Cards: Have them readily available. Bring more than you think you might require. If a prospective client stops by the booth and does not have a card, use one of yours to write his information down

and keep it with your other prospective client cards collected at the show.

Sales Tips: Show interest in the visitors to your booth. Ask questions that will show your interest and that will generate conversation that may provide you with an opportunity to learn about their business. Stay in control of the questions (and therefore the sales process), speak 20 percent of the time, and facilitate the conversation so the prospective client talks 80 percent of the time. Use the firm's presentations or PowerPoints as guides for communicating with prospects.

As Karen Green, partner in the Litigation Department and a rainmaker from Wilmer Cutler Pickering Hale and Dorr would say, "Have your elevator pitch prepared," that is to say, have something simple to comment about on your firm and then turn the conversation back to the prospect.

Trade shows generally are industry specific. Know who your clients are—they may stop by the booth—and the type of work your firm has done for them.

When using brochures and other sales materials, paper clip the specific information you want the prospect to pay attention to. People collect lots of information at these shows and it's best to draw attention to your firm's materials somehow.

Make sure you get a business card from the prospect, make notes on the back—it's easy to forget details when you speak with a lot of people—to remind you about your conversation.

When the conversation is coming to an end, ask if you may continue to stay in touch through mailings, bulletins, and other firm communication that may be of interest to them.

Eat meals away from your firm's booth—you are not there to have lunch. You are there to greet visitors to the booth who are interested in your/the firm's services. Visitors to your trade show booth or space will find lunch and lunch waste unattractive and uninviting. Your goal is to attract people to meet you and discuss their business and legal issues.

Be alert about who is approaching the booth. Try not to spend too much time engrossed in conversation with the colleagues from your firm, thus creating a potentially uninviting atmosphere at your booth.

Beginning to Forecast Your Potential "Wins"

Developing a monthly forecast based on whom you have met, their needs, and the potential for obtaining business from them can be extremely useful. Anytime there is a request for materials about the firm, the request should generate an entry on the monthly forecast. Why? Because with limited time for selling, most lawyers will find focusing their efforts on those clients and prospects that have the most promise will ultimately pan out to be the most successful time.

Forecasting is simple. Here is a sample of the kind of information you should be tracking. This information can be handwritten on sheets like this and then given to your secretary to input into a spreadsheet. Alternatively, preferably, you create your own spreadsheet for tracking purposes. Whichever way is the most productive for you to use, you will find that keeping a forecast will keep you on track.

Working Tool: Client Development Monthly Forecast

Sales/business development forecasting–know where to spend your time by planning with potential clients.

Client/ Prospect	Practice Group/ Type of Service	Attorneys/ Bus Dev Contact	Ofc.	Anticipated Amount	Next Steps / Person responsible/ Date
Counter Applied Sciences	Opportunity to expand one division's work to all of Counter's small molecule work	Steve Argule	SF	$500K - $2.5M annually	Meet with Counter's corporate counsel. Todd to set up date in early February
Moose Global Enterprises	IPO work / Corporate	Brenda Jones; Ellen Nolan	NY	$300,000	Meet with General Counsel. Demonstrate Patent Portfolio CD. Brenda to follow up in May after GC returns from vacation
Steven Braskell	private client	Jennifer Strong	DV	$15,000	Follow up initial meeting to determine if Jennifer has spoken with her husband re scheduling meeting

The Sales Process: Approach

Here is another forecasting tool that is simplified. Use whichever version you think you will fill out and follow monthly.

WORKING TOOL

CLIENT DEVELOPMENT MONTHLY FORECAST

PROSPECTIVE CLIENT	POTENTIAL SERVICE	REFERRAL SOURCE	PROJECTED CLOSE DATE	PROJECTED LEGAL FEES	TO DO

Expert Perspective: The Art of Networking

Networking and meeting people is not easy. Noted author and lecturer on this topic, Ann Marie Sabath (see her website at www.ateaseinc.com), has generously contributed the following information and tips to help you become a pro.

> There is an art to networking. People who want to stay connected to others make a point of attending certain gatherings, interacting with others, and making people feel good about themselves. Networking is a give and a take process. It includes doing favors for others, acknowledging them for their achievements, and introducing them to those who can be of assistance to them. In return, these people are only a phone call away for you when you need assistance. Whether you already are a master networker or would like to learn how to become one, this tip sheet will be of benefit to you.
>
> ### *This Art of Networking Tip Sheet*
> - Emphasizes the Importance of Goal Setting When Networking
> - Explains How You Can Create a Professional Presence in the Eyes of Others
> - Tells the Time to Arrive and the Hour to Leave to Give Yourself "Presence"
> - Shares the People Skills that Are Crucial for Making Others Feel Good About Themselves
> - Describes How Networking Is also a Listening Activity
> - Gives Ways to Make Networking Work for You!
> - Tells How to Network Without Even Leaving Your Office
> - Emphasizes that Networking Is a Long-Term Process
>
> ### The Importance of Goal Setting When Networking
> Just as it is important to plan your work and then work your plan, it is equally important to plan your networking and then determine if your net is working. The best way to do this is to make a schedule of networking activities and your purpose for attending those particular gatherings.

Before you attend these get-togethers, define your stated purpose for attending them (i.e., my goal is to meet people who typically may not schedule time to meet with me in an office setting). After leaving these networking functions, evaluate the goals that you accomplished (i.e., I met the human resource director of XYZ company).

How You Can Create a Professional Presence in the Eyes of Others

After you have scheduled your activities for networking and the purposes for attending those gatherings, plan a strategy for being seen in the best possible way. For instance, if the organization you represent has a business casual policy and the majority of people you are going to meet will be dressed in a business professional mode, then follow suit. No matter what your position, you should dress for the position you want rather than for the one you have. Whatever you do, never dress so that you have to justify your appearance (i.e., "Excuse the way I look. My company encourages business casual dress on Fridays").

Be prepared. Always take plenty of business cards. Only offer a card to those individuals who appear to want one. If you receive a person's business card, be sure to make a point of looking at it for a moment and then commenting on the logo, the person's title, etc.

Be more interested in what others tell you than in what you have to say. You can show others that you are a good conversationalist by listening more than talking and then commenting on what you are told rather than associating what you heard with something that has happened to you.

Let people know that they left an impression with you. Following the networking function, take a few minutes to jot down one thing that you learned about the individuals you met.

Within 48 hours, write a note to each individual with whom you spoke. Your note should include that you enjoyed meeting them. It also should mention something you learned about the person during the conversation.

When to Arrive and the Hour to Leave to Give Yourself "Presence"

Unless you are hosting a networking gathering, it is perfectly acceptable to arrive within 15 to 20 minutes from the time it begins. By doing so, you will be able to mix and mingle immediately with individuals who arrived before you. You also will be able to introduce those people who arrive after you.

Just as when you arrived, the appropriate time to depart is 15 to 20 minutes before the gathering is scheduled to end. By making a point of leaving around this time, the individuals present will see that you manage your time rather than waste it by lingering.

Skills That Make Others Feel Good

Compliment, compliment, compliment! When you meet someone, listen intently to the person. Find a reason to compliment another based on what you may have read about the person, his or her organization, etc. If you are meeting someone for the first time and are unfamiliar with the person, base your comments on what you are learning at that moment. For instance, if you learn that someone has been with a company for several years, compliment the person on his or her longevity with that organization.

Networking Is Also Listening

Did you know that more than three quarters of your networking should be through listening? By being a good listener, you will be demonstrating your interest in others. You can show you are listening by focusing on what is being said and by maintaining eye contact with the person speaking. You also can demonstrate you are listening by jotting down what you heard and by paraphrasing what was said to you.

Ways to Empower People

Empowerment is defined as "giving power or authority to another." When you are in a networking situation, you can empower others by mentioning their achievements to others. For example, acknowledging recent press, a project with which the person has been involved, etc., can open a door for the person you are empowering to speak about himself or herself to another contact you are introducing him or her to. By empowering others, the door will open for you. People always want to help people who have helped them.

How to Make Networking Work for You

Networking is a two-way street. Not only should you be good to others by opening doors for them, be sure to be good to yourself. One way to do this is by making known the goals that you want to achieve. For instance, when jotting someone a note, let the person know of your interest in volunteering to write an article for his or her professional organization's newsletter. Mention to another that you have time to volunteer on a particular committee. Recognize the long-term goal that you want to achieve by accomplishing these short-term goals.

How to Network Without Leaving Your Office

Believe it or not, there are ways to network without leaving your office. You can do this by scanning the local, regional, and national newspapers and magazines. Anytime you see an article that pertains to someone you know, clip it, attach a note, and send it. By doing this, you will be letting the receiver know that he or she is on your mind. You also will remain on the mind of that person. In many ways, this interchange is as powerful as having an actual meeting with the person. It is also more time efficient.

Recognize that you do not even have to know a person to acknowledge an article that you read about him or her. Sometimes this small gesture can act as the beginning of a long-term business relationship. How? More often than not the person receiving your note will respond. This sets the stage for continuing to communicate with the person in the future.

Networking Is a Long-Term Process

Just as it takes seeds time to sprout, it also can take time for networking to reap benefits for you. Recognize that the more you network and the more consistently you follow up with notes, the more likely it will be that you will see results. When you least expect it, "Your net will be working!"

Working Tool: Approach Tip Sheet: The Art of Mixing and Mingling

You have just been promoted to a more senior position or partner in the firm. Alternatively, you have decided to go out on your own. As you are learning of your responsibilities, you find that your new role in your career will require you to attend several business receptions and social gatherings that will require you to mix and mingle. Just realizing this makes your palms sweat! Your fear may be that instead of being in control, you may LOSE control in these situations. Here are three key ways for overcoming mingle-phobia:

1. *Before going to a business/social gathering, create your itinerary.* In other words, go with a purpose. Think of individuals whom you would like to make a point of meeting. Decide what you would like to learn about them (i.e., their last golf outing, the vacation you heard they enjoyed from someone else, etc.). By attending this type of function with a purpose, you will enter a room full of strangers with an added touch of confidence.

2. *If you arrive at the get-together and find that you do not know anyone, be honest, be up front, and be the first to say "Hello."* For example, when approaching a group of people whose body language appears to be open to having others join them, say, "I don't know anyone here and wanted to introduce myself. My name is _____."

Most polished professionals who understand what it is like to enter a room filled with unfamiliar faces will welcome you into their group—at least for a few minutes.

The Sales Process: Approach

3. *If appetizers are available, it may also be a good time to enjoy them.* Take note of the time before going back into the field. Decide how long you will continue to "work the room" before giving yourself another break or perhaps even make your escape, I mean, departure. Unless you are part of the clean-up committee, do not be one of the last to leave. Wouldn't you rather have others be sorry to see you leave rather than sorry that you overextended your stay?—*Ann Marie Sabath*

How to Establish Instant Rapport with Others
When you are making "small talk," be sincerely interested in the questions you are asking others. Most people can spot a phony a mile away.

When a person has answered your question(s), paraphrase what you heard with terms like: "It appears that . . ." "It sounds like . . ." "I understand that . . ."

Finally, during this interaction, use the person's name with whom you are interacting a few times during the conversation. Using others' names appears to be the exception rather than the rule in business today.

How to Politely Get Rid of a Bore
It's all perspective. While certain people may be interesting to some, the same individuals may be perceived as nuisances to others. If you find yourself involved in a conversation with someone whom you consider less than interesting, good manners dictate that politeness prevail.

The key rule for ridding yourself of a bore is to excuse yourself after you have said something referring to the other person. Example: "Good luck with your upcoming project."

On the other hand, be sure that you are not perceived as the bore. When you see that the other person's attention is beginning to waver, it is probably time to move on.

The Four Key Ways to Feeling Comfortable in a Room Full of Strangers

Believe it or not, entering a room full of strangers is difficult for even the most outgoing person. The main difference between individuals entering a room with confidence and those walking into a function timidly is mastery of the situation. Here are the four key rules:

1. *Approach individuals who are standing alone.* In many instances, these people will be as pleased that you approached them as you may be to have someone to talk with.

2. *Treat everyone you meet as though he or she is the most important person there.* By being more sincerely INTERESTED in others, you will be perceived as more INTERESTING. The most painless way is to ask questions to elicit responses and put the person at ease.

3. *Listen more than you speak!* People will welcome your company if you are more interested in what they have to say than in what you have to share. The same individuals will be more attentive to what you have to say if they have asked you a question than if you offer the same information without being asked.

4. *Stay within an arm's length distance of individuals whom you have just met.* One way of making strangers feel comfortable being around you is by respecting their territory. That means maintaining an arm's length as you are conversing. If you get any closer, you may be perceived as invading the person's space.

Phrases to Use When Interacting with Someone You Have Just Met

Some call it first impressions. Others call it rapport building. When interacting with individuals whom you have just met, your initial comments will assist others in forming opinions about you.

When talking with others, position your questions by using interrogatives. For example, ask, "How are you enjoying this conference?" rather than "Is this your first time at this conference?" By asking open-ended questions rather than close-ended ones, the person you have just met will probably offer more information about himself or herself.

Another phrase that usually opens conversation is "How's business?" The benefit of using this phrase is that you do not need to know anything about a person's field to encourage conversation.

How to Begin Enjoying Those Dreaded Business Functions
Schedule a limited amount of time to attend certain business functions. Designate both an arrival and departure time. You may enjoy yourself more if you know you only have a limited amount of time to be there.

Realize that others may feel as inhibited as you do. By recognizing that, it may be easier to approach groups and to initiate conversation.

Make a point of learning one new thing about each person you meet (i.e., company affiliation, mutual acquaintance, etc.).

Last and certainly not least, have fun! The functions that you may dread going to the most can sometimes be the most enjoyable.

Once you have mastered the art of mixing and mingling, use these skills each time you are in a situation where networking is required. For example, speaking opportunities provide a great forum for testing your newly learned skills. Following are some tips that will help after the networking:

Making the Most of Your Speaking Opportunities and Presentations
Example Opportunity #1: Speaking before a group of investment bankers
- Obtain list of attendees

The Woman Lawyer's Rainmaking Game

- Write a follow-up letter to each
- Enter list of attendees into the firm's contact management system or your own database—make a note of where/when you met the individual
- Call attendees to schedule a follow-up meeting, breakfast/lunch—learn about their interests, needs, etc.
- Invite existing clients and prospective clients to attend all your seminars
- Send handout materials to clients and prospective clients who will not be able to attend
- Leverage the work product you prepared for the seminar by using handout materials prepared for the program as a basis for writing an article to submit to a publication
- Distribute seminar information to members of your firm. This will help educate others about what you/your firm offers for services

Example Opportunity #2: Conducting an in-house seminar for a client

- Distribute handout materials provided by the company
- Take the presentation "on the road" for other similar clients or prospects
- Send materials to in-house clients and prospects who cannot attend
- Use materials prepared for the program as a basis for articles to publish
- Solicit feedback about other future programs that may be of interest
- Obtain a list of attendees and continue to follow up with individuals so you may broaden your reach of contacts at the client site.

Note that anytime you invest precious time preparing for a seminar or speaking engagement, there will be ways to leverage at the time. Make it a point to take the bit of extra time to make the most of these opportunities, or if you have a marketing department at your firm, ask them to assist with this part of the process. Their professional insight will be of great value.

Working Tool: Seminar Follow-Up Strategies Checklist

- Obtain a list of all participants with names, titles, company, address, and phone numbers
- At a firm-sponsored seminar, ask participants to fill out an evaluation form before leaving the session to solicit feedback about the presentation, the speakers, to identify additional areas of interest for future seminars, and to solicit a one-on-one follow-up meeting to address the company's specific concerns and for referrals to others not in attendance who may need similar assistance.
- When hosting a seminar or attending a seminar given by another organization, exchange business cards but do not try to sell or close business. As with any face-to-face marketing opportunity, try to leave individuals with a good feeling about you and your firm and a reason to remember you—which may not necessarily be related to business (e.g., golf, sailing, tennis, travel, alma mater, community activities, etc.).
- Within a week or two of the seminar or presentation, send a brief personalized letter to each individual thanking him or her for attending and restating your expertise in a specific area of practice. (These can actually be prepared before the seminar.)
- Follow up the thank you letter with a phone call to qualify each participant and suggest a meeting if appropriate.
- Add all names to the firm and/or your personal database and develop a plan to keep in touch. Send something of a market interest from the firm at least every other month (e.g., an article reprint, a letter about a legal issue affecting their industry, or an invitation to another seminar).
- Develop a method of retaining information about each qualified prospect (e.g., memos to the file, index cards, databases, Rolodex™, etc.). Include critical information you have gathered about the decision-makers, in-house counsel, competition, and anticipated future legal needs.
- Consider introductions to other practice areas within the firm or make referrals to complementary organizations such as accountants, bankers, etc.

The Woman Lawyer's Rainmaking Game

The next step of the process is Qualify and Assess Needs. Here's where the real strategy begins to come into play in the sales game.

CHAPTER 4

The Sales Process: Qualify and Assess Needs

Highlights
- Determining Viability of Prospective Clients—How They Work with Outside Counsel
- Needs/Benefits Worksheet
- Stay In Control of the Next Step, It's Your Game to Win
- Sales Case Study 4–1: Qualify and Assess Needs
- Know Your Audience at All Times
- The 80/20 Rule of Listening and the Art of Asking Open-Ended Questions
- Sample Selling Questions to Ask Corporate Decision-Makers (in a Company Setting)
- Sample Selling Questions to Ask Individual Decision-Makers
- Sales Case Study 4–2 and 4–3: Qualify and Assess Needs
- Tips on Effective Listening for Building Relationships
- Understanding the People Part of the Sales Process
- Personalities Play a Key Role in Building Relationships
- Selected Personality Characteristics Chart
- Working Tool: Understanding Personalities
- Team Selling Can Be Successful—Make Sure You Are a Major Member of the Team
- Tips for Team Selling
- What You Learn Now Sets the Stage for Closing
- When You Are on the List of Preferred Outside Counsel

The Woman Lawyer's Rainmaking Game

A need... if satisfied, imparts a sensation of well being. —Abraham H. Maslow

Determining Viability of Prospective Clients— How They Work with Outside Counsel

Qualifying and assessing a prospective client's needs is the most important part of the sales process. If there's a mistake to be made with the sales process, it's at this stage. No matter how well you know the prospective client or existing client, when selling services, building relationships, or introducing new practice areas to existing clients, it's important to begin at this step of the sales process. For example, think of your top clients —do you know what their three-year goals are for their businesses? Or, as we inquired recently of a team of banking lawyers, "Do you know the bank's three-year acquisition strategy for expansion?" Most likely the answer is no. So before you begin to tell your clients and prospective clients what they should or should not be buying in terms of legal services from you or your firm, begin by asking them some of their goals and needs. The worst thing you can do is to walk into a meeting and begin talking about the firm and the practice, in other words, presenting, without first knowing what you say "fits" the buyer's needs.

Much research has been conducted about the buying behaviors of corporations when it comes to hiring outside counsel. One thing that comes up over and over again in the research is the fact that to get in the door of a client, it's assumed you are a good lawyer. However, retaining clients and expanding the work from existing clients is another story. Think about the value proposition your firm offers to the client. What's different about your firm or you when compared to your competition? Are you able to answer that question if asked? Clients often bemoan the fact that choosing legal counsel is difficult since most practitioners have an inability to differentiate themselves from their competition. Left to determine the compelling reasons why you should be selected, buyers of legal services often find the only way to differentiate among a sea of good lawyers is price. So, like you do with your client work, prepare for meetings with potential clients and be prepared to learn about their needs, their businesses, their personal goals before you tell them what you can do for them.

The Sales Process: Qualify and Assess Needs

> **Needs/Benefits Worksheet**
>
> The distinction between needs, features, and benefits are defined as follows:
>
> Need: An opportunity/problem not yet uncovered/solved
>
> Feature: A characteristic of your service
>
> Benefit: A service feature that satisfies the client need or solves a client problem. Here is an example of each to clarify a need from a feature and from a benefit:
>
> Example:
>
> *Need:* Current outside provider does not have an in-house person with employee benefits expertise.
>
> *Feature:* Your list of experience includes over twenty companies for which you provide employee benefits advice and legal counseling.
>
> *Benefit:* The client/prospect is able to present an entire employee benefits plan to his management team that meets the corporation's business goals. He therefore has solved a company problem and you have made him look good within his organization.

Stay In Control of the Next Step, It's Your Game to Win

As a reminder, selling new business can take time. Many lawyers know it is not unusual to meet someone who is a potential client only to find that the road to closing business may take one to five years. Two exceptions to this: referral sources who introduce you to their clients who have an immediate need (but the steps in the sales process must still be followed) and individuals whom you meet at the right time (the stars are aligned factor). Other than these infrequent opportunities, building the relationship takes time and continuous contact with your prospects.

A scenario to illustrate this point follows:

> **Sales Case Study 4-1: Qualify and Assess Needs**
>
> *Situation:* An accounting firm contact's client requires legal advice

The Woman Lawyer's Rainmaking Game

about the potential sale of her company. The accountant scheduled a lunch meeting for the client to meet with one of his contacts at a law firm.

Objective: The client's objective was to meet lawyers who have expertise with M&A transactions. The accountant was requested by the client to introduce her to three law firm contacts of his. After meeting with three people, she would then make a hiring decision.

Action: Avoid assuming you are the only lawyer to whom someone is speaking just because a good friend at an accounting firm has arranged a meeting. In this scenario, the lawyer was coached to ask specifically whom else the contact is meeting and about the timeframe in which she anticipates she will make her selection.

Begin with a brief introduction about yourself. Then, ask questions like: "Who else will you be meeting with?" "What criteria will you be using for making your decision?" "What's your timeframe for making this decision?" Other good examples of questions follow in this chapter. The client does not need to hear all about your expertise, but rather, how businesses like hers have worked with you to achieve their goals. The actual lawyering part of this is of no interest to her, nor will she necessarily understand the legal specifics.

Outcome: During the luncheon it was revealed that the CEO would be talking with three lawyers. She indicated that she was seeking a firm on which she could rely throughout the process of either selling her business or taking on additional partners with equity contributions. Her pet peeve was errors in documents. Her current law firm made too many mistakes and she was interested in a large firm with an excellent reputation. Price was not the key issue, experience and quality of work product was.

The lawyer was able to discuss how she specifically assisted companies like the CEO's. She offered three references of existing clients with whom she had assisted in similar dispositions of their businesses. (References will address the quality of your work product.)

The Expert: The other two lawyers with whom the CEO met made the mistake of thinking they were the only one to whom she was talking. They discussed their firm and their practice with little at-

The Sales Process: Qualify and Assess Needs

> tention to the detail about the buyer's needs and interests. In this lucky scenario, the first lawyer with whom the CEO met, won the business.

Another example that illustrates qualifying and assessing needs follows. It will be your job to ask questions and to listen carefully for opportunities to discuss the things you'd like to emphasize. It's easy to talk about you. It's much more difficult (as you begin to focus more on selling, you'll experience this) to actively listen. But only when you actively listen, will you realize great results. To actively listen does not mean you never get the chance to discuss your firm or services. It simply means to listen for opportunities and information that allows you to tie your information to what they are saying.

During a coaching session, a client said "I have an opportunity to meet the in-house counsel at a significant insurance company. They are not totally satisfied, according to one of my contacts at the company, with their current counsel for this type of work. I'm not going to tell them I know that, but rather, if in the future I may be of assistance, or if a conflict arises, please give us a call."

We are sure this situation sounds familiar to some of you. But this is precisely the wrong thing to do in this case. Here's a much stronger approach:

At the meeting, introduce yourself and anyone else from your firm. Make sure you review the agenda, which is: "To hear about your needs in the area of employee benefits; to discuss your goals as a group and what you seek from outside counsel assistance; the plans your company currently provides, and the type of relationship you seek to have with your outside counsel. We'd also like to discuss how we might assist you with your benefits programs at the company. In short, we'd welcome the opportunity to work with you."

This approach is honest, strong, and impressive. Try to make a strong impression, but do not subordinate yourself. The key is to remember that you are being watched for your strength. Subconsciously an assessment is occurring as to whether or not you and your team are the right lawyers for the prospect. Be strong, but not overbearing. Be aggressive, but not pushy. Strong people (many decision-makers) like other strong people!

Know Your Audience at All Times
When developing a relationship the first task is to make sure the person with whom you come into contact for your "pitch" (not really our preferred word – some clients/prospects do not want to catch!) is the decision-maker. Ask something like: "How are decisions with respect to legal services made in your organization?" Many perceived decision-makers delegate their authority to others. For example, a bank may have a large in-house department, but in its regional offices the lenders may hire local outside counsel without going through the in-house department. Or, in some organizations, a vice president of human resources may hire outside labor and employment counsel, bypassing the law department. For these reasons, it is important to find out how decisions are made. When a prospect comes directly to you, this is still considered the Approach Stage and the sales process is the same. You must learn about the prospective client's needs, who ultimately retains outside counsel, what their criteria is for choosing outside counsel, and so on.

Discuss with the prospect the fact that you are interested in hearing more about his business needs. Ask about his business; show your interest. It's surprising how people will talk if you let them! This bears repeating: *The golden rule of client development and selling is to listen 80 percent of the time and talk 20 percent of the time.* In order to do this, take charge of the questions. More information than can be imagined will be gleaned from good listening. How does this work? Let's take the cocktail party or business networking lunch or breakfast as examples.

Someone asks: "So what do you do?" Take control of the conversation. Let people know about how successful your business is. When making introductions, it's easy to say, "I run one of the most successful private equity practices on the East Coast." Or, "I have one of the most successful real estate practices in Ohio." Why this boasting? Because people like doing business with successful people. And, this type of response shows strength. It's okay to say good things about yourself, your

The Sales Process: Qualify and Assess Needs

practice, and your firm. Many women lawyers think this is bragging. We ask you, what's wrong with that!

The 80/20 Rule of Listening and the Art of Asking Open-Ended Questions

The objective of the Assess Needs stage is to LEARN about the prospective client's needs. Specifically, you want to control the conversation by *asking questions* versus talking. In other words, LISTEN 80 percent of the time and speak 20 percent of the time (really, this does bear repeating). Many lawyers have the most difficulty with this concept because they often feel they need to have the answers. Selling is about controlling the conversation and leading a prospect to closing business. If you are speaking, you are not in control—the prospective client is. Here's where the negotiation skills you have learned come into play in the sales world. You are in charge of the questions and the prospect is in charge of the answers. By staying in control of the process and the questions, you stay in control of the sale. How often do *you* stay and listen to someone who chats on and on? Not often we're sure.

So how does this work best? Think of some opening questions that will allow someone to talk. The questions you ask should facilitate a discussion that will allow you to seamlessly mention your practice, how you approach the legal issues involved, the firm's or practice group's experience in the field. Although this sounds fairly straight forward, very few people do this well. The ones who do this well are those who listen carefully and demonstrate their interest in the prospective client's attitude, opinions, and business.

These people go on to become the biggest rainmakers of the firm, the best salespeople in an organization.

In addition to these types of questions, you will also want to ask questions specific to any particular area of interest.

Sample Selling Questions to Ask Corporate Decision-Makers (in a Company Setting)

Here are some examples of good open-ended questions:
- When was the company founded?

- What do you see are the greatest challenges facing your business?
- Which business problems are you dealing with now?
- Who is the competition for your business?
- What are your goals for the next three years? How may we assist you in achieving those?
- How many firms is the company currently using? Will you be examining that in the near future?
- Have you been able to take advantage of the Internet for selling your company's products?
- What are your decision-making criteria for hiring outside counsel?
- Is there anyone else involved with the legal decisions at your company?
- What are your expectations or needs for electronically communicating with your outside counsel?
- How much is your current budget for outside counsel and for which services is most of it being spent?

Sample Selling Questions to Ask Individual Decision-Makers
- Who will be making the decision to hire an attorney?
- What specifically were you seeking in a lawyer to assist you with this issue?
- What criteria will you be using to make your decision?
- What is the time frame by which you will make a decision?
- What is your budget, what were you anticipating on spending?
- Have you had the opportunity to work with lawyers in this area before? If so, what was your experience, what worked for you what are you seeking this time around?

The Sales Process: Qualify and Assess Needs

> - What is the best way for me to keep in touch with you?

Note that there are various meeting opportunities to ask the above and other questions and all questions are not necessarily appropriate for all meetings. Use best judgment when ascertaining which questions to ask. The key is to create a dialog that provides an opportunity for the prospective client to talk about their business goals or personal goals if that's the case. You then begin to pave the way for providing solutions and taking a proactive approach to the legal side of their business, rather than waiting for the phone to ring.

Obviously, there are many more questions one may ask and a useful exercise is to jot down questions conducive to your business and your type of clients, or even more specific, the decision-maker.

> ### Sales Case Study 4-2: Qualify and Assess Needs
> *Situation:* An existing client, interested in consolidating the number of outside counsel with whom his company does business asked to meet with members of the firm's litigation team. The firm was competing against one other large regional firm for the business. The general counsel was prepared to select one firm to handle all of the company's litigation, which required a substantial amount of work.
> *Objective:* Demonstrate the firm's capabilities in the litigation area and ask for the business.
> *Action:* The litigation team (three people) met with the in-house counsel for about an hour. They identified areas in which they provided similar litigation work and were able to demonstrate their abilities. They agreed to follow up the meeting with a phone call to the general counsel about one week later.
> *Outcome:* During the follow-up phone call with the general counsel, the firm's contact was told that they had not been the selected outside counsel for the business. The partner thanked the general counsel for his time and ended the call.

The Woman Lawyer's Rainmaking Game

At the urging of the firm's marketing director, the partner phoned the general counsel back within a few days to find out why the firm was not selected. He was told that he and his in-house team hold the firm in high regard. He added that he was very surprised that there was little preparation on the part of the litigation team prior to visiting him at the company and that further, they spent the entire hour talking about themselves and the practice. "I would have expected [firm name] to be far better prepared and was discouraged that there was little actual interest in what I was seeking from outside counsel and my relationship with them. I found the meeting to be one-sided and thought the approach of your partners was arrogant. In fact," he added, "I wouldn't be surprised it they hadn't met at all about this until they were in the car on their way to the company."

A lesson well learned.

The Expert: Preparing for a meeting with a client or prospective client requires focus and attention to the detail to be discussed at the meeting. Reminder: It's about the client, not about you. By attending this meeting intent on what to say instead of what they might learn from the client about his legal and business needs showed a lack of attention to detail and preparation, thus, insulting the client.

Be prepared: Understand that no matter how well someone on the team knows the client, it's always important when targeting for new areas of opportunity and potential work to begin at the Approach Stage and ask lots of questions before speaking. The outcome will always tip in your favor.

Sales Case Study 4-3: Qualify and Assess Needs

Situation: A meeting took place at which three litigators—two women, one man—were discussing how best to connect with an existing client who is the general counsel of a large company that does a substantial amount of work with the government. The general counsel, with whom they were planning to meet, can be a bit persnickety especially when it comes to sales meetings.

Objective: The objective was to cross-sell the firm's corporate services, and to obtain, when the opportunity presented itself, additional litigation business.

Action: In this situation, it's best to take it from the top — even though they know the individual and have worked with him for three years. So, once again, we start at the Approach Stage of the sales process and take the meeting as an opportunity to get to know the general counsel from another perspective. It was determined that the person with the most contact, the male partner, would take the general counsel out to dinner and thank him for his business and continued support of the firm. In this more comfortable and relaxed setting, it's often easier to soften the relationship if it's been primarily all business. Ahead of time, with the planning team, determine what questions might be appropriate to ask the general counsel at dinner. It's also a good idea to inform him that you would like additional business in the future and would like to discuss how things have been going and what is the best way to keep in touch to obtain further business, introduce other firm members, etc.

Outcome: The meeting went well and they continue to receive new business from the corporation. The company has begun to send corporate work to the firm.

The Expert: I firmly believe had they gone into the general counsel's office and began talking about other areas in which the firm may be of assistance the meeting would have not turned out well. (This type of action of making appointments to tell clients what else you/your firm can do for them often does not work and is not perceived as sincere.)

Tips on Effective Listening for Building Relationships

Look at the person to whom you are speaking. Looking down or away conveys a lack of confidence or lack of interest to the decision-maker. When looking at the person speaking, show interest and try not to stare at the person. Use facial expressions to convey you are listening and interested. Try to focus on the person and not on what they are wearing, jewelry, etc. Staring at other parts of their person rather than their face can make him feel uncomfortable

The Woman Lawyer's Rainmaking Game

and he will wonder what you are looking at. Keep them focused by your staying focused.
- Remember to smile—it creates warmth and makes people feel comfortable.
- Try to listen and let some time go by before responding; otherwise, you might interrupt a thought.
- Never interrupt.
- Other than taking notes, don't doodle on paper. It's distracting and rude.
- Listen. Listen. Listen. If you do all the talking, you aren't building your relationship or learning about the decision-maker's needs.
- Don't compete with the buyer. Remember to review the personality charts so you have a better sense of the type of person you are dealing with.
- Lean in to show you are actively listening. Being distant makes it appear you are withdrawn. Don't cross your arms either—it is a defensive mechanism whether the prospective client knows it or not.
- Don't one up someone. Competing is distasteful. Make your prospects and clients the winners!
- Worrying about time is not endearing. Let your prospect know what time you need to leave the meeting and then don't worry about it. Try not to be a clock-watcher.
- Engage in feeding back another's comments to clarify your understanding
- Listen 200 percent—your role is to listen for understanding (not planning your rebuttal!)
- Restate what you've heard in your own words and seek for underlying meaning. Listening to understand does not mean you necessarily agree! A "discount" is any action, body language, or verbal behavior that one perceives as a put-down. Validating or crediting one another keeps the conversation open, each fully engaged in solving problems rather than defending. Validation has the effect of energizing the discussion, "spin" ideas into rich thoughts, and keep all group members participating. Enforcing ground rules

> and modeling healthy communication skills can divert discounting behaviors

[For more information about active listening, and discounting versus validation, see Active Listening and Feedback by Dr. M.B. Handspicker in Article Resources at the back of this book.]

Understanding the People Part of the Sales Process
As the case studies above demonstrate, people are the key to the successful selling of services. Selling legal services means selling intangibles. When there is no ability to differentiate on the part of the buyer, then price becomes the differentiating factor, and that's the last type of discussion in which you want to get involved. Begin to differentiate you and your firm's services by focusing on the decision-maker and her needs as early in the relationship as possible. Due to the strong relationship ties that have occurred over the years many lawyers have become friends with their clients.

During the Approach Stage of the sales process, you have a great opportunity to begin to differentiate yourself from your competitors or your firm from the competing firms. By building strong relationships and exhibiting a style that shows you are attentive to the buyer's needs, the relationship begins to build and grow between the buyer and the seller—so-to-speak. As Harry Beckwith points out in his book, *Selling the Invisible*, "Your prospects have one basic question, 'What makes you so different that I should do business with you?'"

The RFP (request for proposal) process that many in-house counsel now use, unfortunately does not allow one to build a strong relationship from the beginning, thus creating an even more difficult situation in terms of differentiation.

The sooner you begin to understand how you come across to others, the stronger your relationship-building skills will become. In addition, the more you learn and understand about the role personality and behavior play in building relationships, the higher the success rate will be on closing new business.

The Woman Lawyer's Rainmaking Game

Personalities Play a Key Role in Building Relationships

A group of psychologists once taught sales teams at various companies that there are four key personality characteristics we all share. The four primary characteristics to identify and sell to are: dominant/driving, ego/expressive, complacent/amiable, and stable/analytic. On page 4–16 is a chart that outlines some of the characteristics of these profiles. There are also some companies that provide additional information about learning to sell to specific personalities and the role that this plays in the business development process. References to these resources are provided on page 4–17. To drive this point home, lawyers sell to individuals, not to faceless organizations. If you have ever built a relationship with an individual in an organization who left for another company, you know quite well that you have to begin the process of building a relationship all over again with the new contact at the company.

Recognize that not everyone will like you nor will you like everyone. Personalities can clash. By understanding the key profiles, you have a better chance of succeeding at building relationships.

The first thing people say when they learn about this concept is: "I need to be myself, I can't change who I am and be fake just to build business." Everyone has some ability to understand who they are and how they come across to others. We change our behavior in relation to others all the time. Think of how you are with someone very young, or someone very old. Certain judges, clients, co-counsel cause you to relate to them differently than you do others. We intuitively adjust our style without thinking about it. In the case of sales, you begin to think about your style in relation to those whom you meet.

Take a look at the chart on page 4–17. Do you recognize characteristics of some of your clients? How about yourself? The profiles have stood the test of time. Think of the chart as a useful tool in your sales toolbox. Just like any tool, use it if it will help. How will these apply to you or your clients? Do you have clients who, when handed a document say, "Just show me where to sign"? And other clients who need time to review the document and have yellow stickers pointing to areas

The Sales Process: Qualify and Assess Needs

for discussion? Those are two types of personalities: one is dominant/driving and one is stable/analytic.

Here's how this particular tool works. Psychologists tell us that within fifteen seconds of meeting someone, we subconsciously assess an individual based on many factors. The assessment is usually based on the obvious - appearance. By taking a closer look and assessing the type of person with whom you are meeting, you will have a better chance of "connecting" with that individual. Take a look at the chart. The key for three of the personalities is to mirror the personality.

If someone is dominant/driving, that is, bottom line-oriented, a strong decision-maker, you will want to come across confident, bottom line, and decisive. In other words net it out. This type of individual is not afraid to make decisions so is therefore not afraid to try new things, new law firms. If it doesn't work out, she changes counsel again. You most likely won't get a second shot whether it's in the sales process or with handling work.

The complacent/amiable person is one who likes to talk and "visit." They might spend time talking about family, vacation, and other interests. They are often not the decision-maker but rather an influencer in the process. In some cases, these folks are the ones who shepherd the RFP process with outside firms. They collect the data and prepare it for the decision-makers. When dealing with a complacent/amiable, it's important to remember to advise like a coach. You may suggest items to focus on. In some cases, it may be necessary to help make the final decision for them. This is particularly true if the decision-maker you face is a consumer-minded person; in particular for practices focusing on estate planning, plaintiff's work, matrimonial work, and other areas relative to consumers and individuals.

The stable/analytic profile is one commonly held by many lawyers. Stable/analytics are known for their need to have as much information as possible in order to make a decision. Individuals who research every last review before making major purchases exhibit the stable/analytic profile. Therefore, it's imperative not to deliver piles of information to this person. They will want to read through everything. Since everyone is busy most of the day, it's difficult to find the time to read through lots of material and therefore, the decision is delayed. So, again, provide as little as necessary to inform someone about the practice. It's important to demonstrate experience to a stable/analytic profile. The best way to do this is create one-page charts that show results achieved for clients or number of deals, or number of litigation wins. These quick reference sheets are invaluable ways to demonstrate your client successes and get to the point quickly.

Last, but not least, is the ego/expressive profile. This is a profile of many entrepreneurs and decision-makers. The key to building a relationship with a high ego individual is to compliment the ego but not in a patronizing way. Make the conversation about them and they will talk for hours about themselves. If you are an ego/expressive person, you will need to take a back seat to this decision-maker. Remember, it's not about you it's about them. To do this successfully is difficult since ego/expressive people often compete for attention. They are lively, fun, and exciting people.

Since ego/expressive people are concerned about how they appear to others, they are less inclined to take risks with unknown firms, small firms, or individuals. The best way to develop this relationship is to offer strong references and obtain testimonials from other happy clients. You might even include third-party information such as media mentions about big cases or deals that occurred in which you played a major role.

Again, this profiling part of building relationships may seem to some as manipulative. Bear in mind that we adjust our approach to others all the time, not always as consciously however. For those readers who deal with judges, you know what we mean. A different judge causes you to act in a different style depending on her style and personality. (The same goes for jurors.)

These and other tools designed to assist with relationship building are useful and often critical resources as you build your own set of skills in the sales world.

The Sales Process: Qualify and Assess Needs

Selected Personality Characteristics Chart

Note: This chart is just a tool—think of people you know—judges; other lawyers; friends when reviewing the chart and see if you can match types to people you know.

	DOMINANT	ENTREPRENEURIAL / EGO	AMIABLE	ANALYTICAL
DRESS	Expensive but conservative, classic silk ties or blouse	Flashy, latest style, European, bold, draws attention	Casual, relaxed, comfortable	Ultra-conservative, sensible
JEWELRY	Expensive brand-name watch, conservative but high-quality jewelry, pearls	Fancy watch, ring(s), cufflinks, "pinky" rings, diamonds; latest trend jewelry	Sensible and inexpensive watch	Digital or functional watch, tie clasp, (very little jewelry)
BUSINESS STYLE	Takes control, punctual, intimidates, goal-oriented, risk-taker	"I, I, I," storyteller, center of attention, adventurous	Slow, laid back, indecisive, quiet, likable	Precise, calculates words, shy, consistent, standoffish
OFFICE	An "organized mess," high quality furniture	Ornate, flashy, expensive, neat, clean	Steel or wood, inexpensive, semi-messy	Very old, messy but organized, practical
OUTSIDE INTERESTS	Golf, tennis, handball, boating, spectator sports	Tennis, racquetball, body-building, jogging, scuba-diving	Fishing, hunting, spectator sports, family, camping	Jogging, tennis, hiking, biking, backpacking
AUTOMOBILE	Mercedes, BMW, Jaguar, Cadillac	Flashy, but sporty, convertible, Porsche, Ferrari	Honda, Subaru, Ford Taurus, compacts, four-wheelers	Mid-size Chrysler, Acura, Volvo
FAVORITE WORDS	"Bottom Line," "Goal," "Drive," "Winner"	"I, I, I, I," (concerned about how he/she is viewed by others)	"Do your own thing," "No sweat," "No problem"	"Invest," "Wise"
TYPICAL POSITION	CEO, CFO, General Counsel	V.P., Division G.M., Sr.-Level management, marketing; Entrepreneur	Claims manager, Personnel manager, Department attorney	Controller, Attorney, Asst. Division Counsel, Lending Officer, Engineering Manager
HOW TO SELL TO EACH PERSONALITY	Be brief, show you understand their needs, communicate the bottom line	Know their needs, cater to them, convince them the decision will make them look good	Provide definition, make decisions for them, develop a personal relationship	Provide lots of detail present an executive summary

Working Tool: Understanding Personalities

People do business with people they like; therefore, it is important to learn the dynamics of building a relationship. Consider these questions to help you understand yourself and your contacts and how you will interact with these individuals.

1. Of the four personalities, which one best identifies you? (Think about your existing clients and prospects; into which of these categories do they fall?)
2. List your top three existing clients, identify the appropriate contacts, and identify (best guess) which personality best describes each one.

Company Name   **Contact Name/s**   **Personality Type**

_____

_____

2B. How would you "sell" to each of these individuals whom you know based on what you now have learned about personalities?

1. _____
2. _____
3. _____

3A. List your top three prospective clients and identify which personality best describes each one.

Prospective Company Name   **Contact Name/s**   **Personality Type**

1. _____
2. _____
3. _____

3B. How would you "sell" to each of these individuals?

1. _____
2. _____
3. _____

The Sales Process: Qualify and Assess Needs

Team Selling Can Be Successful — Make Sure You Are a Major Member of the Team

More often than not, you may find yourself at a meeting with a decision-maker along with other members from your firm. In-house counsel caution that the most effective team is a team with people who have roles. If diversity is an issue and you were invited to be the female or minority member of the team, make sure ahead of time that you are an active member of the team. Here are some quick steps to remember to be the most effective member of the team as possible.

A well-known Fortune 50 general counsel provides this advice: "I prefer to meet with people who are engaged in the discussion. With each meeting, I am also assessing how the members of the firm work together as a team, what it will be like working with the individuals, and how well they get along with one another. It's difficult to assess this from my end if people invited to the meeting are not active members at the meeting. I see a number of firms, given our work with outside counsel, that come to our meetings. Partners can take over the discussion, leaving others on their team feeling inadequate at the meeting. This behavior does not go over well with our in house team." His comments provide good insight for being prepared to meet with clients and prospective clients. It will be wise to follow the advice.

When participating in a meeting with other members of your firm, insist beforehand that you meet with them to rehearse how your team will be presenting or, better yet, if this is a meeting where the objective is to learn as much as possible about the prospective client or client, be sure everyone is comfortable with the fact they may jump in if they see an opportunity to do so.

Tips for Team Selling

- Be the catalyst, if necessary, for your team to meet prior to the client/prospective client meeting.
- Develop a set of questions you and the team members will ask (keep in mind the 80/20 rule).
- Discuss the role each team member will play at the meeting. This is particularly important if a dominating member of the

> team is present. It's also important if one of the team members has the primary relationship with the client (if at a client meeting). This is also important if you are an associate or if you have associates as part of the team. Appoint a team leader to begin discussions, to review the agenda, and to discuss objectives of the meeting. This overview should not take longer than five minutes so it is best to plan this to insure the client has an immediate role in the discussion. The primary objective is to ask questions, learn about the prospect's business, and to move the sales process along to the next step.
>
> - Everyone in the meeting (from the client side) is important. Remind members from your team that attention and focus will need to be given to everyone in the room, not just the strongest individual, or the decision-maker. Discuss what the stated objectives will be at the meeting. For example, "We are delighted to be here today and what we'd like to achieve is to hear more about [the specific situation] [criteria you have for hiring outside counsel] [the business objectives you wish to achieve], etc.
>
> - Remember the 80/20 rule. At this stage of the process, it's worth taking the time to build the relationship, ask lots of questions and learn about the prospect. In other words, invest time, and they will invest time.
>
> - Leave the meeting with a follow-up question: "What is our next step?" and then mark your calendar to follow up as appropriate

What You Learn Now Sets the Stage for Closing

Learning about the buyer, the company, and the needs of both will help determine how to shape the strategy for continuing to build relationships with the individual and his organization.

In most law firm scenarios, a lawyer or group of lawyers will obtain an appointment to meet with a decision-maker. The next thing that usually happens—that we hope you will avoid doing after reading this—is the lawyer(s) go to their firm's marketing department and develop a package of information to bring to the meeting, including sometimes enough material to read on a six-hour flight uninterrupted. In other

The Sales Process: Qualify and Assess Needs

words, too much information, which can actually do more harm than good, since it may be received as more than a little arrogant for you to presume to know what the prospective client wants before actually meeting with her.

Presentation packages belong in a different stage of the sales process. They are closing tools and should be assembled only after sufficient information about the buyer has been obtained. Then and only then, is it appropriate to present a package of materials. In the meantime, your job during this phase of the process is to ask questions, listen, and learn. If you feel you must bring something to the meeting, then bring a firm overview and your bio. That's it. Anything else will be a waste of effort.

During this fact-gathering stage of the sales process, try to be clear about what your goals are, communicate those goals to your audience, and move the sales process along to the next step. The next step could mean meeting with others to facilitate development of business within the organization.

When You Are on the List of Preferred Outside Counsel
A small group of lawyers recently met with members of the law department at a Fortune 100 company. At the meeting, the lawyers learned they are on the company's "preferred provider" list for outside counsel. This means the law department members may use the firm (or any other firms that are on this list) without seeking additional approval from the general counsel or the board of the company. When reviewing the billings for this client prior to the client visit, they noted that over the past year they had received about $700,000 in fees from this client. Yet, the client's total expenditure on outside counsel was over $50,000,000! What happened? There are several things to learn from this true scenario.

First, just because your firm is on the preferred provider list, doesn't mean you will automatically receive business. You still need to develop relationships with in-house counsel and other senior management members of the company who are responsible for hiring outside counsel.

Second, schedule one or two meetings a year to show your interest in the company. This is critical to maintain your preferred provider status and to insure you are on track with what is happening at the organization.

Third, as seasoned salespeople know quite well, to be on the list is one thing, to go after and close business is quite another. Take the initiative to drive the business development effort. If there is a "billing partner," a "responsible partner," or other partner who "owns" the client relationship, treat this partner as though she is a referral source. Schedule a meeting with the partner to develop a strategy for introducing yourself into the company organization. Regardless of the politics at your firm, there is no one partner who knows the client organization as well as those within the client organization. There are few clients who consider their law firms their primary firm (when is the last time you asked that question of your client?) and even fewer who have loyal relationships with their clients.

The above scenario illustrates the importance of keeping in touch on a regular basis with clients and prospective clients to learn about their business goals, their outside expenditure and activities with other law firms, and the importance of staying connected.

If you contacted one client or contact every day (with a little bit of organization, this is not too difficult even on your busiest days to take one minute to make a phone call and leave a message or send an email) there would most likely be no need for a sales team at most firms. Imagine if every lawyer at your firm made one call a week, the possibilities of acquiring new business is profound.

Just like preparing for a trial, preparing for a sales presentation is important. Without preparation, your chances of winning the business are not the same. Much of sales is negotiating to reach a result you want. Once your sales strategy and objectives are clear, plan on using your negotiation skills to reach a good outcome. A good business development or sales director will be of value here—try to listen to her advice.

The Sales Process: Qualify and Assess Needs

After all this listening and assessment of prospective client's business goals and needs, it may occur to you that the fit with your firm is not a good one. That's okay. Remain in touch with this contact, and think of ways in which you may be of assistance to them through referral relationships or otherwise. Building advocacy into every relationship will help you reach your business goals.

Read on and you'll see how everything you learn from the prospect during these stages, sets the foundation for you to negotiate the sale. The next chapter will explore the next step of the sales process. Strategize is what to do during the relationship-building process when there is no immediate need at hand; but, nevertheless, is important to remain in contact and build on the relationship you've started to develop.

CHAPTER 5

The Sales Process: Strategize

Highlights

- Keeping in Touch with Contacts Is a Key to Building Business
- Using Those Tickets, Dinners, and Golf Games to Your Advantage
- Sample Schedule for Keeping in Touch
- Setting the Stage for Closing the Business
- Personality Fit: A Sales Case Study
- Strategizing for a Real Opportunity
- Practicing Makes Perfect

For God's sake, don't give up writing to me simply because I don't write to you.—Robert Frost

Keeping in Touch With Contacts Is a Key to Building Business

Until now, the sales process has been one in which there is a great deal of listening to understand the buyer and his or her legal needs. You may have spent quite a bit of time developing the relationship so far and it will be important to ensure you continue to remain "top of mind." This means you are the first one the buyer thinks about when a legal need occurs, or a business peer of his or hers asks for a referral to a lawyer. Until a need occurs, and the prospect is able to send business the way of the firm, it is important to maintain contact. With some buyers or corporations, it may be one, two, or more years before he or she actually might send a piece of business your way.

The Woman Lawyer's Rainmaking Game

A good example of this involves a major coffee company on the West Coast. It was not satisfied with its existing litigation counsel and was seeking new firms with which to develop relationships. One large firm was in the running to meet with the in-house team for consideration. After a well-prepared and rehearsed meeting and presentation of the firm's credentials, the firm received an email from the in-house team indicating it had met with many firms and this firm in particular was the most prepared and thoughtful about its approach to the meeting. This stresses what we have written about so far. In contrast, the in-house team also indicated that currently there is no open litigation and promised the firm that the next time the company needs litigation counsel, it will work with their firm.

Keeping in touch to stay top of mind is part of the strategy you must now employ. To accomplish keeping in touch, the partners decided that on a bi-monthly basis they would either meet with or call the in-house team. One of the partners is a golfer and another is a sailor so invitations for summer golfing and sailing will be part of the keep-in-touch strategy to continue to develop a relationship with the in-house team. Invitations to baseball games, ski trips, etc., may also be part of the process. Clearly, inviting members of the team to the firm's continuing legal education events and seminars is an important way to demonstrate the firm's skill set. The in-house team is always pleased to hear from the lawyers.

So, keep in touch on a regular basis.

Using Those Tickets, Dinners, and Golf Games to Your Advantage

Entertaining clients is an important contact and client retention tool used by many practitioners who have established strong relationships with their contacts and clients. The same holds true for prospective clients. Keeping in touch is critical to developing new business. By staying in touch with people, you begin to build a relationship with them, and in turn, they begin to develop trust, an essential part of any lawyer/client relationship. Entertaining prospective clients is also the key to maintaining and building new relationships. Think of the tools available to you at your firm. Alternatively, if you have a smaller firm or solo practice consider the time you have available outside of the practice for

The Sales Process: Strategize

lunches, breakfasts, association events, and interesting seminars. These are all opportunities in which prospects may have an interest—so invite them. People appreciate invitations. No large firm is without a number of events it sponsors and, along with the sponsorships, tables to fill. Rather than try to fill a table with 10 people from your firm, invite clients. They appreciate the invitation and often readily accept since they do not have the opportunity to attend as many of these events as you do. Even if they cannot attend, they appreciate the invitation.

Anne Whittemore, a partner at Virginia's McGuire Woods, recommends, "Forwarding articles and reports of interest; inviting to functions and developing a personal relationship, is a great way to keep in touch with anyone I've met. People appreciate knowing you are thinking of them. I stay in touch with people I meet at seminars this way. It builds relationships."

Kirkpatrick's Janice Hartman agrees with this approach, "Regular attendance at meetings of relevant business groups. Prompt forwarding of client alerts on topics I know will be of interest with a personal note. Visits when I am in a city for other reasons are all ways I keep the relationship going and let the prospective client (and existing clients for that matter) know I'm thinking of them."

Determining ways to keep in touch with a prospect on a regular basis and balancing those contact times so as not to appear too overbearing and in touch too often can be a challenge. In contrast, here is a sample schedule for keeping in touch that maintains the right number of touch points with a key prospect.

Often, marketing and sales people are asked by attorneys, "How can I best leverage my nonprofit board membership contacts?" In the same manner you will keep in touch with business contacts, you may keep in touch with your board-related contacts. Clearly it may be difficult to try to develop business during a board of directors' meeting. In contrast, most people who share the board seats with you are also in business. These are people who may or may not be able to hire you for legal work, but who do share experiences with other business people and may be able to refer business to you. Use the same activities for keeping in touch with your board contacts that you would for any other contacts—be sure to include them on your mailing lists and seminar invitations. If you are looking for ways to further leverage contacts like this, do not do it at the board meetings, but use that time to indicate that you may call them in between board meetings at their office. Then, be sure to follow up with the call or the next time they see you they will remember you did not.

Sample Schedule for Keeping in Touch

Original meeting date:	March 20
First follow-up to schedule meeting and begin building relationship:	March 27
Meeting:	April 8
Meeting follow-up: Letter with appropriate firm marketing enclosures:	April 12
Follow-up invitation to an association breakfast:	May 21
Follow-up note with an article of interest:	July 21
Golf game/concert invitation:	September
Holiday card:	Nov./Dec.

Whether or not the prospective client accepts invitations to dinners, breakfasts, events, or golf games, he or she will always appreciate the offer and remember that you asked. Consider rather than invite a contact of yours to attend a sports game, asking the contact if he or she would appreciate two tickets to the game to take his or her son or daughter? They will remember they are at the game because of your generosity and, again, the gesture will go a long way toward building a strong relationship. It has been proven over and over again that we do business with people who stay in touch with us, who have made a valid attempt to gain our business, and who remain aware of our business needs. It will be a lot easier to continue to develop your existing contacts than to try to build new ones over and over again.

For Susan Paish common activities are a means by which she keeps in contact and builds relationships. "I keep in touch.... not just on business, but on personal notes: i.e., calls to people who have young kids at

The Sales Process: Strategize

the start of school to see how they are doing in the 'back to school chaos,' invitations to others to share the 'joy' of parenting teenagers etc."

Susan Paish has these other tips on how to stay in touch:
- "Finding out what contacts and clients like is key. I have given camping tips to a prospective client (never thinking that she would actually follow them). Boy was I surprised when she and her family showed up at the campsite. She says that she will never forget that and I have heard her talk about this to others.... it was a bit like falling off a log because I love to camp and this gets back to the sincerity point: if you like what you are doing it will show and your guests will soon become your friends in your pursuit of whatever the activity is. (P.S. this woman has been in a couple of general counsel roles and has become a client each step of the way!!)"
- "Constant invitations to the endless dinners and lunches in town. I try to match the topic and 'purpose' of the event to the interests of the individual, but I am quite relentless at attending these events as not only do I get to have fun with my guest, but I usually bump into several other people at the event too. The keys here in my view are to match the event to the interests of the person (tip: make sure you know what they like first), and then to make the invitation completely open ended: no guilt in saying no."
- "I fish and guess what, so do other women! I was actually surprised to find out how many women like to fish and I am pursuing this with some of them as we speak. Of course fishing derbies have long been a close second to golf games for the guys when it comes to relationship building and as I can lose a big fish as good as anyone, I am not shy about gender issues (here or on any other topic)"

Jane Potter believes, "Follow-up can be done as partly discussed above; I also keep in touch with people in other cities and offer to visit when I am traveling to that city on vacation or on business. I invite people to events, such as the Northwest Women's Law Center dinners in Seattle that are partly social but also benefit the local community. I offer to introduce them to people who may be of help in their business.

The Woman Lawyer's Rainmaking Game

I try to get to know them outside the context of their current employment, so that whether or not they stay with that position, they will have reasons to keep in touch."

Debbie Horwitz from Goulston discusses her methods for follow up: "I've taken full advantage of the firm's support for a wide variety of community and philanthropic efforts. I almost never go to an event where the firm has purchased a table without inviting one or more prospect along. I also use the firm's tickets to cultural and sporting events (from Jimmy Buffett to the Boston Symphony Orchestra) to build relationships with prospects in a pleasant setting. Also, whenever I have the opportunity to put someone on a panel or otherwise provide someone with a public speaking opportunity, I try to offer it to someone high on my prospect list. Again, helping someone else to grow their business tends to create substantial goodwill and a desire to reciprocate."

Baker & McKenzie's McBreen provides additional insight about follow-up strategies: "Just as clients respect attention to detail on their legal matters—contract review, legislative updates, timely counsel—they appreciate personal attention. I think of myself as a 'high touch' attorney. If I'm on the phone with a potential client and he mentions his birthday, I take note of it and follow up on the date with a birthday card. If there is cause for a celebration, I send a bottle of champagne. If the prospect is a golfer, I am sure to set up a golf game. It's so much easier when your clients, potential clients, and referral sources are your friends. That's why I like to think of them as my friends. I have found clients and prospective clients want to voice their opinions. Intellectual reciprocity is important. I love the give-and-take of a brainstorming session. I routinely call potential clients as well as clients to discuss issues with them on a promotional basis. If a client has asked me how others are handling a particular legal concern, I will use the opportunity to survey potential clients as well as clients. In this way, I have a reason to call the potential client. I can solicit her views and at the same time share useful information with her; and the potential client will 'take away' the fact that I have this expertise."

The Sales Process: Strategize

Setting the Stage for Closing the Business

At some point all the activities that you plan to stay in touch with clients and prospective clients will pay off. The most difficult aspect of selling anything is actually getting the business. The waiting time may be long, but the payoff, in terms of new business or new clients, will be worth the wait. Remember that a side benefit of keeping in touch with your contacts is that they may not do business directly with you but may refer you to colleagues of theirs who also seek legal counsel.

Meeting a potential client and getting to the stage where you are finally hired to do the work takes time. At some point, you will be in conversation with your contact about a specific legal issue he or she has. Knowing your prospect or client as well as you do and keeping in mind what specifically they look for from their outside counsel relationships (from the Assess Needs stage originally), you are in a key position to be retained.

At this point, go back to the Assess Needs stage and begin the questioning process specific to this issue. Frame your questions to solicit information that will allow you to discuss what you would like your contact to know. Make this conversation about them not about you. Remember the personality profile and determine if you believe there is "chemistry" between you and the prospective client or if it will be necessary to bring in someone else from your firm to round out the personalities involved. When introducing contacts to other members of your firm or team, always think about the personality fit. Even though you may have a strong relationship with your contact, when the time comes for them to meet your partner, if there is a lack of "chemistry" between the two of them, your relationship may not be strong enough to overcome feelings of discomfort.

The Woman Lawyer's Rainmaking Game

Personality Fit: A Sales Case Study

Situation: A large technology company in Cambridge, Massachusetts, did a significant amount of work with three major firms. One firm that handled a significant amount of the company's corporate and litigation work focused on this corporation as a key client and built a team of lawyers around the client. One of the first steps to take is obviously to meet with the client and hear how things are going and to learn about the client's business goals. The information gleaned from a meeting like this provides an opportunity to cross-sell additional services into the client. The key is making sure the relationships will work. The team learned that the client was willing to give the firm a try with the company's labor and employment work.

The Opportunity: The client team and, in particular, the relationship partner introduced one of the firm's labor and employment lawyers to the client. Despite the fact that he provided excellent client support and handled the client's work efficiently, the team soon learned that the labor and employment work was still going to another firm. When asked what the issue was, the general counsel called a meeting with her employment counsel and heard that she did not "click" with the employment lawyer and was not comfortable working with him. This scenario now creates two issues: first, the relationship counsel must inform his partner that the fit was not right and they need to try again with another lawyer. Second, the lawyer needed to be responsible immediately to the client's issue with the team member who did not work out.

The Solution: The team leader spoke with his partner and discussed the situation. The partner understood and made a recommendation to another lawyer in the labor and employment group who he thought would be a better fit.

The Outcome: The chemistry was right this time and the team was expanded to include the labor and employment attorney. By listening to the client and responding with a solution the firm's outcome was a win.

The Expert: This is a scenario that happens in many firms—good lawyer but no chemistry with someone who is used to dealing

5-8

The Sales Process: Strategize

> with another partner in the firm. Often this scenario is interpreted poorly within the firm and the lawyer who was not a hit with the client is perceived unfairly. The best outcome is to deal with the situation and to recognize that like all relationships chemistry matters.

Strategizing for a Real Opportunity

During the Strategize stage of the process keeping in touch is important and becomes the strategy until such time you are invited in to present your solution to a real opportunity. Once the opportunity to present is imminent, the strategy changes from one of keeping in touch, to one aimed specifically at the opportunity. Here is an example.

A large firm's real estate team was invited to present to a significant client of the firm for whom the firm did corporate work. The company, a large pharmaceutical firm, was opening a new location in the U.S. and needed real estate lawyers to help negotiate its acquisition of a significant piece of land on which it would develop its new facility, along with other key development issues, zoning issues, and related real estate development issues. (It had been determined earlier, by the way, that the real estate group within the firm would focus on the firm's existing clients as its target market, which is how it eventually arrived at this stage.)

The first thing the partner responsible for leading the process did was to determine who else should be at the meeting. He selected the individual team members (four in all) and they spent a great deal of time reviewing with the partner who had the most contact with the client, the type of personalities to whom they would be presenting, the background of the company, and the goals the company has for this facility, including deadlines and timeframes for completion of the project and staffing the facility. With this background information understood, the team's next step was to discuss what they would be presenting, to pull together examples of past successes with similar types of facilities, and to prepare a PowerPoint presentation to hand out at the meeting. Being prepared and practicing their presentation paid off. The group was selected as counsel for the project and realized a fee of nearly $2 million.

Practice Makes Perfect

Now that you have kept in touch, an opportunity to present arises. If you will be formally presenting either alone or with a team from your firm, practice! Most lawyers hate the thought of doing this, but statistics from the corporate sales world show that the best-prepared scenarios are also the winning scenarios (for context and reference, think about litigators who usually have mock trials before a big trial). Team members are also more confident when they have a defined role and an opportunity to rehearse. Evidence of this becomes more apparent if you talk to your peers and ask how many of them practice prior to presenting to clients. The number of individuals working with personal presentation coaches is on the rise and the investment of time and dollars pays off.

The next chapter discusses how to refine your presentation and where in the sales process it becomes okay for you to talk about you and your services.

CHAPTER 6

The Sales Process: Address Needs and Present

Highlights

- When You Talk, You Are Presenting
- A Role-Playing Case Study
- Checking In So Your Prospect Does Not Check Out
- The RFP Response and Determining the Response Strategy
- Tips for Mastering the Request for Proposal Process
- Take the Bull by the Horns
- Where the Marketing Team Fits In
- How Much Is too Much?
- RFP Logistical Tips
- Sample Presentation Power Point

Get to the Point or You Will Never Get to the Close. —Harry Beckwith, Selling the Invisible

When You Talk, You Are Presenting

"Imagine the audience with clickers in their hands." This was sage advice from Arnold Zenker, a Boston-based presentations skills expert. Any time a situation presents itself where a face-to-face meeting takes place—be it at a networking event, a corporate visit, a dinner meeting—when you speak, you present. Likewise, at any time, the audience can "change the channel" and zone out. The person on the listening end is always weighing what he or she is hearing against what he or she is interested in and tunes in to the information that fits into his or her

The Woman Lawyer's Rainmaking Game

world. All this means one thing: When you wish to talk about your firm, it comes late in the sales process. (Reminder: the sales process can take an hour or years of time. It's the process on which you need to focus.)

In Chapter Four we mentioned that in the Assess Needs stage, you should listen 80 percent of the time. Now, at the Address Needs stage, you present more than you listen. The business can be won or lost at this stage because anything you say about your services, about the firm, or about you is irrelevant to the listener (the prospect) unless what you are saying directly applies to what is important to them. What is important to them is what you found out about during the Assess Needs stage. For example, if daily updates on an active matter are important to the client, then discuss in your presentation how you intend to keep the client updated. Relate your presentation or the points you are making back to the information the person told you was important. The lawyer who best accomplishes this will absolutely win the business. This is the reason you must uncover needs (not always just substantive legal needs). Once there is an understanding of how this particular individual likes to do business, what type of personality he or she is, and the type of relationship with others he or she likes, only then are you able to succinctly present or as we call it address the needs of the prospect.

Think of times when a strong relationship with an individual has developed only to have that person leave, retire, or get promoted. You then have to develop a whole new relationship with someone else, right? That is because it is not the company overall buying from you but an individual.

Once you have reached this stage of the process with your contact, you may begin to discuss in detail and with knowledge how your services, your firm, and you or your team might best meet their needs as legal counsel.

Anne Marie Whittemore believes, "Personal impressions, experience, and commitment to the client" are key points to get across and help create a successful presentation. Kirkpatrick's Janice Hartmann adds, "Preparation is also very key. Both in presentation materials and in study of the client's expressed requirements and business."

The Sales Process: Address Needs and Present

Recall the Assess Needs step of the sales process in Chapter 4. Whatever the listener is hearing must apply to something important to them or addresses a need they indicated they have. If not, it is hot air and wasted time. People always politely listen, but we want to make sure the relationship is solidifying and that they are clear you are interested in their needs and in them. By providing a lot of what YOU think is valuable information, you may not be addressing specific issues previously identified.

Goulston & Storr's Debbie Horwitz discusses her style of presenting: "During your presentation, listen and ask questions about the prospect's business and perceived needs." Debbie's suggestion ensures that the prospective client is *involved* at all times during the presentation. "Again, I believe strongly that most women are naturally good at this. Our ability to empathize and project concern/interest in others is a very effective sales tool."

Horwitz adds another piece of advice: "Another approach that's worked for us has been to raise the awareness of all professionals at the firm of the importance of mirroring the demographics of our target market. Since some of the people putting together meetings with prospects began to realize that many of the important decision-makers at those prospects are women, and that, in general, businesses want to work with a law firm that 'feels' like and is therefore comfortable to them, more women have been included in every presentation the firm puts together."

Fasken, Martineau, DuMoulin's Parish adds some sound steps that work for her during the presentation stage: "Being prepared, prepared, prepared, prepared, prepared, prepared, prepared (and not repeating myself!!) Seriously though: the key points in a presentation from my perspective are:
- Be prepared
- Be on time
- Keep to the client's (or prospective client's) schedule
- Answer the question asked (not the one you wished had been asked)
- Be sincere

The Woman Lawyer's Rainmaking Game

- Be yourself"

A Role-Playing Case Study

Below are a couple of role-playing scenarios to illustrate this point. A luncheon-networking event (based on a real situation):

You: Hi, I'm Sarah Colgate, how are you? (Approach Stage)

Prospect: I'm Jim Stevens, and I'm well.

You: I'm a partner at Kramer & Evans Law Firm, and you? (*In charge of the questions, taking control, beginning Assess Needs stage*)

Jim: I am the CFO at Gradner Electric Worldwide. What type of law practice are you in?

You: I'm a patent lawyer (*Take control back here and begin to assess needs*) What markets is Gradner Electric in?

Jim: We are in major industrial markets in the U.S. and Europe.

You: Sounds interesting. Has your distribution channel changed much with the Internet and globalization? (*Assessing needs stage*)

Jim: Yes, our competition has certainly increased but we are holding on to market share.

You: Does Gradner use intellectual property counsel? If so, I'd welcome the opportunity to tell you more about Kramer & Evans.

Jim: We do use IP counsel. We work with a firm in Phoenix.

You: Our firm is local and handles international work (*Begin to address needs*) for patents. Would you mind if I came to visit your offices to meet the general counsel and you for coffee?

Jim: Please give us a call. Here's my card.

This scenario actually happened (names changed for confidentiality purposes) at a CEO luncheon. Notice that in the Assess Needs stage, we are not asking too much yet about legal needs, but are seeking out general information. The objective here is to close an appointment, not the engagement. By the way in the real scenario, the CEO joined the CFO shortly after the conversation began. Notice that Sarah does not actually get into a lot about her firm, but, rather, asks questions and only "presents" information when asked, leaving open the opportunity for a future meeting and, thus, begins to build the relationship for potential business.

The Sales Process: Address Needs and Present

Here is another scenario, more formal, and again, an actual case study:

The scene: An on-site presentation with three law firm colleagues and a general counsel and assistant general counsel of a manufacturing facility. The lawyers were asked to come speak about their litigation practice. One other large regional firm was also asked to present. This will be the firm's first meeting with the general counsel other than a nonrelated legal issue dealt with a few years prior to this meeting.

Since no relationship has been built to date with the general counsel, it is necessary to begin this meeting at the beginning of the sales process. The Approach stage was actually made by the prospect. The attorneys therefore are now in the Assess Needs stage.

After brief hellos:

GC: We are seeking outside counsel to handle all of our litigation matters. We have a current matter that we will assign as soon as we have selected counsel.

Lawyers: We brought information about our firm and our litigation experience. Before we present this material, it will be helpful to us if we could hear about your department, the company's general needs, experience in dealing with outside counsel, and more about the type of relationship you anticipate. In this scenario, the need to determine as quickly as possible what the GC likes and dislikes are with respect to handling and staffing of matters, reporting, etc., is critical. Once the GC is finished speaking, ask any pertinent questions that come to mind to: 1) demonstrate good listening skills (affirms "we heard you"); 2) clarifies further any related information that will be addressed once the presentation from the three lawyers begins; and 3) shows interest and understanding.

Avoid: Asking specifics about current matters that he mentioned. You are there to sell the litigation work for all outside needs, not just one matter. Stay focused on the big picture.

Lawyers: To address some of the key points on which you focused, we would like to begin by providing an overview of how we manage and staff cases at Blumenthal & Brogster and then get into specifics about the staffing and other issues you raised. Please let us know during our discussion if there is any further information you require about a specific topic we address.

Checking In So Your Prospect Does Not Check Out

During the presentation, be sure to maximize the opportunity by "checking in" and asking from time to time if he or she has any questions, especially if the particular information you just discussed addresses a point which he or she made. It is critical at this juncture to get the GC and others (if there are others) involved in the presentation you and your colleagues are making. Involving them means they are investing time with you and your colleagues.

The presentation is also the appropriate opportunity to lay the groundwork for asking for the business: closing the deal. By gaining agreement from the decision-maker throughout the presentation, there is a psychological benefit that sets the stage for you to ask for the business and receive an affirmative answer from the other side.

In this scenario, it will be helpful to ask questions that include some of these key points so you are fully aware of the circumstances at hand. This situation is fairly close in format to a negotiation.

Here are some questions for which to make sure you have answers. All presentations should incorporate questions like these. They set the stage for closing business. The answers are critical to how you will shape your presentation and provide invaluable insight into the competition.

1. When will you be making this decision? What is your timeframe?
2. May we ask who is our competition? How many other firms are you interviewing? (This is important to know. The decision-makers will tell you.)
3. On which criteria will you be basing your decision? (Again, you need to know which path to steer down. This information puts you in control of the sales process and provides valuable insight.)

4. Is price an issue?
5. What would you change now about your existing relationships if you were able to change something?

Make sure the message fits. It is about the prospect, not about you.

This above advice is key, advises Jane Potter, "I think that enthusiasm for the underlying work is very helpful, instead of focusing only on the legal issues you can help solve. Also, if you have worked in the lab, or in a corporation that helps the potential client realize that you have been in their work situation and have a better understanding of the pressures and challenges they meet. One comment we've heard from in-house counsel is that they want their outside counsel to help them look good to their supervisors, and so it helps to ask how we can help them accomplish their own career goals. We think this is especially true for women attorneys relating to women clients, as there can be an unspoken recognition of the need to help each other in our careers."

Baker's Maura Ann McBreen agrees, "My success is due in large part to my level of preparation and my enthusiasm; I simply love what I do. I focus the sales presentation on the prospect or client. I want to hear about their business. What are they looking for in a relationship with the firm? What issues keep them up at night? How can I assist them and make them look like heroes to their bosses? In other words, I listen to them. Then, I tailor my sales presentation to what I have heard. I keep the focus on them and their requirements/needs."

Another type of presentation, which many of us do not immediately think of as a presentation, is the response to a request for proposal. Requests for Proposals are often referred to as RFPs and many companies, large and small, use the RFP process for selecting outside counsel.

The RFP Response and Determining the Response Strategy

Responding to Request for Proposals (RFPs) is a presentation opportunity. In relation to the sales process, an RFP is an *approach* to you/your firm. Your response is at the Address Needs and Present stage. Because RFPs are written documents, it creates no opportunity (or very little opportunity) to build a relationship. Further, many companies issue RFPs to manage the expenditures on outside legal counsel more effectively.

The Woman Lawyer's Rainmaking Game

Many times, a company initiates an RFP process for one of four primary reasons: 1) to confirm for senior management or the corporation's board that the corporation has performed due diligence with respect to obtaining the most cost-effective methods for managing outside legal expenditures; 2) to change from its primary one or two law firms due to a strain on the relationship of some sort; 3) to obtain new counsel for specific areas of the corporation's business, e.g., IP, litigation, corporate finance, labor and employment, etc.; and 4) to consolidate the number of outside firms with which the corporation does business and to create a more effective means by which to manage outside legal expenditures.

More in-house counsel are using the RFP process so it is best to respond when you are invited to do so. The RFP process does provide an opportunity to get in the door, so-to-speak, where your firm has not had the opportunity previously. With consolidation of their outside providers happening at a rate faster than expected, in-house counsel are using the RFP process more as a useful tool to assess one firm from the next. Unfortunately, throughout the process, the common differentiator remains price. We all know basing decisions on price and alternative fee arrangements alone can be a slippery slope. Focus on other factors that will differentiate your firm. Here are some useful tips for responding to RFPs.

Tips for Mastering the Request for Proposal Process

1. Upon receipt of the RFP, read it over carefully and note important deadlines. Deadlines are given for asking questions about the RFP (which as you will read is a critical opportunity to connect with an otherwise unknown recipient of the RFPs on the corporation's RFP team).

2. If you have a salesperson at your firm who assists with selling, get him or her involved as soon as you receive the RFP. Make sure you leave the sales person voicemail to alert him or her of the receipt of the RFP as soon as you receive it. Sometimes these documents get lost on desks or in interoffice mail. This means that critical deadlines (and therefore sales and relationship-building opportunities) are lost as well. It is important to understand that preparing an RFP or any sales pitch for that matter is as critical as preparing for a trial or other significant

The Sales Process: Address Needs and Present

client matters. To dismiss RFPs as not as important as your legal work is to dismiss an important opportunity to connect with your clients and prospects.

3. Review the RFP carefully to understand what the company is looking for in the way of services. Assemble a team as soon as possible to develop a game plan. The team should always include the following people:
   - A person from each substantive area of the law who will work on the specific areas of the RFP seeking information about the practice.
   - A sales person or director of marketing from your firm's marketing and business development department. He or she may also invite someone on his or her team responsible for taking the lead on gathering information and preparing the final document to join this RFP response-planning group.
   - The director of finance, or director of billing, to answer all sections relative to fees.
   - The individual at your firm responsible for conflicts. There is no point in wasting resources responding to a RFP is you can't work with the prospective client due to a client.
   - The director of information technology. Most of today's RFPs have sections pertaining to the technology and how it will be used to communicate with your firm (extranets, client portals, electronic billing, etc.).

4. Take the time to go through the RFP point by point and assign an individual from the group who will be responsible for each section. In some cases, the response asked for will be one that is similar to another RFP response and existing boiler plate may be edited to fit this RFP as well. A good example of this is that now is typical for RFPs to ask about your firm's process improvement and project management programs; having a standard response to this question is a good idea.

5. Set a realistic time frame (usually at least one week before the RFP deadline) to have all information handed in to either the secretary preparing the final response or to the marketing de-

partment's designee. A copy of the RFP draft should go out to everyone as soon as possible for review and editing.

6. A cover letter and proposal cover should be prepared and copy center people should be notified that the RFP is coming their way for copying and binding. Many RFP requests ask that multiple hard copies be submitted as back-up to email submissions.

Note of Caution: The RFP response itself should be in the exact format the questions were asked. Generally this is an outline format. It is critical not to get creative and use your own formatting. The in-house counsel or his or her administrative person who prepared and sent the RFP is familiar with the format. It is important to follow it point by point. Adding additional headings and information not requested is harmful to your chances of being asked to present, which is the next stage.

Take the Bull by the Horns

The common thinking by many lawyers who receive RFPs is that the decision about which firm to award the work to has already been made and the RFP process is just that, a process to show senior management at the company that the selection was made thoughtfully. This may be true in some cases; however, a seasoned sales person knows that once given the invitation, the opportunity does exist to take the business away from another firm, even if the odds are high against your firm. Part of the reason the opportunity exists is the RFP process opens the door to what once might have seemed a tightly shut door. This is the sales side of the RFP.

Take every opportunity to speak with the decision-maker or with the person who will be reviewing the RFP responses. Your goal here is to get to the next step of the process: to present to the in-house team making the decision. While nothing is guaranteed, you will want to give yourself and your firm the best opportunity for being at that final meeting, competing in person.

Upon receipt of the RFP, and after the first review with the response team, come up with questions to which you require answers and designate someone to make the call. If your firm does have a salesperson who assists with business development, he or she is the best person to make this call along with the lawyer who has some connection to the

The Sales Process: Address Needs and Present

company and the decision-makers. Some questions, in addition to those you may have from reading the RFP, follow:

1. What criteria will you be using for your final selection? (This is critical information to have. On what basis will the RFPs be judged?)
2. Who is the competition? How many firms are in the running and who are they? (You must know against which firms you are competing. This may shape your message or your sales strategy.)
3. Who will be making the final decision? (Get specific names and titles.)
4. Is it possible to present our RFP response in person? (It's worth the trip if you can be in front of the decision-maker.)
5. How significant will price be in the final analysis of firms invited back to present?

Where the Marketing Team Fits In

The marketing department of most firms has information about the various practice areas of the firm. This information often provides at least a strong start to describing the areas about which the RFP seeks information. If no descriptions exist, or they are outdated, which is the case with many firms' practice descriptions, then this process provides a good opportunity for updating all this information. Remember, the people who can best describe the practice areas and update new case information are the lawyers, not the marketers. The marketers will take this information and help you to make it compelling to the readers of the RFP.

How Much Is Too Much?

Responding to an RFP is best kept to a simple, easy-to-read amount of information. We reviewed an RFP that included 42 bios of firm members! This is overload. Few people have time to read lengthy descriptions. Keep it simple. The easier you make your response to read, the better shot you have at having it read. Apply the same principle to the RFP as to a resume. Saying everything you want to say is fine for an in-person meeting. Keep paper/electronic responses to a concise minimum and you will differentiate your firm's response from others from that aspect alone.

One more tip: Try to include information only about what the RFP requests. Often, lawyers will want to tell all. Again, too much is not a good thing. In addition, too much means too much to read. Any information outside of what is being requested does not respond to what is important to the in-house folks who review the responses. On point is best.

RFP Logistical Tips

1. Check out the latest RFP software that may be available to simplify the process or have the marketing department at the firm create one.
2. Know the criteria for selection.
3. Keep it simple. Too many words mean too much time to read.
4. Tie what is presented in the RFP to needs that have been identified in the RFP. In other words, relate the benefits of your pitch directly to the prospect.
5. Deliver the response one day before the deadline if possible. Responsiveness is everything to clients. Handing the RFP early will make a good impression.
6. Follow the format used by the company in the RFP to create your response.
7. Add partner and associate bios as an addendum and keep it to a manageable few. Again, too much to read means it will not get read.
8. Use client logos for the cover sheet of the RFP response.
9. Tie in other points of interest such as service initiatives, IT initiatives as addenda and point out how these are of benefit to the company.
10. Follow up the RFP with a phone call on the day the company indicated it would make a decision. If no date appears, then follow up within 10 days to learn where the decision-making is at.

The Sales Process: Address Needs and Present

Sample Presentation PowerPoint

This presentation is based on a real example. I have changed the name of the company. The scenarios in the example are real and the comment from the in-house counsel is also real. She sent it about an hour after the meeting.

Background: The company had worked with a significant IP Litigation firm. They were happy with the results but unhappy with the way the relationship was handled. They felt they were taken for granted and that the lead litigator never took the time to check in and make sure the client was happy—in other words, good client management. The firm that created the following presentation had been calling on the in-house law department for a couple of years and finally got an audience. The lead attorney from the firm did his homework, asked all the questions up front (assessed needs), and learned about what was important to the in-house team. Basically, given that the firm has excellent IP litigation skills, the in-house team was then concerned with the way the firm managed the relationship—the service side of the relationship—and made it clear that the decision was based on three things: 1) proven track record with IP litigation; 2) consistent management of the case and the client relationship; and 3) lead attorneys would be present for the handling of the case.

Here is the presentation based on those objectives:

The Woman Lawyer's Rainmaking Game

SMITH & NORFOLK LLP

FIRM

Patent Litigation Group:

Providing legal services to enforce patent rights and defend against claims of patent infringement.

PRACTICE

EXPERIENCE

The Company

April 2004

PARTNER WITH SMITH & NORFOLK

Company
- Communicate your business needs
- Share your business goals and strategies
- Provide level of involvement you want for each decision in the case.

+

Smith Norfolk
- Understand your business goals and needs.
- Commit our Seattle resources to your success
- Anticipate your legal needs and commit to "no surprises"!

= **Your Success**

The Sales Process: Address Needs and Present

WHY SMITH & NORFOLK LLP?

- Experienced
- Hands-on, Seattle-based Experience
- Understand Your Business (at our expense)
- No Surprises!

HANDS ON APPROACH
- We assign a team of attorneys to meet your needs and the partners don't disappear once the case is landed

WE'RE LARGE ENOUGH
- We're a nationally ranked patent litigation firm and our Seattle office is one of our most active IP litigation offices.

TEAMWORK – "NO COMMUNICATION SURPRISES"
- If we know it, you will know it
- Teamwork is critical to delivering results you want
- We will understand your business at our expense
- We enable the in-house counsel to keep the business executives well informed
- We employ technology to deliver on teamwork including, Blackberry's and client extranets to store case documents

TEAMWORK – "NO FINANCIAL SURPRISES"
- We provide a budget for litigation so financial planning is possible.

SEATTLE OFFICE AND FIRM OVERVIEW

- Smith & Norfolk is a full-service U.S. law firm with the breadth and depth required by emerging and established companies of all sizes and industries.
- The Seattle Office has over 70 attorneys, including:
    - Over 25 General Litigators, and
    - Six full time Patent/IP Litigators
- The Seattle Office also has patent prosecution attorneys who provide technical expertise and litigation support to the Patent Litigation Group.
- The Seattle Office has full-service technical and litigation support personnel, including library and paralegal staff specifically trained in researching patents, prosecution histories, and prior art.
- Smith is among the 35 largest law firms in the U.S. with over 800 lawyers worldwide.

The Woman Lawyer's Rainmaking Game

PATENT LITIGATION AT SMITH & NORFOLK SEATTLE OFFICE AND BEYOND

Smith ranked 2nd in the number of patent lawsuits filed on behalf of plaintiffs, and 10th in combined plaintiff and defendant patent lawsuits filed in the United States during 2002.

IP Law & Business

Smith is among the firms most mentioned for prosecuting patents of best quality, as rated by Patent Rankings, in 2002.

*"Power Prosecutors,"
IP Law & Business*

PATENT LITIGATION DEPTH

ß More than 40 Smith attorneys specialize in IP litigation; some of Smith's most experienced patent litigators are in *Seattle*.

ß Many of Smith's more than 80 registered patent attorneys and agents provide litigation support; the *Seattle Office* has 8 registered patent attorneys.

PATENT LITIGATION EXPERTISE

ß Smith & Norfolk's trial lawyers have worked closely with our intellectual property lawyers to provide intellectual property litigation services that combine the real courtroom experience of our trial lawyers with the depth of technical and substantive law expertise of our patent group. We understand the technology, the substantive law, and the courtroom, and we pride ourselves on our ability to present complex technical issues to a judge or jury in a clear and persuasive manner.

ß Smith's patent litigation attorneys successfully try cases to a verdict or decision before both juries and judges. Because we know how and are not afraid to try complex cases, we have the credibility and savvy to often obtain favorable out-of-court resolutions to difficult disputes.

ß We recognize the cost and uncertainty that litigation presents to our clients, and we strive to achieve the most cost-beneficial results possible for them. Smith is a member of the CPR Institute for Dispute Resolution, and our lawyers have used the full range of alternative dispute resolution

SMITH & NORFOLK IS NATIONALLY RANKED FOR ITS REPRESENTATION OF CLIENTS IN PATENT LITIGATION

Smith's Seattle office is one of our *most active* patent litigation groups

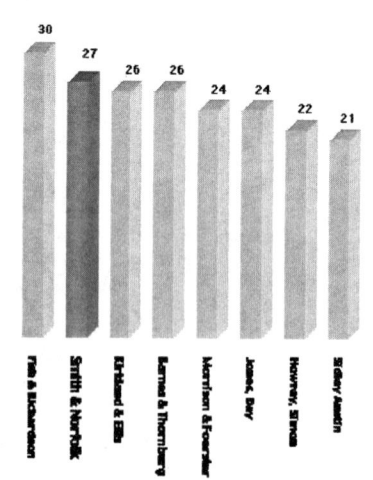

Firm	Count
Fish & Richardson	30
Smith & Norfolk	27
Kirkland & Ellis	26
Karmel & Thornburg	26
Morrison & Foerster	24
Jones, Day	24
Howrey, Simon	22
Sidley Austin	21

In a survey by IP Law & Business, Smith ranked 2nd in the number of patent lawsuits filed on behalf of plaintiffs, and 10th in combined plaintiff and defendant patent lawsuits filed in the United States during the year.

IP Law & Business

The Sales Process: Address Needs and Present

SMITH & NORFOLK PATENT & IP LITIGATION TEAM – SEATTLE OFFICE

TRACK RECORD

- We have represented clients:
    - in most jurisdictions across the country
    - before the Federal Circuit
    - prosecuting, and defending against, patent-related *antitrust claims*.

PERSPECTIVE

- Our attorneys are experienced representing clients in patent litigation on both the plaintiff's side and the defendant's side.
    - Our experience obtaining injunctions and damages for patent owners improves our ability to attack patents and defend against claims of infringement.
    - Our experience attacking the infringement, validity, and enforceability of patents makes us better at analyzing effective and economical patent enforcement strategies.

Our goal is to deliver the business results you want

We devise strategies with clients to minimize risk, win lawsuits, and — if possible — keep clients out of court altogether.

SMITH & NORFOLK PATENT & IP LITIGATION TEAM – SEATTLE OFFICE

EXPERIENCE

- The patent litigators in Smith & Norfolk's Seattle Office are among the most experienced and successful in the Pacific Northwest.
    - Four attorneys have been practicing in the litigation and/or patent law areas for 30 years.
    - Several attorneys have experience handling patent litigation *from the Court's perspective* as judicial clerks.
    - The Seattle patent litigation team includes *lawyers who teach patent litigation at the University of Washington* and to other lawyers.
    - Our lawyers have experience litigating utility and design patents covering diverse technologies and business methods.
    - Many of our litigators have analyzed patents *from the U.S. Patent and Trademark Office's perspective* as patent prosecutors.

TECHNOLOGY TO INTEGRATE OUR TEAMS

- Our team is an extension of your team
- Global technology integration
  - Team collaboration tools
  - Extranet
  - Video, Web and teleconferencing
  - Client accessible databases

CLIENT INTERFACE

Notice how the entire presentation is focused on the client's objectives. In this case, the client was quite pleased with the legal work from another firm. What they were very unhappy about was the relationship part of the engagement. Shortly after the meeting, on the same day, the attorneys who presented received an email stating, "Your presentation was the best presentation we have seen. You stayed on point and addressed our concerns. We thank you and look forward to working with your team."

The next chapter discusses the closing stage of the process, which is about asking for the business, obtaining the engagement. Assuming all has gone well up to this point, it should happen seamlessly.

CHAPTER 7

The Sales Process: Asking for the Business and Closing

Highlights
- How *Do* I Go About Getting the Business?
- In Sales, Never Put Anything Off to Tomorrow
- No Follow-Up Often Means No Business
- Big Bank Case Study
- There's No Magic - Don't Beat Around the Bush, Take Control
- Trials and Demos Work for Law too
- The Prospect's Investment — Making Them Use Their Time Wisely, While Investing It in YOU
- In-Person Is Always Stronger than By Mail or Phone
- Overcoming Objections
- Addressing the "Price" Objection
- Working Tool: Objections Worksheet
- The Myth of Closing
- Tip Sheet: A Brief Primer on Professional Selling

Business is never so healthy as when, like a chicken, it must do a certain amount of scratching for what it gets. —Henry Ford

How *Do* I Go About Getting the Business?

One of the most commonly asked questions I hear is: "How do I ask for the business?" My answer: "Just ask!" If you don't ask, you don't get, right?

When it comes to obtaining new business, Fasken Martineau's Susan Paish says, "How do I ask for the business? Often, not at all. I, personally, don't see business development as a 'task' where a box is ticked off at the end of the day. It is all about building relationships and part of who I am is to get to know the people whom I would like to work with (or to get to know better the people whom I am working with). In most cases, they call me for help long before I ever think of 'making a pitch'." She adds, "*However*, if there is a pitch needed, I am straight up and direct. No beating about the bush: 'If you are going to do x then we have the best people for you on that and you should call them, or do you want me to get them to give you a call?' (Tip: never say that you have the best in something if it's not true. That's another thing I am very clear on with a prospect. I don't ever oversell)."

Anne Marie Whittemore advises, "I directly ask for business during a beauty contest to expressly state that we would like to undertake the representation."

Again, no beating around the bush. Direct is the best approach.

In Sales, Never Put Anything Off to Tomorrow

"I sent the proposal a month ago and have heard nothing" is a common lawyer regret heard by many marketers and sales directors. Not hearing from a prospective client does not mean a "no." Simply, it means you have heard nothing. But, why leave fate in the prospect's hands? Once the opportunity arises to present to a group of prospects, submit information or a proposal about your firm to the client/prospect, make sure you attach a follow-up date. Part of the process is to note in your calendar when you will next follow up with your contacts.

The Sales Process: Asking for the Business and Closing

No Follow-Up Often Means No Business

"I don't want to be a pain," or "appear too aggressive" is something I hear all the time from lawyers as an excuse for not following up on a regular basis. It is important to know that if you are out of sight, you are out of mind. Clearly, if you phoned every day or more often than the prospective client asked of you, it would be too much. Not following up means that someone else may receive business from an individual with whom you've spent time cultivating a relationship.

Aggressive is phoning every day to learn about what's taking so long to "close" the deal. If you are actively pursuing a piece of business and you are competing against other firms, follow up by email or phone at least once every two weeks. Every week might be better. Common sense should dictate the timing. Ask your client/prospective client: "When should I call you next?" Then, try to phone in at least a day or two before that since that's the date they most likely have in mind for making the final decision. Not doing so may mean losing business or learning about a new twist in the situation too late. The easiest way to accomplish regular follow-up is to ask: "May I phone you in another week to hear about where you are at with your decision-making process?" A decision-maker will be happy to let you know how often is often enough.

If you have followed up at least three or four times and still nothing is going on, ask point blank, "Is there more to the process I should know about, such as another person with whom I need to meet?" If you ask, you will probably learn something new that will help you to obtain the engagement. If you do not ask, it's very likely you will learn nothing.

Here's a cast study that demonstrates a recent example of this.

Big Bank Case Study

A female senior partner from a large global firm was asked to provide information about her firm's benefits services. She arranged for a small team to meet with her contact, a deputy in-house counsel. She asked lots of questions and learned the bank was also interested in possibly moving its corporate securities work from its existing counsel to another firm.

She left the meeting and indicated she would send information about both the benefits services and the corporate securities work. Excited, she phoned the marketing director of the firm to review what had happened. She also let the head of corporate securities know about the opportunity.

After carefully preparing a brief, to-the-point proposal about the benefits and executive compensation services, she sent the information off to the in-house counsel, along with a letter explaining how the firm may also provide services, at the appropriate time, for the corporate work. It seemed imminent that the benefits business was coming her way.

Three weeks later, after two follow-up calls to no avail, advice from the marketing director urged her to phone every day at either 8:00 a.m. or 5:30 p.m. until she reached the in-house counsel directly.

The partner connected on the second call. Asking for more information, the senior partner learned that although he and one of his in-house colleagues was interested in getting new counsel for the benefits area as soon as possible, it was not ultimately their decision, but in fact, that of the senior counsel of the bank.

The sales strategy was adjusted and the managing partner for the law firm along with another contact of the senior in-house counsel paid a visit to the bank to learn about what was happening. Surprisingly, the senior in-house counsel knew nothing about the senior partner's visit to his bank or about the proposal. She indicated that although they were going to change counsel, this would be accomplished through an RFP process later in the year.

And so it goes. The deal is not lost, but until she asked, the senior partner was unaware that another step in the process was necessary (or two steps for that matter). Since the deal is still in play at the

The Sales Process: Asking for the Business and Closing

> writing of this book, we don't know what will happen, but the sales opportunity is once again on track, due to the resourcefulness of the senior partner and her willingness to work with others as a team to take the right steps. By asking for the business, she learned that the bank was not yet ready. By asking what next steps she should take, she learned about another layer of decision-making. My guess? She'll get the business but like lots of sales opportunities, it will take longer than anticipated. It will happen on the prospect's timeline, not on the lawyer's timeline!

There's No Magic—Don't Beat Around the Bush, Take Control

To be successful at rainmaking, learn to be comfortable asking for the business. Goulston & Storr's Debbie Horwitz is comfortable asking for business and advises, "Ask for the business very directly. I always express my appreciation for someone to have taken the time to meet with me/us and ask what the next step is. Under certain circumstances, I even assume that we're going to be working together and ask how they want to get started on the most immediate task(s)."

Kirkpatrick & Lockhart's Janice Hartman notes, "I ask for business by engaging in dialogues about problems and issues facing their companies, and looking for opportunities to suggest we can help where I know we can outperform."

"I ask for business by indicating my enthusiasm for what the client is doing," comments Davis Wright's Jane Potter. "This is easy to do in the biotechnology field, where you can share with the client your experiences with healthcare, for yourself, or perhaps a friend or relative. I tell them I would like to help in any way I can to get their product or healthcare idea to the market so that people suffering from that disease or condition can receive treatment. That way your motives for working with them are more genuine, as opposed to simply trying to get the work for its own sake."

"For me, I'm not sure 'asking for business' is as effective as directly sharing with a client that we have a way to solve their legal problems," shares Baker's Maura Ann. She confidently offers this advice: "Lawyers are problem solvers. Brainstorming ideas, even on a promotional basis, gives me an opportunity to work together with a prospective client. That's my foot in the door because to work with me is to want to work with me again."

Trials and Demos Work for Law too

I distinctly remember the day when I suggested we "demo" the lawyer. We tried and tried to get a large litigation client's corporate work. Unfortunately, another firm had a lock on the work. Once before I suggested sending in a lawyer to do free work on our dime. A partner quickly looked at me and said, "We are not selling toothpaste." A few weeks later, a more senior member of the management team at the firm suggested sending one of the firm's best associates in to the client site for a period of time. I replied, "We are going to demo a lawyer!" The partner looked at me surprised at my language and replied, "Yes, demoing a lawyer."

Quite simply what I mean by this is if you have a strong relationship and can't seem to break through to actually close new business either with an existing client or with a prospective client, offer them a chance to try you or your firm at either a reduced fee for only one matter (obviously something straight-forward other than litigation) or for some portion of a matter. Once the client is committed to you, they will work hard to make the relationship work and strive for a favorable result. Going back to the example referenced above, the client was willing to allow the firm to place one of their top corporate associates at the client's site for three months to work in an area where the law department needed assistance. The result for both the client and the firm was favorable.

Once a client has committed to trying the law firm—either by having one of the firm's attorneys on site or by sending one or two matters to the firm to see how they are handled—a buyer of legal services will find many ways to try to make the relationship work. Taking on new business at a reduced rate, showcasing the legal talent somehow will turn to your advantage.

The guidelines for doing this must be strict. Some firms have had the clients hire their lawyers. This obviously has caused problems for the firm. One firm dealt with this by letting its clients know up front that

The Sales Process: Asking for the Business and Closing

if they hired one of its attorneys away from the firm, they had to pay a search fee. While that approach was extreme, some other agreement between you and the client is necessary in case this type of thing happens. Clients agree with most of these guidelines. Again, the better you know your client or prospective client and the tighter you fit your services to their needs, the stronger the relationship. The key is to ultimately build loyal clients—those who won't be swayed by competitors' marketing and sales teams.

The Prospect's Investment—Making Them Use Their Time Wisely, While Investing It in YOU

Recall in Chapter 4 that I discuss assessing needs. A key factor in presenting to the prospect is to tie prospect's needs along with other information learned during the questions phase of the sales process to your presentation. The presentation is an opportunity to show you listened and heard what the prospect said. By randomly discussing the firm's services, without fitting them to clearly defined client/prospect objectives, you will lose the opportunity at the negotiating table to win and leave the door open for competitors to do the job.

Here's an example: A large pharmaceutical client in New England works with several outside law firms. A firm that had no business with the client approached the chief patent counsel to learn more about whom he used outside the corporation for his patent work and to manage his patent portfolio. He started the meeting by saying he was quite happy with the firms he was currently using. Not taking no for an answer, the lawyer (from San Francisco) asked, "Is there anything from a business perspective that you believe you could better accomplish with your patent process?" (*Assessing needs with open-ended questions*) Upon thinking about this, the patent counsel responded by saying he had no way of managing his portfolio of patents and also no way of tracking his patent application process. The lawyer asked, "If there was a way we could provide you with a solution to this, would you consider using our firm?" The in-house counsel thought and responded by saying, "I would absolutely consider using your firm if you were able to assist with this."

The lawyer made a call that day to the firm's chief information officer to schedule a time to discuss how he might achieve this for the client using the firm's technology and by building an extranet. (The lawyer, by the way, was also an engineer and understood how to accomplish part of this task through programming a simple solution for tracking patents). Once completed, another meeting was set up with the in-house counsel to show the firm's solution. During the presentation, the lawyer was clear to begin the conversation by recalling the business problem that was discussed during his first meeting. Now, presenting the solution and linking it directly to the needs of the patent counsel, there is a clearer opportunity for closing the business.

Oh, by the way, the firm is now the outside counsel to the corporation for all its patent work. This example may seem simple, but it's exactly how the situation occurred. Primarily, it's about the client and not about the firm and what you are trying to sell. Try it. You will be solving a need. Don't forget to *ask* for the business though!

In Person Is Always Stronger than By Mail or Phone

To the extent possible, once a "live" opportunity presents itself for possible retention on a project, following up meetings by in-person visits is the best way to continue to show strong interest in obtaining the business. These visits also go a long way toward developing closer relationships between the client and the firm. As in the previous example, the lawyer was from San Francisco and the prospective client from New England. It was worth the trip to meet in person both times, wasn't it?

Since many opportunities are with clients who are not across town in-person follow-up may not be feasible. In this case, regular telephone calls are the next best way to being there. One question that comes up often is: "How often is too often? I don't want to seem too intrusive or be a pest." When an opportunity is hot, once a week is not too often to call. If there is no response to your calls, try calling early in the morning between 7:30 and 8:00 or after 5:00 when people are usually at their desks planning for the next day or winding down for the day. If you try a few times and don't reach the person, no need to leave a voicemail, just keep trying until you get her on the phone. Don't give up!

Overcoming Objections

An objection is anything that prevents you from moving to the next stage of the sales process or from obtaining a new engagement from a client.

The Sales Process: Asking for the Business and Closing

Objections often provide opportunities for closing business. Again, back to the previous example, the objection was, "I already have outside patent counsel with whom I work." This provided the lawyer the opportunity to ask, "Are there any business issues you have that are unsolved?" To deal effectively with objections, use your negotiation skills. The process of dealing with objections is the same as the process of negotiation. Know where you are going and do what it takes to get there.

To handle objections learn to: Isolate, validate, negotiate. To wit:

Isolate: Restate the objection and ask for clarification.

Validate: Determine the source of the objection—validate its objective. Is it a stall tactic or a valid objection? (There are few valid objections.)

Negotiate: Relate objections to previously identified needs, restate how these are addressed by you/your firm, ask if your response addresses the concern.

Here are a few simple examples to make the point:

Objection: We've used [name of competition] for most of our services and we've been quite happy with them.

Isolate: Are you saying that your company prefers working only with [name of competition]? Under what circumstances do you work with firms other than [name of competition]? (This is an open-ended question; meaning the buyer has to speak and say something other than yes or no.)

Validate: So are you open to working with other firms under the right circumstances?

Negotiate: What approach do you recommend for us to become an approved outside firm? Or: What should we do to be considered for your next matter in an area you don't feel your current firm handles?

Basically, don't take no for an answer and try to determine what steps (by asking) will get you to a position that will allow you to be considered outside counsel.

Objection: Your pricing is too high.

Isolate: What specifically do you mean? (Remember, never assume, get them to say more.)

Validate: If pricing were not the issue, would your decision to be to choose our firm? (This will allow you to determine if price, in fact, is the issue.)

Negotiate: What type of pricing are you proposing?

Continue to negotiate and, again, remember to ask for the business.

Addressing the "Price" Objection

Neil Rackham, well-known author and sales coach to Fortune 100 companies' sales teams, advises in his book *Major Account Sales Strategy*, "Price is the 'respectable' way to express Consequences. [Clients] find it much easier to tell you they've decided not to buy because of cost than to explain issues such as mistrust, politics, hassle, or risk. And, because price-based decisions have business respectability, they can also be a convenient explanation within the buyer's own company. As a result, price is often used as a smoke screen for other concerns."

Price is seldom a valid objection. It's one we hear more and more when competing for business in the legal world. I read a letter from an in-house counsel who stated that given the inability to differentiate among "your four fine firms, I used price as the differentiator to make my decision." Two things come to mind with this response. First, the buyer was looking for someone to tell him why her firm was the best choice. For buyers of legal services, whether the services are divorce law, securities litigation or personal injury, a buyer needs information that will allow her to make a decision. The information must be tied (as I've stressed before) to an outcome or goal the buyer wants to achieve. Even for a simple estate plan being purchased by a person inexperienced with working with lawyers, there is something that you could connect with that person on. It's as simple as asking enough questions to build a relationship so the person builds trust with you. In this case, the services were labor and employment and the buyer was sophisticated. But for some reason, the lawyers presenting all talked at the buyer as opposed to with the buyer to

The Sales Process: Asking for the Business and Closing

help him make a decision based on a firm providing information to solve business goals. Your competition will also have trouble with connecting buyer needs to his firm's solutions (in other words—differentiating his firm from other firms). So by rehearsing this style and learning to listen before you present, you will have a competitive advantage.

Once you are able to differentiate your firm from a competitor's firm, by linking your firm's approach and legal solutions to the buyer's business needs, you will become better at obtaining more business for your firm. Refer to the PowerPoint in Chapter 6. The company's needs were clearly stated and the information in the presentation by the law firm was directly tied to those needs.

Differentiating factors include unique examples of how your firm is different. For example, a firm boasting experience with technology markets and can say it has over fifty lawyers with masters or doctoral degrees in engineering, differentiates itself from a firm that does not have these unique qualifications. A firm that has won several awards for the highest level of merger and acquisition deals differentiates itself from its competition. You use these examples when clients and prospects indicate experience in their type of business is critical for working with their company. Think of ways you can address the prospect's needs that relate to their business goals you uncovered in the Assess Needs stage of the sales process.

The opportunity to win business is everywhere.

Think of developing business as though you were out to win the best deal for your client, except the client in this case is YOU! You would not take no for an answer on behalf of your client. Try not to take no for an answer when it comes to winning business against your competition. The Working Tool on the following page will help you be prepared.
The constant cycle of presenting and following up can be tedious, but tenacity prevails.

> **Working Tool: Objections Worksheet**
>
> List the three most common objections you hear from prospects and clients.
>
> 1. _____
> 2. _____
> 3. _____
>
> Write down the ways in which you would restate the objection for clarification (as opposed to responding immediately).
>
> 1. _____
> 2. _____
> 3. _____
>
> Write responses to the objections that you can use when faced with any of these objections in the future.
>
> 1. _____
> 2. _____
> 3. _____

The constant cycle of presenting and following up can be tedious, but tenacity prevails.

The Myth of Closing

Michael O'Horo, an expert in legal sales and coach to many lawyers, has written much about legal sales. Following is a part of one of his articles. I believe this information will be very helpful for you, the reader, to think about how you approach prospective clients.

The Sales Process: Asking for the Business and Closing

I wish I had a dollar for every time a lawyer took me aside and said, very confidentially, "I really am a good salesman, but I could use a little help with closing the sale. Any tips you can give me?" Maybe they've been reading too many "Ten Tips to Effective Selling" airline magazine articles, but lawyers, like many other professionals, spend an inordinate amount of time and energy worrying about closing the sale.

They miss one of the most important truths of successful selling: Just as in the law, the secret to a successful outcome is in the preparation—the setup. Whether preparing to do battle in the courtroom or the boardroom, successful lawyers know the importance of preparation. This includes understanding the substantive issues to be contemplated as well as the politics and personalities involved.

Yet, when preparing to match wits in sales competition, most lawyers seem to suffer a form of strategic and tactical amnesia, abandoning preparation altogether and narrowing their focus prematurely on closing. Professional salespeople know that, if the setup or preparation is done correctly, closing is easy, almost a non-event. Rainmakers seem to sense this; they know that they can't rush the sale.

Conversely, poor preparation and setup guarantee failure in selling just as surely as in court-no matter how good the closing technique or argument. Rushing to judgment in the courtroom often means a negative verdict. It is likewise in selling.

Whenever sales professionals call me at the 11th hour to ask for help saving an endangered sale, I start by having them describe each event and discussion from Day One of the opportunity. Invariably, the "closing problem" turns out to be a breakdown in early stage preparation: an important question wasn't asked or a red flag was ignored. It's always something they already know how to do, but didn't. They cut an important corner on the way to sales success.

Okay, so how does it work? Contrary to what some people fear, closing does not mean coercing the unconvinced or the unwill-

The Woman Lawyer's Rainmaking Game

ing into doing what we want them to do. Such an approach is long discredited even among exploiters, and never had any standing among professionals. Also, contrary to popular myth, closing does not occur at a decision point.

Reluctance to close arises from the perception that it is the Moment of Truth when the prospect decides to accept or reject the sales proposition. Moments of Truth are risky: If the prospect says "No," our effort was wasted. No wonder most untrained salespeople devise so many ways to avoid closing.

Ironically, the feared Big Decision is comfortably and effectively avoided by asking for a number of little decisions, i.e., getting agreement and confirmation as each point is established, just as a trial lawyer does when examining a witness.

A professional salesperson closes only when the prospect has acknowledged that the salesperson has made his "case." Then the salesperson "concludes," along with the prospect, at the only sensible course is to buy, just as a lawyer establishes a series of related points which, taken together, makes his conclusion inescapable. A lawyer makes a closing argument or statement only after making the case and convincing the jury to "buy" his interpretation of the evidence.

Even in the simplified model below (A Brief Primer on Professional Selling), you can see that selling draws on the very skills that made you a successful lawyer, and that closing is merely the wrap-up after we have agreement on the validity of a course of action.

Watch successful rainmakers. You never see the expected deep breath and shifting of gears as they move in for a "kill." Instead, they simply ask the client to deliver the relevant documents so the firm can begin working on the new matter. There is no need to make closing a separate event. It's merely a confirmation of the agreement already reached.

The Sales Process: Asking for the Business and Closing

Closing is an important part of the selling process, just as making the summation or final argument is in the law. But, as in the law, any argument will fail without careful and thoughtful preparation. In today's highly competitive legal marketplace, what lawyer can afford to squander even one selling opportunity?

1. Excerpt from "Sales Results" newsletter by Michael O'Horo, November 2003.

Tip Sheet: A Brief Primer on Professional Selling

- Understand the conditions under which your service can be of help to the prospective client.
- Know what evidence you need to get the prospect to conclude that he or she might need you or your firm in particular.
- Confirm that the suspected conditions apply and that the need is one that you or your firm can fulfill.
- Identify and develop relationships with each person in that organization who influences the purchase of legal services.
- Figure out who the real buyer is—the one person in this group of influencers with the authority to release funds for legal services.
- Find out how important the underlying problem is to each of these influencers, the value of solving it, and the cost of doing nothing.
- Determine what result the organization wants and how each influencer will personally benefit from using your services.
- Differentiate yourself from competitors by showing a unique value obtainable only from your firm.
- Confirm that each influencer favors your solution as the best means of obtaining the necessary results, and that the value offered is most attractive.
- Close by confirming the details of implementation.

—Michael O'Horo

The Woman Lawyer's Rainmaking Game

Spending the time to create a strong business argument for hiring your law firm that is tied to specific information you uncovered during your assess needs ("research") phase of the sales process will guarantee you strong results each and every time. The next chapter will help you retain clients once you've landed the big one!

CHAPTER 8

Maintaining Client and Contact Relationships

Highlights:

- Keep In Touch—It's Critical to Your Long-Term Success as a Professional
- Who, What, and How Often to Connect with Contacts
- CRM—What it Means to Your Client Maintenance Program
- As Soon as You Obtain a Client, They Become Someone Else's Prospect
- Clients Consider You Their Lawyer Even when They Aren't Actively Working with You
- Key Tips for Staying in Touch with Inactive Clients

We can learn to soar only in direct proportion to our determination to rise above the doubt and transcend the limitations. —David McNally, Even Eagles Need a Push

Keep In Touch—It's Critical to Your Long-Term Success as a Professional

Keeping in touch is not difficult. At the beginning of the year, develop a game plan for keeping in touch with your contacts at least four times a year. If you don't, they will develop relationships with other lawyers and you may be the last to find out. Clients and contacts will seldom provide you with the opportunity to renew relationships. They will instead turn away and build new relationships rather than call or email to inform you they haven't heard from you in a while.

The Woman Lawyer's Rainmaking Game

Here is an easy way to do this. Think of the calendar year in quarters. During the first quarter, after all the holiday mail has cleared, usually mid-February, send out a newsletter (by email, clients often don't read "snail" mail) to everyone letting them know how you are doing, how the firm, if applicable, is doing. If you had a great previous year with some successes, share these. People want to stay in touch with successful people and if you don't tell them about your success, who will? During the second quarter, say mid-May, before summer vacations begin, send out another update. This time, do something fun. I've heard great stories about what lawyers (men and women) send to their clients. Clients and contacts love it!

Some examples: a favorite recipe (at the end of your update/ newsletter), a certificate to a plant nursery with a note that reads, "Thanks for helping our business grow," a list of two or three books you've read or heard are terrific (or buy a number of books and send a copy to everyone). All these things work. People are people, even lawyers! A couple of firms have published cookbooks and send them to their entire client and contact database. The response is terrific and enthusiastic.

During the third quarter (end of September) when everyone is back to work, send an update. Perhaps this time, invite a referral source to include some information about her practice or business. Inviting someone else who markets to the same audiences to contribute to your communiqué gives you the opportunity for your newsletter to be sent to your contributor's contact list in addition to yours. For the fourth quarter send out holiday cards to every one of your clients and contacts. Begin this process early, write them by hand. People appreciate the time and effort it takes.

Who, What, and How Often to Connect with Contacts

There are at least four groups of people with whom you need to stay in contact: 1) your business contacts; 2) your active clients; 3) your inactive clients; and, 4) those clients who did not hire you, but could become clients down the road. (A prospect is always a prospect until she becomes a client.)

A 700-lawyer firm recently asked several lawyers from the firm to identify ten people from each of the four groups above (business con-

Maintaining Client and Contact Relationships

tacts, active clients, inactive clients, and clients who did not hire them but are still prospective clients) and had them call these forty people. *Within a few days each attorney received at least one new engagement!* This technique is often referred to contact "mining."

1. Contacts

Your contacts are people with whom you've built valuable relationships. They, for the most part, are happy to refer business to you. The key to obtaining business from your contacts is to keep in touch regularly. This can be done by phone, email, or in person. Let them know that you are interested in providing them with referrals should the opportunities present themselves and that you also want them to keep you in mind for referrals as well.

Like many situations in life, if you don't ask, you won't receive. It's not that people don't want to help you with your business; it's more the case that everyone these days is busy. Unless you keep in touch, you simply are not top of mind. Stay in touch with valuable contacts. For some of you this may take extra effort. For some folks contacting outside a familiar circle does not come easily as it might for others. Because reaching out is important to your business, you need to jot it down on your to-do list. It is a great feeling to check it off.

2. Active Clients

We hear all the time from attorneys that they don't want to bother their clients while they are in the middle of litigation, a deal, or a closing. First, it is important for you to stop thinking you are bothering your clients. They expect that you show interest in their business and will let you know if it's not the right time to pursue other introductions. While you are closely working with your in-house colleague or client, ask them who on the legal team may be the best contact for one of your partners in another area of the firm's practice. It's a simple question and you can be sure your competitors are asking it too.

By taking the time to learn more about your clients' businesses, they will feel as though you are more connected to their company. Perhaps your request is to determine whom the right person is to invite to your firm's seminar that is in a specialty different than yours. Education is high on the list of in-house counsels. Try asking a few of your clients. You might be surprised at the results.

3. Inactive Clients

For those with practices that cater to individuals, such as estate planning, real estate closings, family law, the same mantra applies. Keep in touch with a note, an email, or a phone call. There may be changes in the law that cause you to connect to update an old estate plan, a holiday that provides a good reason to send a note, whatever the occasion, *keep in touch.*

Former clients (who believe you are their lawyer even though nothing new has happened) will be pleased to hear from you. They might even have something they are working on that might be sent your way. An AmLaw 100 firm conducted a market research study of emerging businesses. The study's information showed when clients change lawyers is when they have a need for a lawyer, think of you (their lawyer) and realize they have not heard from you. If they have not heard from you… well, out of sight, out of mind.

4. Contacts who did not hire you, but could become clients.

When the time came for you to bid or compete for a new piece of business and you lost the competition, don't forget about the contact. There will be more opportunities and many times rainmakers have found that these individuals will try to hand you more business in the future. Be strong if you lost the first time or even the second time around. Show that you are a good sport about the process. Keep in touch.

A partner based in the New Jersey branch of a large national firm tells a great story that is pertinent here. He lost business to the competition. After five or six months he followed up with his contact to keep in touch and "see how things are going." He was totally surprised by the answer he received. The prospect told him he was very happy to hear from him, that the firm he selected was not working out as well as he anticipated and he would, after all, like to give him the business.

Maintaining Client and Contact Relationships

Would the lawyer from New Jersey get the business if he had not made the call? My guess is maybe not. If there were other contenders, it may have gone to the first person who called. Again, it's the old out of sight out of mind syndrome. Keep in touch with ALL your contacts. By doing so, you will receive new business either directly or through referrals.

CRM—What It Means to Your Client Maintenance Program

Contact Relationship Management (CRM) is a fancy way of referring to "a keep in touch system." Many firms and individuals use products such as Microsoft's Outlook to store a contact list. Larger firms use sophisticated database tools that offer various reporting and updating capabilities. Many individuals use a spreadsheet. Social networking has built in CRM functions that make it easy to stay connected with your contacts as well.

No rainmaker is without her list of prospects, contacts, and clients saved in some organized format.

How will you keep in touch with all your contacts without a system? If you are a sole practitioner or member of a small firm, contact a college near you to find out about its internship programs in IT. Hiring a summer intern is not expensive and is a resource to help you input and/or edit your database. This should be done at least once a year.

If you are with a large firm that has IT support, have your assistant print out your database of contacts or obtain a printout from the firm's marketing team. Take the time to review your list. Titles, jobs, and business addresses change. No one will know this information except for you. It's critical you keep your list current. One way to accomplish this is to have your secretary call each contact (a few a day and it will be finished in no time). Email is also okay as well. Your contacts will appreciate the fact that you are taking the time to insure their information is correct. By checking on the accuracy of the information, you also have an opportunity to learn of any new positions, titles, changes in their job, etc. All information needs to be verified for accuracy, including spelling of name, title, address, phone—business and cell—fax, and email.

The Woman Lawyer's Rainmaking Game

When you return from a speaking engagement, networking event, a seminar, or sponsored event take the business cards you acquired and write on the back of the card where you met the individual and then record the information in the database.

Once a quarter, make it a point to phone each person on your list—even if it means making 200 calls! This is how you develop business—by keeping in touch. It's acceptable to send an email to keep in touch or to leave a voicemail. It's not necessary that you speak directly with the individual. Just leave a message or send a note to let them know you are thinking of them. This method works well for those of you who don't have the time to network or for those who are not particularly social. Anyone can build a book of business—how you do it should fit with your personality and style. Make the effort and keep your contact lists in order and current.

As Soon as You Obtain a Client, They Become Someone Else's Prospect

Recall the story about the New Jersey lawyer who phoned his prospect after he lost the business. This positive outcome can happen to you too. Your clients are another lawyer's prospects. The competitiveness of today's environment should dictate to you that constant and unprompted telephone calls and contact with your clients are critical to building *loyal* client relationships as opposed to simply, satisfied clients.

Many studies show there are lots of opportunities to interact with clients and build loyalty. Current clients like to be thanked for their business. How often do you do that? Believe it or not, an extremely effective way of doing this is to write a personal, handwritten note. The managing partner of a large firm does this regularly and receives many notes back from his clients thanking him for acknowledging the relationship. Why does this work? Because clients recognize that writing a note like this takes time. And, taking the time to show you care is appreciated. Clients also desire an expression of interest in their business goals by their outside counsel. Each year examine your top clients lists in your database and meet with your clients to ask them about the upcoming year's goals. They will appreciate it. For practices where the client is an individual rather than a company, take the time to thank

Maintaining Client and Contact Relationships

them for their business and remind them that if they or others in their lives have a need for legal services to phone you. Include a card to make it easy for them (or better yet, even a refrigerator magnet).

When was the last time you called a client during an engagement and asked her how things are going? Is she happy with the service from you, your partners, your associates, and team? Most lawyers do not do this. If you are looking for ways to differentiate yourself and your firm from the competition, this is certainly a strong way to achieve that. It does not cost much in time and is genuinely appreciated and recognized by clients.

The following is an example of what might happen if you *don't* stay in touch:

A chief litigation counsel from one of the largest insurance companies in the U.S. recently told a colleague of our that although he has used the same primary outside firm for litigation for the past three years, he has not heard from them other than when he calls them with a new matter or when the firm calls or meets specifically about a case. He expressed his surprise and dismay that after three years no one had come to see him just for the sake of sitting down and discussing how he was doing, his perspective about what could be better about the relationship, if anything. And, worse, he lamented the fact that they had never come to see him to talk about year end/new year goals. His parting comments were, "Time for new counsel, don't you think?"

How simple is it to make an appointment and visit with important clients? Yet, few lawyers take the time to make the effort.

Clients Consider You Their Lawyer Even When They Aren't Actively Working with You

Keeping in touch with existing clients who have current matters that you are handling for them is fairly straightforward. Through phone call updates and meetings, your clients see or speak with you on a fairly regular basis. But what about your inactive clients? They still consider you their counsel. Make a list or check your own client lists and make it a point to email/phone each one. It's best to try to reach them. Let them know you were simply calling to say hello and to hear how things

The Woman Lawyer's Rainmaking Game

are going. This simple task reaps many rewards. It reminds clients that YOU are their lawyer. Often times, lawyers who routinely keep contact with inactive clients find that they receive new business from those clients as a result of the telephone call, email, or visit.

A lawyer from a large American Lawyer 50 firm phoned several of her inactive clients and received four new pieces of business. She was quite surprised and pleased. These results should spur you on to do make more phone calls and keep your prospective client pipeline filled with new opportunities. Plus it's fun to connect with people.

Key Tips for Staying in Touch with Inactive Clients

- Create a list of the clients for whom you have worked over the past ten years or review your list of clients and make sure it is up to date. Send everyone a note, along with your business card. The note should say something like, "I was thinking of you and thought I'd drop you a line. I hope you and your family [if appropriate] are doing well. I would welcome the opportunity to catch up and have enclosed my card. Best wishes, or Warm regards." This simple note is a nice way of keeping in touch and making others feel as though they matter to you as a client/former client.

- Send holiday cards. It is critical. First, it's a great opportunity for keeping in touch without inventing a reason to contact people. Second, clients appreciate the thought. Make the time to write out the cards. We know a lawyer who has her secretary make out the holiday cards in July of each year so they are completed during a less busy time. The lawyer then writes out the cards with personal notes at the time she sends them for the holidays.

- Create a newsletter or update about your practice. Include success stories (you don't have to include client names) about your practice. People like to know their lawyer is successful so don't be shy about it. Women lawyers have often told me they don't like to appear aggressive or self-congratulating. You will appear to be neither of these. Sending out updates about your practice provides examples of what you do and what you have achieved for others. If you remind people about you and your

Maintaining Client and Contact Relationships

practice, they will most likely provide your name to a friend or colleague who is seeking a referral to a lawyer. If you make case law history, say so.

- Attend networking events where you will likely meet existing/inactive clients and contacts. Even if you are not the networking type, from time to time, try to make the effort to attend an event or two. A breakfast or cocktail reception around a women's agenda is always a good way to connect with others.
- If you love networking, create your own event. Invite all your contacts and colleagues and hand out a favorite book of yours to those who attend. You will be remembered long after the event. Making an event an annual function will provide your contacts with reminders about the opportunity to work with you.
- Send inactive clients who were once good clients tickets to something you know they and their family would like: a ball game, a play, movie tickets, or a concert. Better yet, join in if you are able.

In the next chapter we discuss how to maintain relationships and grow the business with your top existing clients. To prepare, examine your accounting records and determine who your top fifty clients are and you can use the tips in Chapter 9 to help maintain and grow those client lists.

CHAPTER 9

Key Client Strategies for Retention and Growth

Highlights:
- What Is a Key Client?
- Why Care About Key Clients?—What's the Opportunity?
- Establishing Ten Key Client Sales Initiatives at Your Firm

There will always be another summit to climb, another difficult route to do... but we must always keep in mind the style and means by which we achieve our goals is as important as the summit. —Sir George Mallory

What Is a Key Client?
Key clients for purposes of this book are defined as the top fifty to top one hundred revenue-producing clients of your firm. Generally, firms examine (through their billing systems) the list of the top one hundred largest fees generated for a given calendar year. There are other ways to assess key clients, but this is the most common and is a strong and productive approach to take.

Once the client list is established, examine the names of the clients. If there are any clients you don't want on the list, replace them with other clients whom you believe have further potential. If you have the type of clients at the firm who are individuals versus businesses, this approach still makes sense. These clients are clients who have developed a trusting relationship with their counsel—you or your partners. The strategy for targeting these individuals and leveraging your relationship with them will be a bit different than the strategies used by businesses, but still, any strategy that will focus on the relationship you have with your clients is a key client strategy. Again, the important thing to remember is that sales and client retention is about developing relationships with individuals not companies. Leveraging the strongest relationships and clients you and your firm have is the most important aspect of business development.

Why Care About Key Clients?—What's the Opportunity?
Surveys like the BTI Client Service Study, Martindale Hubbell's studies, and the ACCA Serengetti Study, along with law firms' independent findings, show over and over again that loyal clients spend more on your law firm than non-loyal clients. When asked if they are loyal to any one firm, the Fortune 500 in-house counsel who respond often say no. Building loyal clients (versus merely satisfied clients) is all about the relationship itself. Showing you care to a client is as important to your business as is showing you care to someone close to you in your personal life. It's necessary to say so, to show it, and it builds advocacy on your behalf.

Loyal clients of law firms spend more with one firm and are more likely to tolerate problems (in other words, give you another chance, if the occasion arises to do so); tell others about you and your firm (spread the word and become your advocates). Reasons enough to focus on top clients. And, top clients may not always be the top in billings. They may be potential top clients, so it behooves you to go through the client list and assess potential key clients as well. Billing numbers alone should not always be your selection criterion. If your firm has performed work for a significant company and the matter was small, you still have a new client who could potentially be a significant client if you focus on building the relationship.

A recent study conducted by a global 50 firm, unveiled the same type of information the BTI Consulting reports show. The firm found that understanding the clients' business was one of the top priorities. Why? Because if the lawyers understand their clients' business then they are in a far better position to help their clients *achieve* their business goals, *anticipate* their legal needs, and *partner* with the company

Key Client Strategies for Retention and Growth

to reach successful outcomes for the business (and in many cases, the shareholders). The firm hired a professional research firm to help with the study and to then assign "metrics" for measuring the future success. To insure the firm's professional and support staff were *aligned* with the clients' goals, they engaged a firm with significant experience helping law firms internally, and conducted another study to determine how "engaged" their attorneys and staff were. The focus of the internal study was to uncover what worked well for the staff and on the flip side, what would make the firm an even better place to work.

Happy lawyers and staff mean better support for clients. The client feedback on the work the firm did was excellent and did much for building team all around. The firm has now created the benchmark for ongoing interaction and feedback with its lawyers and clients. While the firm's initiative focuses on more than just key clients, it is imperative that a firm uses this approach to communicate with *at least* its best clients. How could you possibly build more business if you are not talking with your clients about their goals for growth? If I haven't convinced you to focus on clients, consider this: your competitors are targeting your clients—do you want to be proactive or reactive?

So build a key client program and reap the rewards.

Establishing Ten Key Client Sales Initiatives at Your Firm

Law firms, like businesses, provide a great opportunity to generate revenue. Revenue comes from focusing on existing clients. Existing clients build advocacy for you. They are great referral sources for new business. The goals for your plan: Retention of clients; growth of the business relationship (and thus, the potential for greater revenue), and new business.

Below are the steps to help establish major client initiative for success. Each step of the process will be further defined in this chapter.

- Identify the clients and prospects
- Identify the members of the firm's key client teams and include senior partners, junior partners, and associates
- Meet with all teams
- Conduct major account sales training for all team members

The Woman Lawyer's Rainmaking Game

- Assign revenue goals
- Establish monthly and quarterly meetings
- Adjust compensation credit to benefit all team members
- Track the key clients' company's activities and those of their industry
- Schedule a meeting with the client (or prospect)
- Keep the process moving

To better understand the above steps, let's examine each one in depth.

Identify the clients and prospects: Examine the firm's (or your) client list. Select those clients who have the potential to generate more revenue for the firm and also select the clients who are the firm's or your top 100 clients (the best way to assess this is by total revenue received from these clients). Review all the clients of the firm for consideration. For example, if a significant corporation is one of the firm's clients, even if the total billed to that company was small, they are still a client, the firm has a "foot in the door" and the opportunity is worth pursuing. The critical fact to remember as the firm or you progresses into a sales culture is that sales, like practicing law, is a serious business and one that requires careful analysis, constant focus, and results-oriented goals.

For those of you with private clients, the process will be no different. Perhaps your clients are not repeat clients, but they are still individuals with whom you can maintain a strong relationship and facilitate their ability to build advocacy on your behalf. Word of mouth is a powerful tool in obtaining new clients as you have no doubt experienced with your practice. To begin, review your client list and select the names of the individuals for whom you achieved good results. Think about clients with whom you built or have a strong relationship and you would like to keep in touch. You will be rewarded for following the same process as the lawyers who focus on individuals in larger organizations.

Identify the members of the firm's key client teams and include senior partners, junior partners, and associates for current clients: The lawyers who should be on each client team must be selected carefully.

Key Client Strategies for Retention and Growth

Some firms have not put the "billing partner" or "origination partner" on the team at all. In building the team, it is critical to remember the focus needs to be on what is best for the client and the client's company and not what is best for the lawyer or the firm. Many firms that are building client teams get stuck at this step.

First, select firm members who are team players. A partner who has contacts with the client or the prospect is good to have on the team, but not the most critical person. A note of caution: partners who have contact with clients are not always in touch with the business goals of the company. In many cases, their contact is limited to one or very few people in the law department. It is rare for a partner to have continuous communication with the CEO, CFO, or COO of a client company.

Building the team for prospects: For this discussion, a prospective company is one with which the firm has not been engaged in the past. In some cases a partner or other member of the firm may have a contact at a prospective company. This should not instantly guarantee a place on the team. Why? If there is a contact at the company, why wasn't this developed in the past? Just like practicing law, firm leaders should ask lots of questions prior to making decisions about these important team efforts.

Other team members should include a range of people from the firm, including junior partners and senior associates. It is critical to build a diverse team of people with different personalities and backgrounds who will allow the firm to build-in succession planning to continue long-term client relationships. It is often a mistake to include only partners on the team and the clients will think so as well.

Meet with all teams: Schedule a first meeting with all teams to discuss the firm's objectives for the major account initiative, to set expectations, and to answer questions team members may have about the initiative and their goals.

Conduct major account sales training for all team members: The client and prospect team members must learn new skills—sales skills. To insure teams are able to effectively compete for business, it is wise to build sales training into each team members' annual plan. Three or

The Woman Lawyer's Rainmaking Game

four training programs will not be too many. Lawyers do not have the training that professional salespeople have. (For sales training resources, see Resources.)

A commitment of time to learn these skills is important and not to be underestimated. No matter how busy you are, you are not too busy to take the time to build skills that will help you get and keep business. It is important to learn as much as possible and to be as comfortable with the sales process. Knowledge in this area increases the odds of winning new business. A criterion for moving forward as a member of the team will be to attend at least two training sessions. Attending training requires an investment of time. Two to three days total is not too many; in fact, it's just a start. Anyone who is not willing to invest this time in her training should not be part of the team—she may ultimately hurt the firm's chances of success in sales you win or lose.

Assign revenue goals: For existing clients, this process will be a bit easier since the firm has a track record and a billing history with the client. For prospects, the specific revenue goal will not be easy to determine until one or more meetings with the prospect have taken place. Since most lawyers are goal and deadline driven, knowing what the goal is makes it easier to know what steps to take to achieve it. A corporation's major account team works toward goals that are established by the company at the beginning of each fiscal year. Everyone at the company has a clear understanding of the revenue targets. One way to determine what you are aiming for is to learn from the client about how much his firm spends annually on legal fees. One East Coast firm with a significant West Coast client was surprised to learn that although it received a good deal of business (and thus revenue) from the client, that it was a mere fraction of the client's total expenditure on outside legal fees. There is always information to be learned by speaking with clients.

So, for example, company A spends $20 million annually on outside legal fees. This expenditure is spent on intellectual property lawyers, litigators, and corporate lawyers. The company is growing and expanding. One might assume that there is real estate and labor and employment work as well. One or two lawyers visiting the client's offices may determine this by asking the appropriate questions. It is NOT wise, for example, to bring a labor and employment attorney and real estate attorneys to the client to "pitch" the prospect on this business. It's presumptuous to do that. Once the individual(s) have a better understanding of the client's goals and business objectives from the visit, (and of course they would ask questions about hiring, physical plant expansion, etc.) only then is it wise to follow up with information about other areas of the firm and information about how you might assist the company with its goals.

At this point, you may be able to determine what potential revenue could be earned by providing more of the same services as well as these additional services. The firm would be wise to follow their clients' lead on setting target revenue goals. These goals should be adjusted after the first few client meetings once the opportunities have been assessed.

Establish monthly and quarterly meetings: Right up front ask all teams to plan out a calendar for regular team meetings. Using the firm's calendaring system, enter the dates into everyone's calendar. Teams should meet monthly to stay on target. As long as the majority of team members are available, the team should meet, take notes, and update everyone in writing. Many accounting firms have borrowed from their corporate counterparts and have adapted major account planning formats that are conducive to team updates. Having everyone working from the same documents and task lists is important to insure accurate flow of information across communications channels (which in many cases will be across offices). A glimpse at a sample one-month task list might show the following:

October Tasks for Company X Team
1. Meet with IP counsel to determine who on the in house counsel team is the appropriate labor and employment contact.
   Who: Susan.   Deadline: 10/4
2. Review current and past litigation matters with information resource team/library team.
   Who: Todd.   Deadline: 10/15
3. Schedule meeting with general counsel and other key corporation members (CFO/CEO) and managing partner of the firm.

The Woman Lawyer's Rainmaking Game

Who: Andrea.   Deadline: Schedule meeting before end of month/meeting to take place before 11/15.

Keep tasks each month to a manageable few, make them actionable and demand results from the team. If team members lag in results, change team members. This is about client retention and growth. It will be important for everyone to have retention and growth as part of the underpinnings of their team efforts.

For the effective management of teams (and therefore firm goals and revenue targets), meet quarterly with teams to learn which teams may need assistance with their strategy, team focus, or team members. Firm management has a role in these key client teams as well. Showing management support for the initiative will accomplish two tasks: First, teams will understand that they will be held accountable for their performance; and second, teams will understand the firm expects and applauds the client focus and the team members' efforts.

Adjust compensation credit to benefit all team members: From the management side of the firm adjustments may need to be made to the firm's overall compensation system to facilitate team selling and cross-firm selling. A team is a team, and one individual should not be carrying the weight for the entire team, nor should one individual obtain credit for the whole team. This important adjustment in compensation has already been made to many firm's compensation plans. Adjusting compensation to ensure clients are firm clients and not individual clients will be not only show important support for the team members, but will begin the necessary shift of the firm's culture from individual participation in firm goals to team participation. Firms that have a one firm mindset will surely survive those firms that are made of a group of individuals. Shifting origination credits from a "client" view to a "matter" focus, also can aim emphasis toward expanding the effort to cross-marketing other practice areas to existing clients. Also, most firm accounting/compensation systems can accommodate "tiered" matter or client origination credit reporting, so that a multi-lawyer team can be entered into the system as a single entity that is itself made up of (for example) 25 percent individual credit for each of four attorneys.

Key Client Strategies for Retention and Growth

Hale and Dorr (now Wilmer Cutler Pickering Hale and Dorr) was a leader in designing compensation systems other firms followed. Known for its "Smith System," the firm was watched by other firms as a leader. In the early 1980s the management team at the firm understood that in order to promote the team, to build and retain clients, and to ensure collegiality among its professional and support staff, it transitioned to a compensation structure that supported the enlightened thinking. All clients ultimately became firm clients. Everyone was expected to support the team, work hard for clients, insure financial discipline, and respect everyone in the firm. This model and culture runs strong today throughout the firm and is continuously reinforced and supported by its strong management team. Those who test it and try to run counter to the culture will quickly learn there are no exceptions to the team environment of respect. In this case, everyone wins.

Paul Hastings in California is another firm that upholds these values and reaps client benefits as a result, with a strong system that rewards team-based proliferation of clients across the firm's many offices and practice specialties. Again in the late '80s, management of the firm determined that a strong team approach, internally and externally benefits the clients, the firm's support team and the firm's lawyers. Strong management at the firm rewards the positive culture with a compensation system designed to support the culture the firm wishes to maintain.

Track the key clients' company's activities and those of their industry: Track the company's activities through the firm's information resources (library) group to stay apprised of any recent developments with the company. Some good resources in general for tracking industries and large companies include *Business Week; Fortune; Forbes*; and *Inc.*, along with specialized industry publications and websites.

Schedule a meeting with the client (or prospect): The objective of this initial meeting is NOT to tell the client what the firm can do for the client, but rather, to listen. At this stage of planning, gathering information is the most important part of the sales strategy. If the team loses out on an opportunity, it will be at this critical step of the process where the snag in the sales plan began. This meeting is to take control of the process. The team is in charge of the questions and the client or prospect members are in charge of the answers. This means that the team is listening 80 percent of the time. Try not to schedule any meetings with clients until team members have spent time in sales training and time planning out the strategy for the initial meeting. The team must always be coordinated with its efforts. Tools and resources like your firm's database, client extranets, marketing and information resources and information technology directors may be able to provide valuable services for you—schedule a meeting with them and explain what you are trying to accomplish—their input and ideas and assistance will be valuable to helping you and your team achieve its goals.

When meeting with existing clients, inform them that they have become part of the firm's major client initiative. They will understand what this means and are often pleased to be considered an important firm client. From this point on, the sales process takes over and team members should have a clear vision of what the outcome of this meeting will achieve.

Keep the process moving: Building new business from either existing clients or prospects takes time. Sometimes it takes years. Constant focus and attention to building the team members' relationships with the clients is critical. At this stage of the strategy, consider ways in which to remain in contact in between engagements or when there is no current matter on which to work. Think of ways the team or firm may support the client's business. For example, one large bank made it clear to their client team that they wanted the team to introduce them to their contacts and thus to help them build their private client business at the bank. These kinds of expectations by clients are on the rise as they demand more "partnering" from their lawyers.

Balance all these day-to-day activities with the billable time you need to spend. Once you weave sales activities into your daily plan, they will become second nature. Try to make one call a day to a contact at an existing client or someone who is no longer an active client but important to stay in touch with nonetheless. Even if you leave a voice-mail, you've made the connection and it will be appreciated. Loyal clients are earned and you must work at these relationships to maintain them.

Last, teams must stay action oriented. If you are not generating new or additional revenue from each client, take more training and work with a sales coach.

In the next chapter, gaining the confidence to reach out to clients and to practice the art of rainmaking are discussed.

CHAPTER 10

Sales Confidence— Build It and They Will Come

Highlights:

- The Good News
- Why Being Smart or Working for a Big Firm Just Aren't Enough
- Rainmaking Skills
- The Right Attitude
- Women and Relationship Selling
- Superlearning and the Big Switch
- Feeling Competent Boosts Your Confidence
- The Resilience Factor
- Just Say No to Negatives
- Building Your Confidence
- Find a Good Mentor
- The Dilemma of the Strong Woman
- Feelers and Thinkers
- It's Not Selling, It's Helping

Accept imperfection. Accept it, but keep your eyes on the program's objectives, and keep trying.—August J. Aquila and Bruce W. Marcus, Client at the Core

Can you sell without confidence? Probably not. It is something that you need to develop so that you can remove obstacles to your success.

The Woman Lawyer's Rainmaking Game

Developing the right skills and understanding how to work with your natural strengths help you build the confidence you need.

Besides giving you a foundation for understanding and building your sales confidence, you'll find exercises in this chapter. They will help you to develop tools to become more effective at developing business and to stay on a productive course.

THE GOOD NEWS

Whether you are a strong woman or you feel like a fake, sales confidence affects your business development. No matter where you are on the confidence scale, there is good news: you can relax and be yourself.

There's no question that, for many people, sales can be uncomfortable. Learning about the buying and selling processes helps you feel more at ease, because you understand that there are many different contexts in which you are operating and there are different styles of selling. This comfort and understanding gives way to sales confidence and success. Even the most doubting woman can develop a thriving practice.

WHY BEING SMART OR WORKING FOR A BIG FIRM JUST AREN'T ENOUGH

In some ways, the means by which you received training in law school not only taught you great skills, it also, for many, taught doubt. Losing the case for a client, being at the wrong side of the table and not obtaining the best deal through negotiation are events that cause anxiety and fear in many lawyers.

Law schools don't teach courses on how to promote yourself or develop self-confidence. Since selling is about promoting yourself and overcoming obstacles to get to the engagement, the win of the deal, the closing of the sale, you probably don't feel prepared.

So how do you become confident enough to walk into a room of people you don't know, insert yourself into a conversation, introduce yourself, and begin the relationship-building process? Or, walk into a presentation with other senior partners, some of them older and perhaps more experienced than you, and become a force in the sales opportunity with the confidence you need to obtain new business for your firm? Many resources exist to help you on your way.

RAINMAKING SKILLS

Learning how to sell makes you feel more comfortable, so it is important to look at – and appreciate - the skills you already have. Understanding that selling is something you can learn and do in a way that is comfortable for you directly affect your sales confidence.

Leigh-Ann Patterson, a Boston lawyer who also writes and speaks about business development, says it best: "If you can teach yourself the rule against perpetuities, you can teach yourself rainmaking." Doesn't that immediately give you confidence that this is something you can do?

Studies of rainmakers reveal the skills required for success. Larry Richard, Ph.D. conducted a study of 95 lawyers who were judged by their peers to be "excellent attorneys." He divided the group into two categories: "successful rainmaker" and "service partner."

Richard found statistically significant differences between groups in three areas: Ego drive, Empathy and Resilience. Rainmakers score higher than service partners on each of these measures.

Ego drive is the desire to persuade others "for the sake of persuasion." Empathy is the ability to shift perspective to understand how others perceive the world. Resilience is the ability to "bounce back" from criticism or rejection.

What does this study suggest for women attorneys seeking to develop their practice? First, rainmaking is different from developing a successful practice. You don't need to be a rainmaker to be successful. However, you may need to learn some of the skills noted in the study to be a rainmaker.

Second, many women attorneys already have many of the skills identified in the study. They are naturally empathetic. Just knowing about these skills helps you to zero in on those you need to develop in order to feel more confident.

The Woman Lawyer's Rainmaking Game

THE RIGHT ATTITUDE

In 2005, the Legal Sales and Service Organization (LSSO) set out to discover the key characteristics that define business development and rainmaking success for today's female lawyers. More than 400 attorneys responded to the call, providing candid feedback and insights into sales tactics, referral sources, firm support, personal motivation approaches and client management techniques that help drive business development.

One of the articles written about this survey was "Winning Strategies of the Best Women Rainmakers," by Marcie Boral Shunk and Catherine Alman MacDonagh, as published in The Complete Lawyer (Volume 2, Number 5). They revealed that what the LSSO Survey revealed were "four basic, guiding principles of success: attitude, leadership, client service and investment of time." Since attitude is so connected to confidence, it is worth closer examination than provided in earlier chapters. Shunk and MacDonagh wrote:

> Attitude may not actually be everything, but it certainly counts for a lot. The LSSO study asked questions such as "What do you say to yourself when your business development efforts do not succeed?" and "What do you say to yourself when a sale or business development effort was successful?"
>
> Responses were fairly easy to categorize as demonstrating either a positive or negative attitude. For example, the answers "keep trying," "keep in mind for future - stay in touch," and "I try to understand the rationale behind the loss and learn from it" all indicate a positive attitude. On the other hand, negative attitudes are displayed by responses such as "I have resigned myself to not even trying any more, because there seem to be so many societal and institutional biases which prevent success, no matter how hard you try," or "I am too busy anyway," or even "I become depressed."
>
> There is a certain optimism, an element of persistence, and the ability to be resilient expressed by the women rainmakers who have the right attitude to be rainmakers. And, since attitude is

so often a choice, this is a characteristic that can be developed with some conscious effort.

This discussion on attitude isn't just some feel good topic. In the study, women who reported taking a supportive or evaluative approach to success—and failure—enjoy 16.4% to 35.3% higher originations than a typical female equity partner. On the flip side, female partners who negatively judge their business development failure capture just 61.7% of average originations earned by female partners.

WOMEN AND RELATIONSHIP SELLING
Women lawyers bring unique attributes to the sales processes. In fact, there is plenty of evidence to suggest that, since women are naturals at building relationships, it's entirely likely that, in time, and with the growth of women lawyers in the marketplace, they will outshine men as the rainmakers.

In various measures of personality traits, women consistently score high on interpersonal abilities. They are more likely than men to be accommodating, accepting, empathetic, and compassionate. While the down side of this is that women are sometimes then perceived as not strong enough to make things happen, the truth is that these abilities are requirements for relationship building. And the ability to form and develop relationships is a major strength in business development and selling.

In fact, women are so good at establishing rapport that they can become quite close to the target. The irony is that sometimes they feel that they cannot ask for business from someone so close!

But what if you were to change the way you think of selling? For example, you might just try to be helpful to someone with whom you have a relationship. Wouldn't it be a shame if you didn't help someone you care about with a legal or business problem because you didn't want to "sell" to them? By not opening this door, you're actually keeping the other person from accessing the kind of information and power-

The Woman Lawyer's Rainmaking Game

ful resources you can provide. Business is not distinct from relationships; they are all one and the same.

We love the story of a senior litigator who was well-experienced, well-known as a terrific trial lawyer and who had amazing connections. So why did she lack sales confidence? She said that it was because she was so close to her connections. When asked whether she didn't want to try to help her contacts, she replied, "No, I don't want to abuse the relationship by asking for help."

How did she overcome this? By understanding that her contacts had a way out: they have choices. You can *have* a business conversation. Your contacts will let you know whether they don't want to go there. Why not simply ask what is going on, offer to help, and let the other person make their choice?

You can be the same kind of natural, empathic listener you are for your friends. Much time is spent coaching men on how to ask an open-ended question, and then stop talking and listen. This is the kind of thing women do all the time without thinking of it as a sales skill. Many times, just asking a contact about what is worrying them or what is going on gives you a chance to be helpful.

Sometimes, just figuring out what you will say by writing it down and/or role-playing helps get you beyond your inhibition. We know an outgoing lawyer that had great relationships with other professionals (scientists, accountants, etc.). But she would not ask them to help her get referrals. When it was suggested that she try saying, "we're both trying to develop our careers, let's help each other out," she said, "I'm not comfortable, it's too close."

But isn't that the point?!

Coaching helped this lawyer to be able to talk so that she felt competent and comfortable in this type of conversation. For example, her coach asked, "Why not try having the conversation? You could then apologize, saying you feel bad about talking with her this way because she's your friend?"

Sales Confidence—Build It and They Will Come

She tried this and her friend was so happy! And she never had to apologize either. Besides a happy ending, this was a sales confidence boost for this lawyer, who went on to build an enviable referral network using this approach.

In 1997, the consulting firm Coulter King O'Neill conducted a study of buyers. They set out to learn things like whether buyers prefer dealing with male or female salespeople. What do they find are the differences between the two?

The results were interesting. On balance, most of the buyers interviewed were male decision-makers. They generally felt that women are more honest, quicker to admit that they don't know the answer, and quick to respond with the answer from the right resource at their firm.

Most decision-makers found that men were not as good at listening as were women. However, they also indicated that women were slow to get to the point and that they shouldn't be afraid to ask for the business. Assertiveness is a positive characteristic. Given that most of us are dealing with strong decision-makers and clients on a daily basis, it's a characteristic that is respected.

In the March 2006 issue of the ABA's Law Practice Today, (Volume 32, Number 2), Harry Keshet Ph.D. and Catherine Alman MacDonagh published the first article that discussed the LSSO Women Lawyers Survey entitled "Women Marketers: The Difference Between Good & Great." They examined the differences between very successful ($543,778 average prior year's originations) and the moderately successful ($133,528 in average prior year originations) and found the following:

> To meet prospects, the very successful engage in more activities with both other lawyers and non-lawyers. They follow similar strategies to meet and form relationships with referral sources, too. Overall, they take a planned approach. They draw attention to themselves by taking leadership roles in the nonprofit and other organizations that they join. They also network, offer sponsorships and do speaking engagements. Thus, they position themselves to meet people who can hire them or who can become referral sources. They also become known

in their marketplace by publishing more frequently. The very successful are also more active at internal marketing than are the moderately successful business developers. They join client teams, take leadership positions, participate on committees, co-speak and work on pitch teams. They actively form relationships with their colleagues, are seen, get known and focus on business development activities with their peers.

Relationships are the key to building a thriving practice, and the very successful women in the survey appear to be masters at relationship building. They freely and appropriately ask others—including clients, other lawyers and referral sources—for new work and to introduce them to people who are in a position to hire them.

Many women can take the perspective of others. This allows you to better anticipate the needs of clients and to interact comfortably with prospects. You can easily put people at ease and help carry a conversation or help people feel included and a part of the conversation. These abilities and inclinations are the strengths women bring to building their reputations and getting known with confidence and ease.

Horwitz agrees: "Building relationships is what women do naturally. If we could only get out of our own way and recognize that the key to selling/business development is building and maintaining relationships, I believe the rainmaking potential of women is greater that any of us currently imagines."

So how do you get out of your own way? Becoming more confident helps a great deal. And women have some interesting ways of boosting their confidence, such as "superlearning" to feel really competent, finding a mentor, or looking at things in entirely new ways.

SUPERLEARNING AND THE BIG SWITCH

A woman professional tends to feel like she needs to know so much in order to feel like she is a skilled, competent professional. We call this "superlearning," and it helps women to feel that they know enough. In turn, this helps them to feel more confident.

Sales Confidence—Build It and They Will Come

Lawyer: "I'm not sure I have a right to say that I know what I'm doing, that I'm a bona fide, talented, skilled lawyer."

Coach: "Well, how much do you have to know to sell, to be an authority or to help people?"

When asked what her specialty was and what she was really good at, this woman lawyer said, "compared to other people I know who are really good, I don't even think I can call myself a real expert." When asked why she said that, the lawyer responded, "Because there ARE other people that can do this better than me."

Coach: "How does this relate to business development?"

Lawyer: "Because I need to know 95% to feel like I can say that I want to do your work."

It doesn't matter whether you're an expert; it matters that you can solve a client's problem! If you can, then you are expert ENOUGH to help the client. This is not some abstract idea.

Coach: "So, where does this come from, the need to know so much?"

Lawyer: "It's based on what I think other successful women know. I went to a meeting of them and got the courage there to say that I feel that I'm kind of a fake, that I didn't really know as much as they did. The woman next to me said, 'you stole my line! I don't really know that much...' Well, it turns out that 8 out of the 10 in the room felt that way, even though they were all top-notch professionals."

Finally, one of them told the group: "We're all excellent professionals and we all deserve to be here. Start acting like the skilled professional you are!"

So now you know. "Superlearning" does not help with business development. Here is where the switch happens. It's all about how to use what you know to solve the client's problem. It's about the application of knowledge.

Yes, there is some risk because you don't know everything. But you have the capacity to learn how to get the answers you need. This switch provides a different kind of confidence in the sales process.

FEELING COMPETENT BOOSTS YOUR CONFIDENCE
To get hired, attorneys need to build a great reputation. They also need to get known by existing and potential clients by demonstrating that they have the required expertise to resolve their matters. This means showing knowledge and understanding of issues and using interpersonal skills that builds client trust and confidence. Both technical knowledge and interpersonal skills are required for success.

The following activities help build a reputation and increase exposure to existing clients and prospects. They also boost confidence!

- Do excellent work and find appropriate ways of informing clients, prospects, and referral sources of your accomplishments.
- Write. Contribute to a newsletter or client advisory.
- Publish articles and use them to meet with people who can hire you. Use it as an opening to discussing their needs and problems in such a way that gives them confidence that you can help them.
- Network. Join a business or industry association (don't just talk with lawyers at bar associations!) and be an active participant.
- Speak. Host and speak at seminars with other attorneys and professionals on subjects of interest to specific industries.
- Speak at trade organizational meetings, answering questions and meeting with members of the audience after your talk.
- When engaged in these activities, there is a degree of persuasion required to clearly—and at times, strongly—state your points and give advice. Some women attorneys feel more comfortable and skillful at promoting themselves when they are in the "lime light" and stating their points in a way that conveys competence.

Being in the lime light can be uncomfortable if one thinks of it as being more on display than showing one's competency. Successful women build their confidence at speaking and interacting by taking the

Sales Confidence—Build It and They Will Come

time to be very prepared. They know their subject and the spotlight is on their knowledge. This positions them as knowledge brokers. They can persuade based on the confidence they have in their knowledge and in themselves as problem solvers.

If you can do these things, you will feel you've earned the right to consider yourself an expert. In turn, you will gain sales confidence.

> **THE RESILIENCE FACTOR**
>
> *"To be resilient is to be both strong and flexible. You also have to be willing to examine and understand your experience and take the opportunity to learn from it. You learn about your strengths and weaknesses, your illusions, beliefs and values, relationship patterns, what worked and what didn't work, and you learn about other people and about the world. Knowledge is power. When you take the opportunity to learn all these things each time you stumble in life, you will naturally develop confidence in yourself and in your ability to deal with similar situations in the future."*
>
> - Shirley Vandersteen, Ph.D., C. Psych.

For many people the ability to "bounce back" from criticism or rejection is an acquired skill. Studies of women often note that they often attribute being criticized or rejected as a result of a personal flaw and take such remarks or behaviors as painful indication of inadequacy.

For most people, business development and selling by their very natures are not quick roads to success. It can take a great deal of time before women lawyers understand the sales and buying processes thoroughly enough so that they don't take it personally when a prospect doesn't buy her services. For example, establishing rapport is just one step in the selling process. It is also a step in creating a long and lasting relationship.

Building your reputation and getting known takes time. It is a process of repetition without much immediate reward. Over time, prospects hear people speak many times, read articles they write, see them at meetings and meet them personally. It is from these multiple contacts that a reputation is developed and women attorneys become known.

There will be many times that little or no new business gets generated from a good deal of effort. This is not the fault of the attorney. This is not a criticism or a rejection. This is the reality resulting from a slow and steady process. Neither Rome, nor a law practice, is built in a day.

Lack of success is not a personal failure! And don't attribute the successes you do have as accidents. This undermines your own competency. So, if the sale doesn't happen, you need to de-personalize the failure. This is business, even if it feels personal. It's probably not about you, even if it sometimes feels that way. So, resiliency is important for any woman who will be successful.

Bouncing back is especially relevant to confidence. As Dr. Robert Schuller says, "You are what you think about all day long." You can't hang on to why someone didn't hire you, analyzing to the nth degree why you weren't chosen. This only erodes your feelings of competence and confidence. Remember: you cannot control others, so learn what you need to from an unsuccessful sale and then MOVE ON. Getting stuck in a downward spiral only serves to make you wonder why you weren't good enough, smart enough, or why that person didn't like you.

"Dare to risk public criticism." (Mary Kay Ash) Sometimes, the more successful you are, the more resilient you must be! In the words of the eloquent writer-lawyer John O. Cunningham: "Great people draw great criticism.... Defeat is the inevitable consequence of standing up for character." Think Dr. Martin Luther King, Abraham Lincoln and John F. Kennedy, just to name a few. These are people who displayed tremendous resilience. Their confidence is what helped them to overcome resistance, criticism and all kinds of failure.

So what can you do to boost your resiliency? Since you can't change what has happened, you can only work on your reaction to it. Develop good coping mechanisms and find ways to creatively solve problems (which you are good at!) and you will become resilient.

Sales Confidence—Build It and They Will Come

You can also figure out what helps you to heal when you're feeling rejected. Go do it and get back into action. Keep items of inspiration around you, such as books (read Zander's *The Art of Possibility*) or quotes from people you admire. Do something healthy which makes you feel better, like taking a long walk, working out, or going to yoga class.

Resiliency

Here are some great quotes about resiliency; they're here for you when you need some motivation:

"That which does not kill us makes us stronger."
—Friedrich Nietzsche

"The faster you fail the sooner you succeed."
—Motto of the innovation company, Ideo

"Whether you believe you can or you can't, you're right."
—Henry Ford

"No life is so hard that you can't make it easier by the way you take it."
—Ellen Glasgow

"You don't see the world as *it* is but as *you* are."
—Goethe

JUST SAY NO TO NEGATIVES

In his book "Even Eagles Need a Push," David McNally writes, "Clearly what distinguishes truly successful people is that they are contributors. They are in love with life and all the possibilities of what it means to be human. Their accomplishments, their successes, are rooted in their desire to grow and be of service to humanity."

Think of the possibilities you have and what they mean to you. By continuing to focus on what is ahead, you will keep moving forward and little can get in the way, including negative people, thoughts, criticisms and fear. You will have greater confidence, which allows you to realize the possibilities and reach your goals.

Positive thinking is much more productive than negative self-doubt. Developing positive thinking doesn't mean that instantly you will not have negative thoughts. What it does mean is that when negative thoughts come, you are able to recognize them and let them go. Over time you will notice a lessening of their effects on you. They become merely thoughts without power or influence. When this happens, they fade and dissolve. Remembering and acting on your positive thoughts weakens the negative and opens up the possibilities of discovery, mastery and confidence.

Even women who are confident, successful and generally positive have to be reminded once in a while to refocus on ourselves and take the time to tune in to WII-FM or What's In It For Me? The more you focus on success the more you will achieve your own. The more success you have, the more confident you'll be.

Getting and keeping clients and doing great work wraps all the positive things together in one package. Find and recognize the things about being a lawyer that you feel passionate about. If it's working with clients and others toward successful outcomes, then go for more of it!

BUILDING YOUR CONFIDENCE

You must want to dedicate time to support the goals of the most important person in your life—you. When you set goals and then achieve them, you will build your self-confidence and your sales confidence.

Exercise 1: Strengths, weaknesses, friends and foes

First, list what you think are your strong points. Identify accomplishments that have made you proud of yourself.

_____
_____
_____

Now list any fears or obstacles you would like to overcome.

_____
_____
_____

Sales Confidence—Build It and They Will Come

Next, list the people in your business and personal life who you trust and who can help you build a successful career. These are people with whom you want to spend more time.

_____

_____

Lastly, list the people in your business and personal life who never seem to be able to ask about you, about what is important to you and the people who are not necessarily fun or productive to be around. In fact, they may be people who can't seem to do anything but criticize. These are people with whom you need to spend less time. The time you save not being with these people is time you can put toward your business development.

_____

_____

Now review your lists, beginning with your achievements. You have probably reached them because you had a goal and, as many would say on a larger scale, a sense of purpose. How long has it been since you felt this way about your career and your needs?

Exercise 2: The feeling of success.

It only takes a minute, but it's very valuable.

Close your eyes and count to 10 and breathe deeply as you count. Now, think about a time in your life when you reached a goal—it could have been a running race you won, a victory in court, trying something you were afraid you would fail at and conquering it, like skiing, hiking or writing a brief.

As you think about your accomplishment (and hopefully it's one that made you smile) picture yourself achieving it. Now, give yourself a sign (a pinch on the hand with the other hand is my sign) that will, at a moment's notice, allow you to recall this great feeling all over again and bring you to that feeling of accomplishment and success.

This may sound corny, but even the most accomplished of you reading this book will find that it's a really great tool to have to boost confidence on a moment's notice.

The Woman Lawyer's Rainmaking Game

OK, so now you've got a secret weapon for recalling your successes and bouncing back. Take this with you when you are in selling situations that cause hesitation for any reason—feeling like a failure, too tired, not outgoing enough, hate networking events—and you will muster up the strength to go the extra mile for that moment.

FIND A GOOD MENTOR
Finding a mentor can really help in a lot of areas besides business development, such as practice management, making your way through your firm's or clients' political mazes and the like. But the best reason to have a mentor is to establish support for you. Your mentor can be your sounding board, supporter, listener, advisor, teacher, and sometimes, though it's not necessary, your friend.

Pick someone you admire, trust and respect, someone you know will offer good, practical advice on the things you can do to develop your sales confidence. Many young women attorneys have learned the art and science of "working a room" while networking alongside a mentor. If you find the right one, your mentor will guide you through the sales process, and just knowing that your mentor is there as a safety net can add to your confidence.

Being a women lawyer means juggling a lot sometimes. For many, work-life balance issues affect their selling confidence, for some simply cannot make time in their busy schedules to attend events either early in the morning or late at night. For others, firm culture plays a role.

The most important thing is to find a mentor who will understand who and where you are in your life. So, no matter what your situation may be, a good mentor will help you to make business development the priority that it should be for you. There are plenty of sales contexts, and many different places and times for business development. A mentor can help identify the right opportunities for you.

THE DILEMMA OF THE STRONG WOMAN
What about the "strong" woman, who seems to have plenty of sales confidence? Her strength plays a role in the selling process, both for her and for her prospect.

The strong woman may have confidence, but what they have in common with those who don't is how to deal with rejection and the need for support. Because when that strong woman doesn't make the sale, she needs to have the same resiliency and support, but others may not see her need for support or give the support because she is strong. This dilemma is real. Talk about a Catch-22!

So strong women, like anyone else, need to seek out others who will give them the pat on the back they need and allow them to be vulnerable, and they need to ask for the support that is needed to get them back on track. Asking for help does not make you weak; it just means you need support. Strength is the power to know what you need when you feel weak or vulnerable and to ask for what you need from someone who has the capacity to support you.

Being a strong woman can be lonely. Spouses, partners, and co-workers may not understand the complex issues of being a strong woman. So, if this is you, try to find other women and men you can turn to who will be understanding of what you are going through and who will accept your pain, let you get it out and let you keep your sense of strength.

Stay resilient and don't let your pain rule your thinking. If you swallow your pain, it will create knee-jerk reactions to things and reduce your strength so that you won't have the space to react thoughtfully and strategically. In turn, this affects your confidence.

Strong women who are able to aggressively go after work may be seen as behaving too much like a man, lacking sensitivity, being too pushy, etc. This can be devastating because it can be used against a woman to push her away, make her feel irrelevant or, worse yet, attacked. So, a counter attack, such as using humor or factual statements can help.

FEELERS AND THINKERS
The Myers Briggs Type Index, which is commonly used to identify personality characteristics, indicates that 65% of women are "Feeling" types, while 35% of men are "Feeling" types."

This demonstrates clearly that women are more empathetic, tender, concerned about the effects of decisions on people and relationships, able to take the role of the other person and more easily see another's point of view, and better anticipate responses. These are wonderful traits for sales because you will be able to see the client's needs more easily than men will. Plus, you are naturally better about continuing to nurture the relationship, which is what client development is all about.

IT'S NOT SELLING, IT'S HELPING
Now that you're listening for it, you will become aware that there are opportunities in conversations where you could be helpful...your ear will change!

You will have confidence in knowing that you have the experience and the knowledge and the connections to other lawyers that would be resources for your clients. By being a problem-solver, you will be HELPFUL, caring and loving. Try this: "Tell me about that, maybe I can be helpful."

Being helpful (rather than trying to sell) helps you to feel GOOD, more confident about yourself. Selling is not about overpowering someone to get what YOU want and it's not about undue influence.

For women lawyers, putting selling into the problem-solving category switches it from being about power to nurturing a relationship. Not only does this give women a leg up over men, it's a sure way to improve sales confidence.

Thinking Out of the Box — "Slay a Dragon"
Long ago, map-makers sketched dragons on maps as a sign to sailors that they would be entering unknown territory at their own risk. Some sailors took this sign literally and were afraid to venture on. Others saw the dragons as a sign of opportunity, a door to virgin territory. Similarly, each of us has a mental map of the world complete with dragons. WHERE DOES FEAR HOLD YOU BACK? WHAT DRAGONS CAN YOU SLAY?

This chapter was written by Catherine Alman MacDonagh and Dr. Harry Keshet.

CHAPTER 11

Connecting with Clients

Highlights:

- Your Clients Are Your Most Valuable Asset… and Another Lawyer's Prospects
- Contact Your Client for Feedback Before Your Client Contacts You
- Proven Methods for Building Good Relationships with Clients
- Using Market Research to Learn About What Works for Clients
- The BTI A Team
- Form 11A—Short Client Survey
- The Proof is in the Pudding
- The In-House Counsel and Senior Decision-Makers Speak on Selling, Legal Services, and Women Lawyers
- Ten Client Development and Service Strategies for Success

Knowing is not enough; We must apply. Willing is not enough . . . We must do. —Johann Goethe

Your Clients Are Your Most Valuable Asset…
and Another Lawyer's Prospects
Your firm's clients are another firm's prospects. Getting clients and keeping clients are two different things. Once you have obtained a new client, the selling cycle and servicing cycle are continuous. Outstanding service begets additional new work. The best way to understand what determines good service is to align yourself and your firm with your clients'

The Woman Lawyer's Rainmaking Game

goals and business strategies and listen carefully to what clients expect. They will be more than happy to tell you, and often are quite pleased you asked. Establish a regular pattern of connecting with clients—quarterly is preferable, annual is a must (at the very least).

A recent meeting between an AmLaw 100 firm's managing partner and one of the firm's largest clients illustrates my point. The managing partner of this global firm was making the rounds and meeting with general counsels and CEOs of the firm's largest clients. When asked how might the firm do things better the general counsel replied, "At this company we have a sales team. Our sales team visits our top customers every quarter. I'd be surprised if I had a visit from one of your lawyers in the last three years! We are not happy about this and you are going to have to work extra hard to keep our business this year."

True story. The managing partner had been hearing this from his marketing folks and now it came true. The good news is that he did visit the client and asked about the relationship, and the other good news is that the client was honest and the firm was able to turn a potentially terrible situation into a stronger relationship. The firm is still working hard at building the relationship back to where it was, but the client account has been saved.

This story is not unique; many firms find out too late that the clients they so carefully worked on to bring to the firm feel abandoned once they become clients of the firm. It is never too late to go talk with clients. More clients today are carefully examining their relationships with outside counsel to ensure they have the best service providers the company's money can buy.

Contact Your Client for Feedback Before Your Client Contacts You

One of the best ways to insure you are on the right track with clients is to ask them. Asking clients is not a novel concept and quite frankly it's expected by them that you will. Most firms struggle way to much over this issue. My recommendation is just do it and don't wait for the firm to conduct something like this on a firm-wide basis. The in-house counsel and officer level members of today's companies are carefully scrutinizing legal bills. Their role in their organizations is to minimize risk to the business and to help increase profits. The cost of litigation is high and with so many firms competing for legal business, the profession is becoming a buyer's market. A large healthcare group that spans the country recently sent out an evaluation to its in-house team. The members of the legal department and others in the company who work with outside counsel were asked to evaluate the law firms they use and the individual lawyers' performance. My own view is it would have been better if the law firm beat the client to the punch on this. Once the evaluation was complete, the company sent the results to their outside lawyers asking them to review their evaluations and to be prepared to respond about the areas where they received lower marks. Many corporations are adopting these and other proven methods from corporations whose expertise in process improvement and customer focus result in higher profits and rewards. One of those models is the DuPont Legal Model.

Proven Methods for Building Good Relationships with Clients
Adapted from Motorola by the DuPont law department team, the DuPont Legal Model process is becoming widely adapted by other corporations. (Log on to DuPont's website www.Dupont.com for specific information about this model and to order its guidelines booklet.)

The process requires law firms to meet a specific set of standards the company has identified as important to the relationship. Corporations are also asking firms to share in the risks they face with litigation; and on the flip side, are willing to share in the wins as well. Overall, the key to successful relationships with clients is to *align* yourself or your firm with the client. Those practitioners and firms who achieve success at enhancing the value of their client relationships will reap stronger rewards than those who do not. The benefits often include more work from the client; advocacy on your behalf by the client; and loyalty from the client. Other, more sophisticated, clients turn to successful models like the ever-increasingly popular DuPont Legal Model.

Jim Michalowicz, provides valuable insight into this model. Michalowicz is a well-known authority on adapting the Motorola Six Sigma standards and practices for the law department. Our work and ever growing experience in this area proves that more clients and firms are applying process improvement methodologies, like Lean and Six Sigma, and

The Woman Lawyer's Rainmaking Game

project management to their work. Jim is a frequent speaker at law firm management conferences. He urges lawyers to keep top of mind that it's all about the client and the company's success and less about the lawyer and how much she can bill. He kindly provided us with an overview of the DuPont Model for this book, which follows. Basic attributes of Jim's Legal Model focus include:

- Reduction of cost. Emphasis is on win-win for client and the firm. Factors other than just billable time include non-billed investment in the relationship (for example training lawyers and law firm staff on understanding the client's industry, studying trade journals and preventative law counseling and education).

- Growing the business. Focus is given to how law firms can "partner" with the client. Key to some of these relationships is the outside firms' commitment to the priorities of their clients' businesses. In some cases the priorities might be commitment to diversity, in others it may be willingness to share risk and in others a strict adherence to a set of values, rates, and other key drivers in the relationships. The critical point here is the client is paying the bill and is keenly aware of this. While many firms and practitioners focus on their own needs, those focusing on the clients' needs gain market share. More and more data are becoming available to learn how to do this successfully.

- Diversity. Market statistics provide a metric against which to measure a firm's success at diversity, including the hiring and retention of women and minorities.

- Technology payback. Law firms that are part of the "virtual law firm" contribute knowledge and work product to a shared knowledge management database that is available not only to the client but to all the provider firms. Law firms are expected to contribute their own technology investment to make the information flow seamlessly. Electronic invoicing, integrated matter management, electronic discovery, document imaging, etc. are crucial to the payback. Law firms create a win-win for themselves by being connected and develop a strong referral network.

- Best in class. Many smaller firms and solos use the simple but complete client survey form such as the one included in this chapter. Whether your firm adopts a more sophisticated approach like the DuPont Legal Model or a strong, effective client survey approach, it is important to connect with clients on a regular basis (certainly not longer than a year) to strengthen the relationship and affirm for your client that indeed, you are appreciative of the business and her input into the working relationship she shares with you and your firm.

More can be learned about the DuPont Model and process improvement, and project management—and should. There are quite a few books about the topic (try a Google search), the Legal Lean Sigma Institute, and seminars for lawyers that include the topics.

Using Market Research to Learn About What Works for Clients

Two organizations regularly interview clients and produce reports highlighting what builds strong relationships. One is the Association of Corporate Counsel (ACC) and the other is BTI Consulting. Other independent firms such as Brand Research, Stephen Brewer, Altman & Weil, and others regularly conduct market studies across industries and geographic regions. (See Resources at the end of this book for contact information on these firms.) The studies all suggest similar themes. Clients want their law firms to understand their business, to anticipate their legal needs and to make unprompted calls to keep them apprised on what's happening. Getting in the door of a new client is easy. Keeping clients is not easy—it takes commitment to the relationship, hard work, and partnering to help clients reach their business goals. Simple to do, but according to ACC and Fortune 500 clients while outstanding service and focus on the value-added aspects of the relationships are at the top of their lists in terms of what they want out of their relationships with outside counsel, they believe fewer than 7 percent of firms and practitioners actually understand these important relationship criteria and step up to the plate.

The BTI "A Team"

BTI asks clients to name lawyers who they believe exemplify service excellence. They call this list each year the "BTI A Team." Here are some highlights from their discussions with clients about what makes an "A" service provider that you will find useful.

The Woman Lawyer's Rainmaking Game

BTI A Service Provider (Service All Stars) Key Attributes:
- Consistently looks at the services they provide from the client's perspective, rather than their own.
- Puts the client's interests ahead of his own and always takes the extra step—advice and responsiveness are baseline requirements.
- Unrelenting commitment to help the client.
- Goes beyond technical skill delivery to add something more.
- Seems to view every case and point of service as a way to build a relationship rather than an isolated case or matter.
- Becomes an extension of the client's team.
- Is on a mission to understand and anticipate their needs and to find the best resources to meet those needs.
- Establishes exceptional understanding of their client's issues circumstances and needs and uses it to develop mutual investment in the relationship.
- Consistently looks at the services they provide from the client's perspective, rather than their own.
- Consistently helps translate legal advice into the business value. These clients benefit from increased time to market, advantage in closing transactions, risk avoidance, and revenue from intellectual property assets.

Firms are now hiring salespeople from industry to assist them with the process of managing their top clients. In most firms the top 100 clients are accountable for 50 percent to 80 percent of the firms' revenues. This is a good reason to make sure these clients are nurtured. We have stressed how important it is to conduct regular client feedback studies. It is a strong relationship building and marketing activity. Client feedback is a way to show you care about what clients think. Clients are quick to let you know how much they appreciate the fact that you've taken the time to ask for their input. A key factor in obtaining client feedback is to *act* on the feedback and not to ignore it. Work out a plan with the client on how you will respond to any specific issues or opportunities the client has identified and follow up. Nothing will damage the relationship more than to ask for feedback and ignore it.

Connecting with Clients

Market research firms are available to assist with client feedback studies. If you have a marketing department at your firm, the members of the department will be more than happy to help you craft a client feedback questionnaire for you to mail to those clients with whom you have contact. Otherwise, Form 11A is a simple format that can be easily adapted to suit your needs and to include questions specific to each client. For those of you who have a practice that is plaintiff oriented or deals with individuals, this survey can be easily adapted and used at the end of a specific client engagement to obtain feedback from your client.

This simple but important survey highlights the key areas clients have indicated are of interest to them. A letter should accompany this survey from you or a managing partner of the firm. Once a client has completed the survey, it will be critical for you to send a handwritten thank you note as soon as you receive the completed survey. At that time, thank your client as well for their business. You may add other questions that you believe will be relevant, but these are straightforward and will provide a good opportunity for dialog and feedback. This is a mini-survey (one page) that covers quality, accessibility, communications, and responsiveness. The survey also elicits ideas from client regarding seminars. It must be one page; ask qualitative and quantitative questions.

Form 11A—Short Client Survey

[Firm Name] appreciates and thanks you for your continued support. As we move forward and plan the future, your feedback and opinions are important to us. We are/I am committed to *meet* and *exceed* our clients' expectations. Please take a moment to complete this survey.

We would like your impressions of our firm

(Please circle your answers)

Overall Quality of Our Services	Excellent	Good	Fair	Poor
Accessibility of Our Lawyers	Excellent	Good	Fair	Poor
Update and Reporting Practices	Excellent	Good	Fair	Poor
Responsiveness Of Firm	Excellent	Good	Fair	Poor

Do We Meet Your
Expectations?   Always   Almost Always   Sometimes   Rarely

Do your think we understand your industry and your business? Please explain.

Would you be interested in attending future seminars provided by the firm? If so, what issues would you like addressed?
What kind of information would you find useful for us to include in our monthly updates?
Do you have any other comments or suggestions for ways the firm can improve its services or relationship with you?

Optional Questions:
Would you like us to follow up with you regarding a particular service issue?
May we use you as a client reference in the future? If so, please provide your name below.

So, start today and create this simple, but effective client feedback survey (edit it to fit your needs) and send it out to your clients. You will be really surprised at how many respond, we promise.

The Proof is in the Pudding

Baker & McKenzie's Maura McBreen leverages her firm's client development committee responsibility with an eye toward client retention: "All firms require partner involvement in administrative and management matters, e.g., attorney recruitment, professional development, pro bono, etc. I am Chair of the Client Development Committee of our Chicago office so I devote my firm administrative time to our client development initiatives. This maximizes my contact with our most significant clients."

As an example of the kinds of questions you might ask your clients when visiting with them, we've asked some in-house counsel to provide their feedback and thoughts about some relationship-specific activities.

The In-House Counsel and Senior Decision Makers Speak on Selling, Legal Services, and Women Lawyers

Women in-house experts speak. Those interviewed included:

Deborah Ackerman, Vice President—General Counsel, Southwest Airlines Co

Louise Firestone, Senior Vice President and General Counsel, LVMH Moet Hennessy Louis Vuitton Inc.

Connecting with Clients

Pat Gray, Senior Vice President, General Counsel and Secretary, Arch Wireless, Inc.

Debra Hunter Johnson, Vice President, Human Resources, American Airlines

Barbara Kolsun, Senior Vice President and General Counsel, Kate Spade LLC

Sandy Roberts, Vice President, Managing Director of Private Financial Services, U.S. Bank

Pauline Waschek, Chief Contracts Counsel, Honeywell.

Here's what was asked and how they responded:

1. As a buyer of legal services, which marketing activities catch your attention. Activities to which I am referring, include: Seminars at your site; off-site, firm-run seminars; advertising; email newsletters; newsletters and updates by mail; articles written by attorneys; direct solicitation; anything else that causes you to pay attention and even try a new firm through a new contact?

    - Offsite firm-run seminars.
    - All kinds of seminars; email newsletters; direct solicitation if it reveals the person has done their homework, is familiar with my company and our issues (not hard to do).
    - Any seminar will catch my attention; advertising and newsletters usually won't. Direct solicitation doesn't work unless I've been introduced by a third party I trust. That's usually how I find new firms—I'll ask someone I trust for a recommendation.
    - Firm-run seminars, email letters, and articles written by attorneys. Some marketing activities come off as too aggressive ("in your face"). Assuming the most appealing clients are the ones with voluminous legal work, whoever the decision maker is for a client with that profile will likely be very pressed for time and be the kind of the person who will lack patience for marketing techniques that push form over substance or address legal services that are only peripherally relevant. The other activities you list tend to fall into those other categories (techniques pushing form over substance, too

aggressive, take too much of the decision maker's time...
with a firm-run seminar, the decision maker has the option
to leave whenever he or she needs to . . .)
- Articles written by attorneys.
- I prefer email newsletters and direct solicitation.
- All of the above. I love seminars—it's been a great marketing tool especially where you get continuing legal education CLE credit and you hear others talking. Direct solicitation, probably not because I use either people who I know or who are recommended to me. For example, we were just summoned by the press due to a lawsuit. We hired a lawyer who was recommended to me by a lawyer at Ralph Lauren. On the other hand I use people who I know a lot. The best way for them to stay in my view is seminars, newsletters.

2. How do you prefer to be contacted by an attorney whom you've met who would like to keep in touch with you? Email, telephone, etc. How often is okay with you?
   - Email is preferable as it allows me respond when I have the time; about once a month would be okay.
   - Email and telephone at least quarterly.
   - Email, telephone—any means is fine. Every 4-5 months will work, but please don't call or write more often than that—I don't have the time!
   - Email is the best. Twice a year
   - If I meet them at a conference and I give them a card, the sooner they get in touch with me afterward, the more likely I am to keep them on their radar screen. Continuing to invite me to things, we are a relatively small company. By letters, by emails and by invitations at least four times a year. We are all so busy in-house.
   - Depends on the context and how the attorney left it with me at our first meeting. An intuitive person can determine if there's the right "chemistry," which would open the possibilities for more frequent contact. A follow-up invite (with short, handwritten note) to events of interest: women's bar

Connecting with Clients

events or events structured around topics of interest is probably the best approach.
- Be yourself. Be genuine about your interest in connecting with the person as a person as opposed to a possible new client, even if you target the in-house counsel with the intent of pursuing a possible client relationship, and make sure you connect on issues of mutual interest. Not that a client relationship has to be a friendship.
- Focus on developing your unique expertise in an area of legal services and make sure you publish, present at seminars and otherwise get recognized for the quality work you do.
- Make contact and keep in contact with periodic calls. Determine where the skill set match is between you and the company and market those skills, be confident and direct—ask for work. Ask what it will take to get work.
- Stay open and positive about pursuing the relationship without being overbearing. Invite the in-house counsel to events of mutual interest so long as he or she is receptive.

3. What three tips can you provide to women lawyers who are interested in meeting in-house counsel with respect to making contact and staying in touch?
   - Ask your male partners who have ongoing relationships with clients to take you along to client meetings especially where female in-house counsel will participate. These women like to see firms developing the careers of women.
   - Join ACCA, MCCA, and ASCA and go to/speak at their local CLE's and events; we are a participant in the Texas Minority Counsel division of the Texas Bar and always attend their annual event
   - Put together a seminar—but please don't make it "women-only"
   - Organize a smaller lunch to introduce me to other women clients in my industry
   - Invite me to non-legal events that are organized around an interesting theme—a wine tasting, for example (as opposed to the ubiquitous sports events males get invited to.)

11-11

The Woman Lawyer's Rainmaking Game

- If the senior male partners in your firm golf (or fish/sail/etc.) with their clients, learn to golf (fish/sail/etc.) and ask to go along when they take clients golfing/fishing/sailing.
- Develop strong expertise in a particular area and do lots of public speaking on the subject; people will notice and bring you work if they perceive you as an expert.

4. What recommendations do you have for lawyers to stay in front of the prospect and remain top of mind?
   - Create value by having a valuable strategy or update to something in their business or personal area to discuss.
   - Follow up.
   - Put together forums for women lawyers. I love events like that. I recently spoke at one like that at Thelen Reid. A cocktail party followed it. It was a women IP panel. I went this week to a breakfast at Fried Frank that discussed how women can help the law school. It's always interesting. The Association of Corporate Counsel had a couple of events like that at its annual meeting. Women in those firms need to get involved in planning those types of events.
   - Key in on topics of interest to women in general not just issues dealing with the law; e.g., women lawyers and menopause and memory loss and the multi-tasking time juggling thing.

5. Do you have a preference, given that skill sets and qualifications are equal, towards working with men or women outside counsel and if so, why?
   - Be professional and confident in your approach. Don't be afraid to mix business with a more personal approach.
   - It's great to know the general counsel but cultivate relationships with other in-house attorneys who are responsible for hiring.
   - I prefer to work with very qualified people. All things being equal I prefer doing business with women as they have always proven to be so on top of everything.
   - With the assumption you have given (equal skill sets), no preference. However, the necessary skill set is pretty com-

Connecting with Clients

prehensive; not just understanding the law, but also understanding relevant business issues, which can be extensive, and understanding the politics of working with people, etc.

- I'm a government contracts attorney and have worked with more male than female outside counsel, simply because there are only a few women who practice in this area of the law. My inclination would be to work with women as I'd like to give them the opportunity to develop relationships with in-house counsel, which, in my opinion, is an important part of rainmaking.
- It depends. In terms of day-to-day activities, I always prefer women. In terms of shark (this is an awful thing to say) for litigation, I might choose a man. It's the emotional factor. I refer women who call me for a matrimonial lawyer a man. There's still kind of an emotional factor that some women, including myself, still suffer from. Perhaps a slight inability to stand back and not look at things personally. Emotional involves money.
- Women are more responsive, they are more efficient because they multi-task as human beings. You can be frank with them.

6. Do you have other, general advice you might give to women partners in law firms who are trying to get the attention of general counsel to ultimately build a book of business?

- I don't believe that women partners need to get the general counsel's attention to develop business. I believe that women partners should focus instead on getting that first piece of work. Once they get their foot in the door, they must provide excellent legal services, develop an ongoing relationship and, in my experience, more work will naturally follow. I believe in-house counsel prefer to work with a relatively small number of competent outside counsel and that they tend to go back to the lawyers who have provided them with good service in the past. I also don't believe that the way to build business is any different for women than it is for men. I suggest studying the rainmaking practices of success-

ful male partners and developing similar practices and keep practicing them.
- Find ways to set yourself apart through your contacts, letterhead—in everything that you do.
- Be consistent. Be professional. Don't be emotional. Don't talk too much—women tend to talk too much—get to the point. Use personal contacts to get in the door. It's still hard to break into that male bastion. Trustworthy. Short, sweet, and professional. Women are less afraid to admit they don't have an answer but they'll find it.
- I think organizations like ISOS could be restructured to serve the purpose. General counsel should be engaged to participate more actively (the last meeting I went to really focused on firm issues and firm input). Also, women partners should network constantly: serve on boards of nonprofits, etc., join golf clubs, tennis clubs.

7. Are there specific activities you enjoy as part of building a relationship and keeping in touch with colleagues from outside law firms? Golf? Tennis? Spa visits? Panel participation at a law firm? Fishing? Mutual time with children? Skiing?
    - Lunch periodically if the in-house attorney and outside counsel live/work in the same city. Dinner occasionally when outside counsel is in town if the two of us don't live in the same city. I appreciate being invited to training sessions at the firms whose attorneys I work with and attend whenever the subject matter is of interest and I have the time. Annually I am invited to an alumni dinner at a firm in Washington where I used to work and attend when I can. I believe it's important to maintain a professional relationship so I don't want to share so many activities that the distinction between personal and professional relationship becomes clouded.
    - Eating lunch. I love to have lunch with outside lawyers in a nice place where I would not normally eat. Meeting at professional meetings like INTA, INCC, where you are away from home. Dinners around those meetings—dinner party. Golf, golf, golf, and then spa visits.

- Panel participation (real, interactive participation at which everyone is truly engaged).

Following are some additional service tips that may also work for you.

Ten Client Development and Service Strategies for Success

1. Care about clients, staff and one another in the organization. The increase in communication and teamwork will translate to increased effectiveness. Client confidence in the team will grow as they perceive your firm to be a cohesive, strong unit.

2. Have vision. Keep an eye on what's happening in the world, and how it can affect clients. Try to anticipate changes in the marketplace and plan on how the firm will meet the challenges that will result from these changes. Have compassion—many world events will affect clients on a personal level, and it's important to be sensitive to their feelings.

3. Organize "key client" teams to nurture important clients and to obtain future growth from them. The clients will appreciate being able to contact any member of the team should they have questions. This will also strengthen the firm's positive image.

4. Reward effort. This could mean rewarding ten years of service to the firm; successful client results; a well-planned seminar; exceptional leadership; community participation. Firm members—professional and service staff—are too valuable to take for granted. The reward can be something as simple as a handwritten note of appreciation, although some firms have the equivalent of a Gold Medal, or Academy Award—whichever you chose, do it! You'll be amazed at the morale boost.

5. Conduct regular client audits and surveys. Not only will you keep current with your clients' needs and priorities, but also you will obtain valuable feedback about your performance.

The Woman Lawyer's Rainmaking Game

> You may also be able to identify new areas for growth, which will expand your client base.
> 6. Solicit feedback from firm members to better define firm sales and service training needs. Who better than the individuals understand their needs? Once an area for training has been identified, don't be resistant to hiring outside consultants to handle the process. They have the expertise and tools to maximize effectiveness. Good training leads to new business and quality service to clients.
> 7. Call two new contacts per week—a MUST for anyone to develop business. Keep in touch with old contacts every two to three months. Ask them for referrals and reciprocate.
> 8. Create a partnering effort. In a professional firm, have each junior partner and senior associate choose three partners to target within the firm. The partners will become prospects for cross-selling opportunities. Encourage the partners and associates to have open-ended discussions to share information about cross-selling opportunities.
> 9. Attend one social or business meeting per week to network. This could be as simple as a cocktail, breakfast or lunch with a business associate.
> 10. Be honest, authentic and unpretentious. Don't imply relationships that do not exist, take credit for others' work, brag about money or accomplishments, or "talk down" to your team. Always be honest. Clients will perceive you as having confidence, dignity, and integrity.
>
> Listen to your clients. You will always win.

Go forth, be confidant and sell to win!

CHAPTER 12

Coaching

Highlights
- Coaching
- What Coaches Do
- The Case for Coaching
- Coaches' Approaches
- Training
- Are Women Lawyers REALLY Different?
- Start Early and Often
- Meeting Challenges
- Are you Coachable?
- Planning
- Impact on Firm Relationships
- Clients and the Future
- Coaching Tools
- Benefits of Coaching
- Organizational Support
- Coaching Resource Guide

So much of *The Woman Lawyer's Rainmaking Game* focuses on concepts, motivation and tips that help lawyers make rain, in much the same ways that you would get from attending a seminar or workshop. Here, we focus on the different roles and benefits that coaching can have in a lawyer's professional and personal development. We also examine how business development efforts impact a lawyer's relation-

The Woman Lawyer's Rainmaking Game

ships in her firm, both with other lawyers and the business professionals who work with them. Finally, we explore how rainmaking efforts are being supported in ways that women lawyers find valuable.

Coaching

At this point, it is well established that being a successful lawyer certainly includes being technically proficient but that doing good work won't be enough for anyone to be successful. It is just as important to be entrepreneurial, in other words, to make rain. In 2001, David Maister published research on success in professional service firms in *Practice What You Preach*, in which he demonstrates the links between financial performance and other factors including training and development, coaching and client and employee satisfaction. Coaching can help you with those factors and the business side of the legal profession, where your legal training likely did not focus in any great depth.

There are different kinds of coaching, such as business development, leadership, and life. Regardless of the focus, coaching's primary purpose is to integrate concepts and tools into an individual's daily practice so that she takes action beyond planning. In this way, she engages in and follows through with activities that are appropriate for her, treating each experience as an opportunity to learn, improve and continue growing.

Besides the lawyers themselves, law firm business professionals believe in coaching. In April 2012, The Institute of Coaching published an interesting study on the *Use of Coaching in Law Firms* by Des O'Connell MA (Cantab), MBA, Solicitor. The paper contains findings based on interviews with "ten human resources and learning and development professionals in nine law firms in the City of London—including two of the world's largest (over £2bn of revenues between them in 2011); and the London offices of two US-based law firms with over 3,000 lawyers between them. It is based on interviews carried out during November and December, 2011." His research reflects our experience with the business professionals who work with lawyers: "respondents are advocates for [coaching]. They trust the coaching process."

Given the focus of our book and our consulting work, we are particularly interested in business development coaching. Essentially, when we coach our clients, we help them to create a plan with a strategic focus, employ tactics that are likely to produce success, expand their comfort zone, stay on track, get out of their own way, try new things, and be accountable (to themselves) for doing what they said they were going to do, when they said they would do it. In short, we help lawyers set and reach (if not exceed!) their goals. One of the ways we support each lawyer is to be very flexible in our approach and ideas so that we can help her select and prioritize activities that leverage her strengths and allow for specific, strategic focus.

What Coaches Do
The International Coaching Federation says that "Professional coaches provide an ongoing partnership designed to help clients produce fulfilling results in their personal and professional lives. Coaches help people improve their performances and enhance the quality of their lives... Coaches are trained to listen, to observe and to customize their approach to individual client needs. They seek to elicit solutions and strategies from the client; they believe the client is naturally creative and resourceful."

We especially like this description of coaching by our friends at Akina, who say they "help professionals 'find their voice' in sales and leadership." Their philosophy is that "successful selling, both externally and internally, is a natural outcome of building authentic relationships in which one person identifies and solves another's problems. [Coaches] help individuals improve their business development skills by coaching them to start, build and sustain authentic relationships and to identify and solve problems."

Here's how Stewart Hirsch of Strategic Relationships, a coaching colleague and former practicing lawyer, describes business development coaching:

- Helping lawyers focus on business development with the same level of intensity and professionalism that they bring to legal work
- Coaching them know what to say in the moment in ways that are comfortable and natural for them

- Helping them create realistic and achievable individual business plans and helping them implement those plans
- Providing strategic and tactical business development advice
- Suggesting action items, designed to successfully enhance relationships and secure long-term clients
- Holding them accountable to their objectives

To the above we add a few more from our own experiences with clients:

- To provide a "safe haven" for discussion about apprehensions, political situations, and business development myths. For example, that one has to be a super gregarious, outgoing, out-every-night, individual to be successful at business development.
- To provide coaching for one's current level of skill. Even the most successful rainmakers, like great prize-winning athletes, can continuously improve their skills and often benefit from having their own coach to talk to on a regular basis.
- To provide a platform and share a set of tools and knowledge to strengthen one's ability to build the sales confidence to drive revenue.

The Case for Coaching

"A friend can help you for a few minutes," says Ed Poll, "but beyond that they have their own career and personal issues to deal with. A partner in today's eat-what-you-kill world is protective of his own book of business and not likely to be very much help. If you're an associate, there are limitations on what you can tell a mentor or partner because their opinion will impact you at compensation time. There's only so much you can tell a spouse without freaking him or her out. Remember that the spouse is a passenger in this vehicle called your career path. Since the passenger never truly knows what's in the mind of the driver, they're more likely to panic at sudden twists or turns... A coach, on the other hand, is your accountability metric—someone who has no vested interest in your outcome other than as a trusted advisor who wants to see you succeed."

Coaching

We agree with Stephen Seckler, who says, "Now more than ever, success in private practice requires an ability to generate business. If you want to have control over your own destiny in private practice, having your own stable of clients is the key." Ed reminds us that "No Olympian athlete has won gold without a coach. So why should attorneys have to do it alone?" Lawyers have a lot at stake; there is no need to make business development more challenging than it already is by trying it without support and resources. Among many other things, coaching can deliver the following benefits:

- Objective perspective and either ongoing or situational assistance
- Enhanced business/client development skills and competencies
- Increased revenue with long-term strategies for sustainability
- Improved self-confidence and self esteem
- Attainment of partnership level
- Organization of and control over personal and professional life
- Enhanced performance and heightened productivity
- Focus and clarity
- Time and space to think, be creative and invest in yourself
- Time management
- Stress reduction
- An enjoyable relationship with a coach who holds you accountable to yourself

Coaches' Approaches

Like other business development coaches, we believe that a "one size fits all" approach is ineffective. We do not suggest that anyone fundamentally change who she or he is or that anyone should ever be disingenuous. Quite the opposite is true—remember, it's about authenticity. We usually won't recommend engaging in activities that you might find terrifying or excruciating. We will, however, ask her to commit to continuous development, improvement and growth. This, by definition, means constantly stretching comfort zones, trying new things and so forth. As with any learned activity, the new skills will become second nature with repetition, consistent effort and coaching to ensure follow up.

The Woman Lawyer's Rainmaking Game

Your work with a coach is always confidential. Your coach should not divulge what takes place in these sessions. At times, where requested, we can develop a reporting format that is integrated into the overall program and that allows the coach to keep the firm apprised of activities and progress generally. In O'Connell's study, respondents indicated that "they have in place careful quality controls—some formal; the majority more free-form (though still rigorous). And they strongly defend the principle of confidentiality, even at the expense of not knowing or being able to report on what is happening in the coaching sessions."

O'Connell also suggests a reasonable approach for balancing the firm's and individual's interests: "One firm uses a standard form to gather feedback at the end of each coaching assignment. The form asks about: [o]bjectives identified, [b]enefits gained, [c]hanged behaviours resulting from the coaching, [re]commendations, feedback for others... The form does not enquire into the details of the coaching session. Sometimes the coach is enlisted to ensure the form is completed and returned; but the coachee always retains control of the feedback. The coach is never asked to report separately from the coachee."

We like to begin coaching relationships by asking the lawyer to take the Myers-Briggs Type Index (MBTI) instrument online; sometimes if they are taken some other assessment, we will use that. The MBTI personality assessment is an excellent starting point for both the lawyer and the coach, since it offers a foundation for understanding individual differences and applying that understanding to the ways people think, communicate, and interact. It is an excellent tool that offers us great insights into how the lawyer is "hardwired" and what their natural preferences are—we hasten to state that no one personality type is better or more likely to succeed than any other. We get a lot of valuable information from the MBTI because it allows us to understand the ways people take in and process information and make decisions.

We use the MBTI assessment to develop the participants' understanding and abilities in such areas as communication, team building, leadership, and business and client development. It allows the coach to assist the lawyer in developing self-knowledge and awareness, understanding strengths and natural preferences that will be used in

Coaching

developing a business plan, selecting activities that have the highest chances of succeeding for this individual, and informing coach as to personality type.

Experiences with business development training and coaching vary. As we mentioned, it can't be one size fits all. What works? What doesn't? Like each lawyer, each coach has a different methodology, toolkit and style. For example, some spend more time focusing on social media, such as LinkedIn and Twitter. Others are more interested in relationship selling and the attendant strategies for it. One thing that seems universal is that coaches are quite adaptable and gauge their success by how well their clients do.

Jessica Block of Block & Ross hired her coach to help her market her law practice. "I had attended a number of marketing seminars sponsored by other professionals, but found it hard to put the concepts into practice, especially in a way that felt comfortable for me. Working with Steve [Seckler] was a revelation. He understood my practice, broke through my roadblocks about marketing, and found a way to make marketing a more organic process that felt comfortable, natural and, to my surprise, fun. Like taking tennis or ski lessons, it took a little while before the concepts I learned from Steve became second nature for me, but eventually they did. I have seen a steady increase in revenues and in my ability to attract the kind of business I really want."

The coaches we know <u>always</u> act in the best interests of their clients. Finding the right coach that works best for one's practice, personality and style is part of the key to a successful coaching experience. Interestingly, Stewart Hirsch and I have had occasion to not only speak together (most recently for a women's bar association), but we also share a law firm client. We have recommended each other to different lawyers in that firm because of our concern for the individual and finding the best fit for them. It should be easy to find a coach that is all about helping you.

Training

Training provides lawyers with the necessary understanding of the processes, concepts and skills that can serve as a great basis for coaching. Individual, confidential coaching is where the practical application of learning, self-accountability, and real progress takes place. It helps the lawyer applies concepts and tactics in ways that leverage their strengths and that make sense given their practice area, market, etc.

Perhaps most importantly, as it applies to coaching, training establishes common language and allows the coach to assist lawyers in:
- Creating and implementing an actionable plan
- Learning how to overcome obstacles
- Realizing successes, and
- Developing both personally and professionally

In the retreats, programs and workshops we deliver for women lawyers, we tailor the topics and activities to achieve the group's particular goals. These might include team-building or kicking off, continuing or concluding an initiative. But always, we are interested in helping women lawyers learn new things or how to apply what they already know in new ways. The great sales representatives in the corporate world will tell you they study sales and will sign up for training programs every year to continue to remind themselves about the basics and to continuously expand and sharpen their skill set. Lawyers should be no different; this is why we think the best organizations encourage and/or provide training for lawyers and business professionals at all phases of their career. Even the best can still get better.

Are Women Lawyers REALLY Different?
The short answer is yes. We know this intuitively and from our years of coaching many different lawyers. The fact is, "whether you are a man or a woman – being a lawyer is a tough job. The expectations are high. The deadlines are brutal. The issues are complex and the hours are long. And, while attorneys demonstrate tremendous competence in their ability to handle a demanding professional life, many lawyers (male or female) struggle with maintaining a sense of balance alongside this often intense career," notes Sonia Stringer on the Life Design for Lawyers blog in September 2009.

She goes on to write, "Nevertheless, women seem to experience a unique and more complex set of challenges working in our field. In

Coaching

our workshops and coaching calls, women lawyers confide they often feel they must sacrifice their own personal needs to meet a never-ending stream of professional responsibilities. Women are almost universally concerned about the reality of achieving professional success—while still having a family and a "life beyond work." Some share fears about gender bias and whether woman (particularly mothers) can really build a practice and succeed at the highest levels in the legal profession—while honoring personal and family responsibilities."

Stringer further cites statistics, which back up what seems obvious. In one of the reports released by the National Association of Women Lawyers, although women graduate from law school at about the same rate as men (48-52%), over 70% of women lawyers have left the profession by their seventh year. For those who remain, only 16% move on to become equity partners in major law firms, the majority of leadership positions still being held by men.

Even though women are naturals when it comes to relationships, women lawyers can be less comfortable with rainmaking. Sometimes this is because they feel like they have to know more than is necessary from a technical perspective (we call this super-learning in the book in our earlier discussions about confidence). This is related to feelings of being what is commonly referred to as an "imposter." Also, women lawyers may be reluctant to make an overt request for business, or may face additional time pressures as a result of balancing professional and personal lives.

Arguably, male lawyers face these challenges as well; however, female lawyers may seek different ways to resolve them. The legal profession is very competitive and revealing one's fears and problems can expose one to risk, perceptions of weakness, etc. Working individually with a coach fills an important gap. It allows for a forum and ongoing opportunities to discuss what is going well and to address the inevitable difficulties that arise in business development. While, as authors of this book, we have a clear bias but there is an abundance of research to support the fact that, yes, women lawyers really are different. They do face unique challenges. Coaching can be an excellent response to what we view as a critical situation in the profession.

The Woman Lawyer's Rainmaking Game

Start Early and Often

The experiences we have had over many years of training, coaching, developing and implementing programs, combined with conducting market research studies on women lawyers as well as our consulting work leads us to what should be an obvious conclusion:

- Formal programs delivered early on in a lawyer's career deliver benefits earlier in a lawyer's career.
- Firm culture, structure and support can be critical (but are not always necessary) to a lawyer's success.
- Developing the necessary skills for building and leveraging key relationships parallel with developing legal skills will result in building stronger confidence about one's ability to build business and strong working relationships well into one's career.

What's so valuable about a formal program that begins early in a lawyer's career? Lisa Mackie, an associate at Alexander Holburn Beaudin & Lang, says that her firm "supported my marketing efforts by facilitating early access to marketing resources, and continued resources to support my professional development plan." She goes on to say, "coaching has been of tremendous assistance to me, and it's a marketing avenue definitely worth talking about."

The support Lisa received was tailored to the professional development plan she wished to pursue. "Shortly after being called to the bar, associates were encouraged to develop a plan that identified our respective practice goals, personal goals, and client development goals. This plan became the platform to build our practice, and ultimately shape the direction we each chose to take." In addition, Alexander Holburn offered a mentorship program, whereby each associate was paired with a partner/mentor in their practice area that could offer assistance and guidance in the early years. Associates were additionally provided financial support to pursue marketing events and initiatives of interest to them.

Perhaps one of the most unique opportunities Alexander Holburn offered its juniors was the opportunity to participate in a year-long coaching program designed by an executive coach, Allison Wolf. The program was comprised of a series of personalized one-on-one sessions with Allison, in addition to monthly "group sessions" with other junior lawyers practicing in similar fields. At each session, participants would add to their personalized professional development plan and set short-term and long-term client development goals. Even after the program concluded, the one-on-one coaching sessions continued to be offered."

Lisa credits her current client development achievements to these early marketing resources. "Many lawyers can attest to the fact that your first years of practice can be your toughest years in the profession. A considerable amount of time is spent learning new practice areas, taking on new challenges, and balancing work/life generally. Having resources, like coaching, at my disposal early on gave me the boost I needed to shape my client development plan. Having continued support (such as partner mentorship and financial support) gives me the support I need to stay on track."

Lauren Jenkins, an associate at Holland & Knight, comments "Luckily, I am in the Rising Stars program, which has had a tremendous impact on my growth as an attorney. In particular, the focus on marketing (especially having my own PERSONAL marketing coach) has provided me with a completely different outlook on marketing and creating my own brand. The Rising Stars program has also introduced me to the support offered within the firm."

Lauren further reports that, through the Rising Stars program, she developed a strong relationship with the marketing professional in her office in Virginia and that she is also working with the marketing professional who concentrates on her practice group. "Thus far, I have found that if you put forth the effort and are interested, our marketing group is more than willing to assist."

"The biggest thing the firm has done is to offer business development courses led by a coach in both a group setting and in individual one-on-one meetings. The group meetings facilitated by the coach were very useful. We were able to share our plans, successes, tips on what is working and what isn't, and generally share best practices. In addition the firm offers many business development related seminars each year." These experiences, from a senior corporate associate who provided comments in confidence, demonstrates the value of combining training and coaching – and starting early in a lawyer's career.

Linda Widdup is a Consultant in Banking and Finance, Ashurst, Australia, who also works with Allison Wolf. She did not wait for her firm to provide her with the support she needed: "I hired my own coach. This way, the work we did was independent and focused on my priorities. I didn't want the coach to also have to have the firm as a client and to have to tow the party line. I wanted to entirely control the agenda. This worked out very well. Later, when I told the senior people at my firm that I had made this investment in coaching they were very impressed that I had taken the initiative to do so."

Meeting Challenges

As one progresses and becomes more senior, the challenges change but they certainly don't abate. In fact, the pace of change has only increased on every front. Thus, coaching isn't just for associates or younger lawyers. As O'Connell's study notes: "Firms have a challenge in changing people's behaviours. Training is not seen as effective here. Coaching may provide an answer... It may open up new opportunities. There are big changes taking place in the legal marketplace / business structures. Partners need to adapt. Coaching may be a valuable tool here—especially for the older ones."

Regardless of practice, firm size, or years of experience, the barriers to women's advancement include lack of mentors and informal networks as well as being overlooked for more challenging assignments. We do know successful women rainmakers who have been able to succeed in spite of these obstacles but have been interested in learning more specifically about business development success. Author Catherine Alman MacDonagh led the Legal Sales and Service Organization's (LSSO) several studies about women lawyers and business development issues. Among other findings, many of which are highlighted in the second edition of this book, more than half of the women rainmakers in LSSO's 2003 study pointed to firm culture and reputation as their primary obstacle to business development.

But we wondered whether "blaming" the firm was a way of escaping personal responsibility. So, to gain insight into this question, in 2008, we asked respondents to tell us about personal barriers to their ability to generate new and repeat business for themselves and their firms. The greatest number of responses indicated apathy: "as a new attorney, rainmaking is not very important at my level." More than 40% reported that they did not intend to stay at their current firm. Of that group, 30% indicated that they no longer wanted to be at their firms. Nearly 30% were frustrated with advancement opportunities.

So, obviously, it can't just be the workplace that must change. Attitudes and mindsets are choices and there is individual responsibility that comes with taking charge of one's business development success. That said, just over 75% of the same respondents indicated the gender makeup of their senior management team (executive or management committee) of their firms were all or mostly men. And, more to the point, two thirds (66%) of the survey respondents reported that their firm had no women's initiative. Thus, if we want women lawyers to be more successful at the rainmaking game, we have to make sure our players are talented, well trained and properly equipped AND that they play on a well-managed team for savvy business owners.

Are You Coachable?
A coach can't help you much if you aren't coachable. In her article, *Maximizing Coaching Outcomes: Identifying the Coachable Executive*, Rachelle J. Canter, Ph.D., says that "many studies and articles have outlined the characteristics of effective coaches and coaching programs." She suggests that "[s]uccessful lawyers often assume that they are automatically successful business people and leaders; so too do executives assume that if they are the best at achieving business results, they also know best about achieving results with people. The truth is that the ability to generate good business results is not the same as the ability to generate good people results. The evidence from the field of emotional intelligence (EQ) demonstrates that EQ is twice as important as IQ and technical skill combined in predicting success and is almost entirely responsible for leadership success… successful coaching requires equal partnership with a coach and a willingness to

learn… By far the most serious impediment to the successful coaching of executives is the issue of coachability.

Coachability is just what it appears—the ability to be coached—and it depends on an affirmative answer to at least three questions: Is there a behavior of yours that you want to change? Is changing your behavior a priority? Are you willing to be held accountable for making changes in your behavior? Absent affirmative responses to all three questions, even the best coach cannot single-handedly produce successful coaching outcomes."

Lauren Jenkins says: "What has worked the most is having a personal marketing coach. The experience has taught me to figure out exactly what I want to achieve, and from there, I am able to determine the best path for success. Before the coaching program, I found marketing/business development overwhelming. It seemed that marketing was solely speaking and writing, with the occasional lunch, and somehow—clients appeared. I can tell you from speaking and writing, I didn't get one single client. Of course, that isn't to say that speaking and writing don't work. Rather, marketing needs to be intentional. Going through the motions rarely results in long term success."

Linda Widdup originally sought out a coach to help with raising her profile and with developing business at a time when she was moving her practice to a new jurisdiction and firm. "The coaching helped me in a lot of ways. In my specialized area of law I do a lot of public speaking. Coaching helped me to gain confidence and shift my focus from my performance to helping the audience. This change in focus contributed to my effectiveness as a speaker. I now have a very high profile as a respected leader in the field and for being an excellent presenter. I receive many invitations to present at leading industry events.

With my coach I also explored my personal strengths and values, and learned an approach to business development that was aligned with these strengths as opposed to trying to fit in with the example set by the big boy rainmakers at the firm who play golf. I appreciated the many tips I was able to incorporate into my business development activities such as the importance of listening as a key business devel-

Coaching

opment skill. I also became a more effective networker. I developed a series of open-ended questions for use at networking events in order to find out more about the people I was meeting. I also became better at introducing myself."

Lisa Mackie believes "to bring in business, you have to mean business. In my experience, business development training and/or coaching will work if you work. Coaching legal professionals is really no different than coaching professional athletes. It's a team effort, and the results that you achieve reflect the time that you devote to the process. It is an investment made by your coach and yourself. The more you invest, the higher the prospective payoff. Coaching worked for me because I was prepared to put in the time and the effort to set a plan, and stick with that plan."

Planning

Planning is usually one of the first things a coach will help lawyers do; a coach can help develop a business plan that is built specifically to leverage an individual lawyer's strengths and interests. This is done in ways and places where the lawyer can best create and seize opportunities in strategically effective ways.

We have a section in the book about planning but for this chapter, it is sufficient to suggest that the development and refinement of business plans are both the roadmap and the foundation for coaching sessions. We assist (note that we do not craft the plan for the lawyer) in the creation and implementation of an actionable plan (emphasis on actionable) and then use every opportunity during execution of it to help the lawyer learn how to overcome obstacles, realize successes, leverage strengths and acknowledge weaknesses.

Linda says: "Coaching worked best when I had my goals in line. If you don't have a goal and clear objective coaching won't be as effective." Lisa Mackie's coach helped her to devise a very seminar-focused marketing plan. "For me, it is far more effective (and efficient!) to connect with a prospective client in person rather than through paper, such as with an article or advertisement. The more I taught, the more I got talked about, and word of mouth is really key when you practice in a niche market (I practice primarily in the areas of strata and residential tenancy law). With the help of my marketing coach, I was able to select which speaking engagements to pursue now, and which opportunities to work towards later."

Whether you decide to hire a consultant-coach, work with a mentor, or engage your firm's marketing and business development professionals, it is helpful to have an experienced person help you as early in your career as is possible. You will develop good business development habits before it is critical for you to be excellent at bringing in business and you will realize success sooner rather than later. With a coach, you will have an individual plan that is designed to accomplish goals that make sense for you and you get someone that helps you integrate your skills and activities in ways that produce results.

The LSSO studies demonstrated that the most successful women rainmakers had a plan. It can be written on a yellow pad or a formal marketing action planning template (provided in the book), but preparing for the upcoming 12 to 18 months and deciding where you focus with your business development goals, will be important. A coach can provide a check and balance against your thoughts and planning goals that can prove to be invaluable feedback. This type of coaching can come from a formal outside coach, an internal mentor or a well-respected business colleague. As we keep suggesting, coaches come in many forms.

Impact on Firm Relationships
Obviously, business development efforts and successes impact the relationships that lawyers have with others in their firms. These impacts can be positive or negative; one of the things we do in our coaching practices is help our clients navigate potential and real political landmines within their firms, practice groups and offices, as well as client, prospect and referral organizations.

A positive outcome that Lauren mentioned is that she is building a stronger relationship with her firm's marketing team. Your marketing and business development professionals can be tremendous resources, none the least of which is encouragement.

Coaching

As Lisa identified: "One of my biggest realizations as a junior associate is that your clients are not just outside of the firm; they are working right down the hall. The more success I had developing business outside of the firm, the more success I had developing connections within the firm. In short, it was about profile-building. The more external marketing activities I pursued, the more internal referrals and cross-marketing opportunities I received. With each connection came increased confidence, and it wasn't long before I felt comfortable approaching both junior and senior colleagues with marketing ideas and initiatives."

Clients and the Future

Clients affect a lawyer's planning for the future. Focusing on retention and growth is even more important than acquisition. As Lauren aptly stated: "I am always trying to attract new clients while retaining the current clients. With every client/potential client experience, I try to do a post-mortem to determine what worked and what didn't work so I can approve my approach in the future." This willingness to learn through an evaluative approach demonstrates an extremely positive attitude. We discuss the importance of attitude in the book because it a choice and it is one of the keys to business development success demonstrated by LSSO's studies.

Lisa shares how her clients affect her future planning. "I think the recent strain in the economy helped improve my perspective on client development, and my future practice plans. All too often, lawyers (myself included) perceive clients as one-dimensional problems needing to be solved—a client who needs a will drafted; a client who needs help commencing a startup business; a client who requires assistance disputing an eviction notice. We forget that the same client who is commencing a startup business may also need that will, or may in fact have a litigation dispute on the go. When the economy slowed down a couple years ago, I was moved to rethink my approach to client development and reconsider not just what I can offer prospective clients, but what my firm can offer them as well. This realization opened up new cross-marketing opportunities, and a professional development plan that was client-focused rather than practice-focused."

The Woman Lawyer's Rainmaking Game

Coaching tools

We use several tools that are very helpful in managing time and focusing on priorities. One of the first tools is the Individual Plan Template.

Another tool we use is the Sales Activity Tracker:

Again we don't put form over substance; this can be kept on in a journal, excel spreadsheet or in a more robust CRM system. For some, it works best if we copy and paste the list into our Outlook calendar coaching invitations. For each meeting or call, we simply update the action item that is to be taken and the date we are targeting for the next step. In this way, we keep a running action item list in one place.

One of the most important things we do is to help lawyers prepare for the events BEFORE they attend them. Imagine how helpful it would be to work with a coach to set your goals for a networking opportunity like a reception or conference, then prepare for it and make sure you are following up as appropriate. Most lawyers we know are only average at networking at the event, fewer still are good at following up. The best of the best know what to do before, during and after any networking event in order to maximize the return on their investment of attendance time.

This excerpt of networking tips from The Legal Mocktail's Event Skill Builder™ provides some excellent suggestions as to how to prepare for an event:

- Establish a goal for yourself—remember, networking is about forging and further relationships that are authentic; a goal of getting 5 business cards is not one that is likely to help you be successful.
- Try to get information about who will be attending. Who do you want to meet? Who can you introduce to whom?
- If you can get the attendee list pick one person to call. "I noticed you were also attending the conference and I was wondering if you were going to the reception as well. I was hoping to take a few minutes and meet you to find out more about you and your company."
- Prepare several questions in advance.

- Practice a self-introduction. Know what you will say when asked, "What do you do?"

This is a good time to use our Elevator Speech Worksheet; while it's good to have a generic version that is flexible enough to use in any situation, you want to refine it for specific use at each and every event you attend.

Benefits of Coaching

Linda says that business development (versus life or work balance focused) coaching has helped her personally and professionally in the following way: "There comes a moment in your development as a lawyer when you realize that in private practice you cannot sit back and let other people find you the work. There are those few lucky people who inherit a practice from a senior lawyer. But many of us have to focus on building something for ourselves. I have seen colleagues leave private practice because they weren't able to successfully build a practice. Also, it is far more satisfying to build something for yourself and build your own relationships than follow in the footsteps of a senior lawyer. When you work with another lawyer's clients the expectations of that client are different from what you would have established early on if they were your own client."

Many of our clients say that carving out the time to debrief, discuss and brainstorm regarding their professional development concerns, challenges and successes is one of the best investments they could make in themselves. This investment of time need not be lengthy in order to deliver a great return, as Pat Sabatale explains of her experience with Stewart Hirsch:

"Following on the two day training sessions, we had several hours of as-needed advising that has made a big difference and been lot of help for most of us to make sure that we internalized what we had learned. The first coaching call was a little intimidating… I really did not know what to expect. But, there was a client call fast approaching and I KNEW I NEEDED HELP. I quickly found out that talking to Stewart Hirsch… was worth the call. He delivered professional coaching beyond expectations and quickly assimilated the information I gave him. We talked about what I had discussed with the client, and then with a few words using the new principles we learned in class, the whole picture fell into place. I realized I had all the pieces needed for my conversation, I knew what was important to the client... Stewart helped me focus on how to say it. The price of admission... a 15 minute phone call. The outcome... a client who recognized that I heard everything she wanted from us and was happy to be engaged in the planning!"

Organizational Support

So, what's a firm to do? LSSO's studies and our experiences lead us to the conclusion that, in order to increase women's commitment, confidence and sales performance, firms should, among other things, support and encourage their women lawyers. By giving them resources to set and achieve—if not exceed—rainmaking minimums and benchmarks, they help their women rainmakers overcome obstacles and seize opportunities.

As of 2008, 66%—nearly two-thirds—of the respondents in the LSSO study reported that their firm had no women's initiative. Of the firms that do have a women's initiative, some, like Holland & Knight's, are real. None were open to all the women in the law firm. Only 25% of those programs offer training and mentoring as part of the program and a mere 18% were categorized by respondents as formal. Other firms claim to have a women's initiative but some seem more like window dressing than anything else. Eventually, we know lawyers will find it out and, we think, clients will too.

Clients care about the substance of these programs. It isn't just a random question that comes up in conversations or that appears in Requests for Proposals. DuPont is an excellent example spending "$42.6 million with minority and women owned law firms" last year, according to Thomas L. Sager, senior vice president and general counsel.

Coach Ellen Ostrow notes that "Firms are increasingly being asked by clients to account for the attrition of women attorneys and their absence from leadership ranks. Rankings of firms in widely read industry publications can bring uncomfortable attention to firms that have had difficulty retaining women lawyers." She goes on to suggest that taking a unique and specialized approach to coaching women lawyers allows them "to overcome unintentional obstacles to advancement… [and] includes strategies that factor in family responsibilities… " to, among other things, help "women lawyers assume leadership positions within institutions accustomed to masculine styles of leading. Providing coaching for women lawyers can make all the difference when it comes to retaining and advancing talent."

Interestingly, O'Connell's 2012 study reports that, in comparison to five years ago, "Most respondents report a marked increase in use of coaching compared with 5 years ago. One respondent expressed disappointment with the firm's investment in coaching over that period; another with the lack of take up of coaching which had been on offer over that period."

Lest you think that coaching is only for lawyers in firms, read what Jennifer Knapp Riggs, Counsel, Litigation, Sprint Law Department, had to say about her coach: "[Coaching] has added significant value to my legal career and my life. In my first occasion to work with Marianne, she helped me to create a business development strategy that combined my experience and my passions. When I became more senior, I worked with [her] to overcome challenges that face women attorneys who work a reduced-hour schedule. When I decided that I wanted to make a professional transition, [my coach] helped me to create a plan that identified my needs and desires. Together, we created a blueprint for obtaining success that I continue to use today… All women attorneys need someone like Marianne in their corner!"

Whether you work in-house or for yourself, in a small or a large organization, you will experience challenges and rewards. Regardless of your situation, it is critical to have focus and resources. Allison Wolf says that a coach is available to provide one-on-one support to lawyers at a time when there is something important to achieve." Here is her list of some of the typical reasons a firm might choose to hire a coach.

- There is something at stake (a challenge, stretch goal, or opportunity), and it is urgent, compelling, exciting, or all of the above
- There is a gap in knowledge, skills, confidence, or resources
- A big stretch is being asked or required, and it is time sensitive
- There is a desire to accelerate results
- There is a need for a course correction in work due to a setback
- One has not identified his or her core strengths and how best to leverage them
- There is a need and a desire to be better organized and more self-managing
- A career is no longer fulfilling and a change is required
- The pressures of work have become overwhelming

Allison points out that "in the case of sole practitioners and small firms there are no in-house support staff available to provide assistance on some of the management challenges of running a law practice." This is where coaching can be helpful. Those practicing in a large firm will face unique challenges and additional special issues for women. For several years, we served on the survey committee for the National Association of Women Lawyers, which has done extraordinary work to enhance the understanding of issues related to retaining and promoting women lawyers.

NAWL's Report Of The Sixth Annual National Survey On Retention And Promotion Of Women In Law Firms published in October 2011 by The NAWL Foundation and the National Association describes the purpose of the NAWL studies: "annually track the professional progress of women in the nation's 200 largest law firms by providing a comparative view of the careers and compensation of men and women lawyers at all levels of private practice, as well as analyzing data about the factors that influence career progression. By annually compiling objective data about firms as whole, the Survey aims to provide (a) an empirical picture of how women forge long-term careers into leadership roles, (b) benchmarking statistics for firms to use in measuring their own progress, and (c) over a multi-year period,

Coaching

longitudinal data for cause-and effect analyses of the factors that enhance or impede the progress of women in firms."

Barbara M. Flom and Stephanie A. Scharf further reported in 2011 on NAWL's behalf that "This sixth year of the Survey presents a sobering picture of the prospects for women in "Biglaw." Not only do women represent a decreasing percentage of lawyers in big firms, they have a far greater chance of occupying positions—like staff attorneys, counsel, and fixed-income equity partners—with diminished opportunity for advancement or participating in firm leadership. We recognize that the current economy has led to continuing challenges for big firms. Nevertheless, those challenges explain neither the uneven progress made by women lawyers compared to their male counterparts nor the backward slide of gender equity in law firms.

Being a rainmaker is more than just bringing in work and having your own clients. Is it the only answer to the many worrisome issues raised by the LSSO and NAWL studies? Maybe not, but it does offer women increased opportunities for advancement, career, leadership, and progress. It is much easier to be successful at rainmaking when you have support; mentoring, training and coaching can make a huge difference.

The anonymous senior associate whom we mentioned earlier in this chapter discusses an important issue—budget. "We also have a designated marketing budget which helps provide financial support. This is both a plus and a minus. It's positive because there are funds available to us for business development activities. The challenge is that budget is not large enough to support regular and active business development. So I cover much of the costs myself," she says.

Which leads us to a final point: if your firm doesn't make the training and coaching investment in you, perhaps you should consider investing in yourself! Spending the right amount of time doing the right things all while maintaining the right attitude requires the right support; you will be stronger with it and weaker without. And who better to invest in than YOU?!

The Woman Lawyer's Rainmaking Game

Coaching Resource Guide

- Akina Corp: www.akina.biz
- Rachelle J. Canter, Ph.D. www.rjcassociates.com
- David Maister: www.davidmaister.com
- FIRM Guidance: www.firmguidance.com
- LawVision Group: www.lawvisiongroup.com
- The Lawyer Coach: www.thelawyercoach.com
- The Legal Mocktail: LegalMocktail.com
- Legal Sales and Service Organization: www.legalsales.org
- Ellen Ostrow: www.Lawyerslifecoach.com
- Seckler Legal Coaching: www.Seckler.com
- Strategic Relationships: www.strategicrelationships.com
- Marianne M. Trost: www.thewomanlawyerscoach.com
- The Women Lawyer's Rainmaking Game – www.Rainmaking-Game.com
- www.lawbiz.com

CHAPTER 13

Retaining and Growing Your Key Clients: SAM-Legal©

Highlights

- Background on key client planning
- Foundational principles of business development (worth repeating if you have not read the book in a while)
- Stages of the Sales Cycle
- Creating value; Value Propositions
- Approaching an existing client
- Soliciting Client input; Assessing Goals and Needs
- Conducting an effective client meeting
- Key components of growing a client
- Developing a client action plan

We have also provided some tools and templates for you to use. The Client Action Plan is a document that is in Appendix A. The various components of creating a key client strategy are outlined in the chapter. You may wish to print out a copy of the Action Plan or download it from our web site: www.RainmakingGame.com.

Background

Key client planning, or, Strategic Account Management ("SAM") as it is called in the business world of sales, is a strategy that not only produces the best results for collaboration with clients and colleagues across the firm, but it is the most effective relationship-building approach for retaining and growing existing client relationships and building strong streams of revenue. Corporate sales organizations recognize the signifi-

The Woman Lawyer's Rainmaking Game

cance of a strong SAM program and today, many law firms are implementing SAM programs and hiring business professionals with sales backgrounds to manage and oversee these programs.

Why Are We Writing about SAM in a Sales Book for Women Lawyers?
Many women lawyers either have key clients or are billing time on firm clients and need to become more involved in building and retaining these important relationships. While getting involved may or may not mean sharing in the origination credit, it's worth the effort to join a team or to begin to build new relationships with existing clients. And, for lawyers who have practices that focus on individuals or consumers, a SAM strategy still works. Think about some of the best successes you've had and turn those clients into potential referral sources by maintaining a strong relationship with them through LinkedIn or Facebook or directly by speaking or meeting with them at least four times a year. The results of your efforts will be impressive. For those of you in a larger firm where the firm helps corporate clients, here's how to begin.

Identify four or five significant firm clients (or your own clients). If you are not the relationship partner, then identify who is the relationship partner and think of him/her as a referral source—someone who can introduce you into the client relationship (obviously this has to be someone who is also a team player!). Take the time to meet with these individuals and build strong relationships with them first. If you run into obstacles, then find another way to reach the goal. As one partner from a Southwest 400-lawyer firm said, "There are challenges to working your way into a client that is "owned" by someone, who frankly, inherited the client. In other words, what I think should be a firm client is overseen by a partner who was a mentee of the partner who developed the client in the first place." She went on to say, "That said, I found a way to involve myself with the client through other relationships I had and now he and I have learned to work as a team. Sometimes, it's easy and sometimes it's not." If you find you have difficulty getting introduced to the firm's key clients, then take a step back and meet with the management team to revisit their goals about cross-selling and client retention and address the topic of working in teams to solidify the client base.

Retaining and Growing

The rest of this section will address how to build effective key client relationships and the process for doing so.

FOUNDATIONAL PRINCIPLES OF BUSINESS DEVELOPMENT

Things come to those who wait, but only those things left by those who hustle.— Abraham Lincoln

Principle #1: Relationships Drive Business

Simply put, people do business with people they like. Of course there are some exceptions but generally speaking, building and maintaining relationships generally happens over time. People may Google some key words to find a lawyer but to maintain that relationship and make it meaningful, they have to connect with you/your firm. So when building key clients, relationships matter—both internal to the firm and external at the client.

Principle #2: Business Development Volume is Critical

Whether formal or informal, a high level of activity is necessary for success. When building relationships across the firm or with prospects and clients, it is important to become "top of mind" as we say. The only way to achieve this is to stay connected. We recommend at least four to six times a year and one of those times at least in person. Follow the sales process the book outlines and remember where you are in the process. Use opportunities to connect with people as stepping stones to closing new business or gaining new referrals.

Principle #3: Value Propositions will Open Doors

Creating value for others is what will help you to open doors. In other words, a value proposition offers a reason for someone to connect with you. More on this later.

Principle #4: Constant and Ongoing Communication is Imperative

Staying top of mind with clients and potential clients will keep you in the loop for obtaining new business. Likewise with internal or external referral sources, staying connected will yield results. Like going to the health club, with repetition comes results.

Principle #5: Add Value, Don't Pitch

Stay away from putting together a presentation that you will give at a meeting. Especially if you have not gone through the needs assessment stage (see Assessing Needs section of the book). Use meetings to uncover what is important to clients rather than to pitch clients about the work you think you could do for them. The former is a much stronger approach, particularly if you are using a value proposition you know will matter to them.

Principle #6: Business is Unpredictable

This we know: if you have a high volume of activity, things begin to happen. Results can't always be traced to a specific business development activity and may seem quite serendipitous; but we can assure you, there is generally a connection to some activity or connection you've made and phone calls you may receive. Like planting seeds, it's very difficult to know which will sprout first, but with time, patience and focus, results will come.

STAGES OF THE SALES CYCLE

The greatest of all mistakes is to do nothing because you can only do a little. Do what you can.— Sydney Smith

We thought these worth repeating (they are in the beginning of the book too). Focusing on key clients does not mean skipping over steps in the sales process. With every new relationship (including the ones with your partners internally at the firm or referral sources external to the firm) remember to follow the steps in the process. Each individual with whom you are building a relationship will have his or her own style, needs, expectations about the relationship and what's in it for them and how connecting with you will help them drive their goals forward.

Getting Organized: Getting and staying organized is very important in the world of selling. Identifying the clients, referral sources and partners who will be important to connect with for your key client planning is a foundational step toward your success. Use an activity tracker to stay connected with everyone at least four times a year.

Retaining and Growing

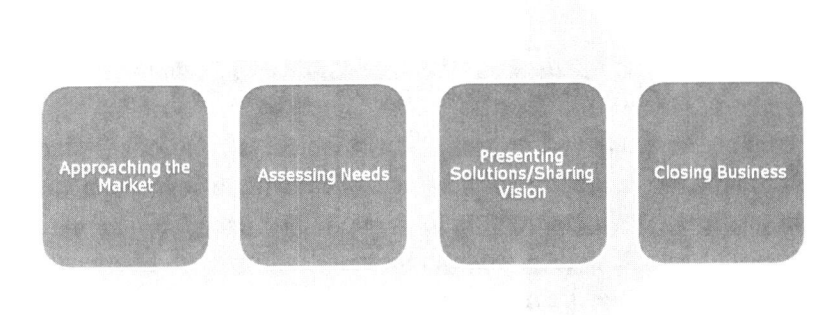

| Approaching the Market | Assessing Needs | Presenting Solutions/Sharing Vision | Closing Business |

Approaching the Market: Getting in front of your contacts will be important. Approaching contacts and clients with something of value to them (more on this in detail further into this chapter) will open doors.

Assessing Needs: Understanding what is important to referral sources and contacts will give you more opportunity for adding value to the relationships. Assessing needs means not only for a given opportunity, but in general, what an individual buyer needs out of his/her relationship with outside counsel.

Presenting Solutions/Sharing Vision: When you speak, you are essentially presenting. Discussing shared visions and how what you have to say bridges to something your buyer has indicated is important to her is a powerful method of getting engaged.

Closing Business: Demonstrating strength and confidence is absolutely critical to obtaining new business. One must make "the ask" as we say. If you do, you'll be further up in the line for getting the business.

Keep the sales process in mind as you work with key clients and contacts and increase your odds of client retention, growth and new business.

CREATING VALUE PROPOSITIONS THAT CREATE VALUE FOR CLIENTS

You don't get paid for the hour. You get paid for the value you bring to an hour.—Jim Rohn

To continue to retain and grow a client it is necessary to offer value. This could come in the form of helping a client with their cost containment goals, or providing training to the non-legal team/business units on topics about which they will require more information. Many partners are hesitant to call clients for a meeting. Yes clients are busy, but they expect their outside counsel to be proactive and call them to catch up, say hello or to schedule a meeting. We've heard this over and over again from clients. Connecting with your contacts will help to differentiate you from others who do not engage in this important relationship-building activity. Think of it this way, have you ever received a phone call from someone who quickly engages you in discussion? Chances are you know them well and/or they called with something of value to you. Perhaps an invitation to a program, or a new way of crafting a deal that will benefit your company or more simply, an invitation to lunch or meeting to connect.

To take client relationships to a level where clients see their relationship with you/your firm in the same manner you view your relationship with them, in other words, "key," adding value to the relationship based on the clients' needs will be very important. How do you know what will be valuable? Ask your clients. Creating value propositions to reach out to contacts is not easy. The more value you offer, the better the chances to meet with contacts and discuss opportunities for working together. Creating value to reach out also provides one with the confidence necessary to have forward-looking conversations about new business opportunities. Buyers tell us they have three primary criteria for hiring outside counsel (not necessarily in this order): relationship; expertise and experience. Other criteria come into play for sure, but without these three or at least two of the three, there is little opportunity. While we are on the topic, price is only of value if you already have expertise and experience. Price alone will not get you in the door, with very few exceptions.

Retaining and Growing

A formula for creating value propositions is helpful. First, what's the attention-grabber? This should be easy to read in 2.4 seconds (think about when you use Google and how quickly you scan the information on the first page that comes up). If the titles don't grab you, you move on quickly. Second, what are the benefits to the reader? Why should she read this information from you? And last, what is the call to action? In other words, as a result of reading this, what do I, the reader, need to do or what will you the sender do as a next step? There should always be a follow up step in your court.

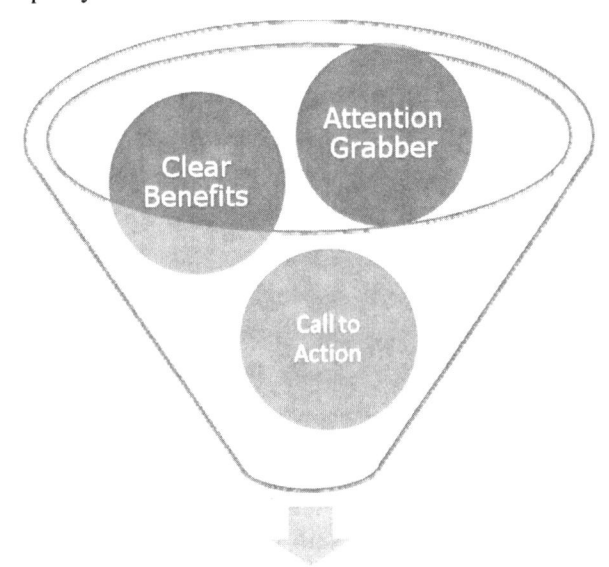

[Funnel diagram containing "Attention Grabber", "Clear Benefits", and "Call to Action" feeding into:]

Value Proposition

Value propositions vary from very important to maybe important. A helpful way to think about the most powerful of value propositions: is it need to know or nice to know? Need to know will definitely open doors. Nice to know can work, but it's not as powerful and especially so if you are not dealing with a contact with whom you have yet to develop a good relationship.

To create need to know value propositions, we have a formula. We say there are three levels of value propositions:

First, **You Know, You Know**." For example, "You Got Sued Today." Most likely they know that. So it has less value.

Second, "**You Know, You Don't Know**." For example, there is a regulatory change that will impact your company. You know about the regulatory change or the fact that you need local permitting, but you don't know how it will impact your company, or where to find local jurisdiction help. The second example below is a good value proposition which demonstrates this level of value.

Last, "**You Don't Know, You Don't Know**." For example, you don't know about a change coming your company's way so you also don't know how it will impact your company; or like our first or fourth value propositions below. This is the most valuable of value propositions. An outstanding example of this was when a client of ours recently saw that a union was organizing against a company in a state where the firm didn't even have offices. He called the general counsel and left a voicemail, "I saw that this union is trying to organize against the company. I have had great experience beating this union." (that's the "You Don't Know") and (Value Prop here): "I would be happy to provide counsel to your existing outside firm handling this for you or to work with you directly." The partner received a call back from the general counsel of this Fortune 100 Company and was hired. Value propositions work.

Here are five value propositions our clients have created and we thought you'd find helpful in thinking about your own value propositions. Read through these and use the Value Proposition Worksheet to craft one for one of your clients.

Value Proposition Examples

1. New Patent Rules Seminar

September 20, 20XX
Kenwick Karten Obst Best
10 Main Street, Irvine, CA 92614
8:00 a.m. – 9:30 a.m.

Value Proposition: New Patent Rules Will Affect Your Company's Patent Strategy

On August 21, 20xx, the U.S. Patent and Trademark Office announced new rules that will affect your company's intellectual property portfolio strategies and the dollars your company spends on patents. The new rules become effective on November 1, 20XX. Join us to learn about short-term strategies that should be implemented well in advance of November 1, 20XX and for long term strategies to maximize the strength and value of your IP portfolio under the new rules.
Presenters:
John Grover, Partner, Kenwick Karten Obst Best
Jarom Kesler, Associate, Kenwick Karten Obst Best

Cost: Complimentary

1.0 hour of MCLE credit will be available for lawyers.
Contact Lauren Ferraro at lauren.ferraro@kkob.com to register

2. Energy Industry, Regulatory Issue

Situation: CYTAM has plans to build a new power plant in Northwest Region. They are located out of the region and are not connected to the regulatory agencies.
Value Proposition: We've had significant success in getting permits approved specifically for these types of power plants in this region. We'd be happy to help CYTAM with the permitting process to get you on a fast track to building the power plant.

3. Market/Economic Opportunity

Hi Silvia,
JP Morgan's buyout of Bear Stearns this morning at $2 a share is only the beginning of the trouble for the storied bank which faces a stream of litigation by bank shareholders and employees, according to **Chuck Casper, class action attorney at Montgomery, McCracken, Walker & Rhoads LLP, in Philadelphia**.
What types of litigation will we see this year stemming from the deepening credit crisis and subprime mortgage fallout? What settlements are we likely to see?

The Woman Lawyer's Rainmaking Game

If you are interested in speaking with Mr. Casper about these questions and other legal ramifications of the unraveling banking crisis, please let me know. I would be glad to arrange.
Regards,
Saskia Sidenfaden
Financial Relations Board

4. Innovative Project

Bob,
I am reaching out to you on a topic I think will be of interest to Acme Corp. I recently completed an innovative financing transaction for a significant client that involves the public offering of hybrid debt security. Benefits include:
Access to growth capital;
No common unit dilution
Access to new group on investors; and
Minimal balance sheet impact relative to traditional debt offerings.
In connection with the transaction described above, we worked through all of the legal and tax hurdles unique to companies in your industry, and I'd welcome the opportunity to share this idea with you. How does your schedule look over the next few weeks for a brief meeting? I will give you a call to follow up or please feel free to reach out to me.

5. Decision

Cynthia,
A recent decision concerning storm water regulation will affect many California companies.
The XX Court ruled that extremely stringent limits in the California Toxic Rule apply to industrial storm water discharges. The California Toxic Rule limits are considerably more stringent than the "benchmarks" which are non-enforceable guidelines many facilities consider to determine when contaminants in storm water are at levels of concern.
It will be important to make sure your facility takes appropriate steps to **monitor for compliance** with the California Toxic Rule to avoid civil penalties from the Regional Water Quality Control

Board or citizen suits from environmental organizations. If this is an issue for you, I would be pleased to send you a brief recap of the decision or answer any questions you may have.

I will give you a call next week to schedule a time to meet.

Creating Your Value Proposition—Worksheet

To create a strong value proposition it is helpful to think about the following:

What changes do you see occurring that may impact clients? _____

How can you turn this experience into a value proposition? Outreach Email; Webinar; Seminar; Article; Phone Call or Meeting to Discuss?

What is your 2.4 second opening statement (the attention grabber) ?_____

What are the Key Benefits to the Client if They Take Your Call; Read Your Email; Agree to Meet?

What action do they need to take?

Trends the firm is monitoring/you are seeing _____

What is Your Action Step in Closing? How Will You Follow Up?

APPROACHING AN EXISTING CLIENT

You have to sow before you reap. You have to give before you can get.—Robert Collier

A successful woman partner with some strong long-standing clients recently lost two of her biggest clients. One was not her fault, the company went bankrupt. The other, however, was a sad story. After 18 years of a successful relationship the client changed firms. After conducting a series of client interviews with the client, we delivered the bad news: the client felt the relationship was taken for granted and that the partner had taken her eye off the ball. They said, "This was theirs to lose and we will not consider working with the firm in the future." So what happened? While they spoke regularly about existing case work (the firm handled many files for this client), the emotional side of the client/attorney relationship suffered. Just like you would tell a child you love them, you must regularly let your client contacts know you appreciate

The Woman Lawyer's Rainmaking Game

the opportunity to work with them. Just doing good work is not enough (although it is critical, obviously). This partner had assigned work to a younger partner who also did a great job, but in so doing, the relationship lawyer took her eye off the ball and did not have regular calls with the client or visit the client enough. It was a very disappointing situation for her, the firm and for the client. The general counsel's comment was "the work product was good but I can get that with other firms. The key for me was that other firms were showing us they thought about the company and our challenges and they were proactive and demonstrated a strong willingness to work with us under our terms."

While this seems extreme, it's not. There are lots of good choices for outside counsel and the loyalty grows with ongoing communication and showing you listen and care about the company and your contacts' needs, challenges and goals.

Keeping in touch on the relationship front with existing clients may seem like a simple concept but there is a lot to it. In major corporations the SAM programs are extensive and top sales executives are in charge of companies' most important customer relationships. We are beginning to see a very slow trend in this direction for law firms as well. To lose a key client will generally have a long-term impact on any firm. To read about how to approach a client to begin to build a long, loyal relationship, read on.

To begin, make a list of your most important clients (three to five is best to start—too many gets overwhelming) and all of the contacts you have at these client organizations. Use the Client and Contact Activity Tracker provided in Appendix B. If you have been more reactive lately than proactive in terms of connecting with the client, schedule meetings with each of your contacts. Simply pick up the phone and let them know you'd like to connect with them about how things are going from their perspective. We call it a year-end review and you can conduct these meetings during the fourth quarter of the year. You will be surprised at how receptive clients are to these meetings. If you miss Q4, then do it during Q1 and you can still call it a year-end, new year planning meeting. We've provided a Year-End Review form with some

Retaining and Growing

sample questions you can ask. You will want to think about your clients and come up with your own specific questions as well.

Conducting a year-end review has high value to clients and it's a good door opener for relationship-building. This is different that a client feedback meeting (although similar in some ways) so if your firm has conducted those with key clients that's fine. This is your one on one opportunity for meeting with the client. It's also a good idea to bring the one or two-year history of the firm's relationship with the client. Just so you are prepared and informed for anything that might come up. There are other ways to approach these important client contacts as well.

Think about a value proposition for each client and reach out with your value proposition. Of course, the value propositions you develop will be stronger if you have a sense of what is going on with the client and therefore how you can add value to each relationship based on their needs.

There is another part of SAM strategy worth mentioning here. We hear often from women lawyers in the larger firms that they are not always part of a key client team or that they themselves don't control any significant clients of the firm. They ask about two things: first, "If I am not going to receive any origination credit for working with this client or even expanding this client, why should I do it?" And, second, "How do I approach my male colleagues about including me as a key relationship lawyer on the client team they manage or for the key clients for whom they are the relationship lawyers?" In these situations our advice is to think of your partners as referral sources and target them for relationship-building in the same manner you would those referral sources outside of the firm. Over time if your involvement with these clients helps to expand the relationship and bring in new business, then it's time to have the origination-sharing conversation. Most larger firms today are really trying to address this origination situation and splitting origination is becoming a more common practice. Again, it's all about doing what's best to retain clients. It's foolish not to let others into these client relationships.

Here are some other ways of approaching existing clients for relationship building:

The Woman Lawyer's Rainmaking Game

- Interview for an article
- Pro bono work
- Invite to speak on a panel
- Sponsor a survey
- Participate in a charitable activity
- Start a roundtable
- Client referral
- Cost saving ideas
- Custom client alert

All these and more are ways to approach clients and offer value. The key is to create your Client/Contract list and pursue building strong relationships with specific individuals. One more note on this: be sure to develop three to five good contacts at each of your client organizations. This is important so if one good contact leaves, you still have others within the organization that will support you and the firm. An added bonus is your contact who left may now bring you into her new company also.

Year-End Review Guide

The last quarter of each year provides an opportune time of year for checking in with both clients and prospective clients (November and December specifically). Consider scheduling meetings to discuss one and/or all of the following:

- ☐☐☐**Year End Review** (an update or recap of important matters worked on during the year)
- ☐☐☐**A Client Service Interview** (formal or informal client satisfaction and service commitment review)
- ☐☐☐**Annual Planning Session** (discuss business plans, initiatives and aspirations for the upcoming year)

This proactive approach achieves the "top of mind" mindshare that we seek and also affords us the ability to be viewed as a trusted business advisor.

Client Service questions to consider:

- How would you describe the relationship with us?

- What would you consider the most important elements of a professional relationship?
- Are there specific areas that we could improve?
- How would you describe the quality of our work?
- Regarding value, how do we compare to other law firms?
- Would you suggest any changes?

Upcoming year planning questions to consider:

- What are your top three priorities this year?
- Can you describe your goals and objectives for the coming year?
- What potential challenges does the company face?
- Where do you see the business going in one, three or five years?
- What are the critical company initiatives for the upcoming year?
- What growth opportunities do you foresee in the future?
- What are the greatest challenges you're facing in the legal dept.?
- What's currently working in the legal dept.? What's not?
- How do you see using outside counsel to help you achieve your goals?
- What criteria are used for selecting outside counsel?
- What areas provide the greatest opportunities for improvement?
- What is the best way for us to stay in touch with you?

Always close with a recap of the meeting and next steps based upon your understanding of the client's needs. Schedule a time to follow up (including dates and times).

SOLICITING CLIENT INPUT; ASSESSING GOALS AND NEEDS

If you think that communication is all talk, then you haven't been listening.—Ashleigh Brilliant

The Woman Lawyer's Rainmaking Game

As we pointed out previously in the Value Proposition section, connecting with clients is the key to success. Creating and packaging value can be difficult. To do so means we truly understand our clients' goals and needs. Often we believe meeting with a client and presenting ideas on how we may further service the client is welcome by the client. If the relationship is very strong, this can be true. But rather than present ideas about new services to offer, it is far better to conduct a needs assessment (discussed in the main section of the book) by asking really good questions. Asking questions allows you to facilitate the dialog in a direction you wish to take it. And, it demonstrates an interest by you in the client's thoughts and ideas and business.

There are three types of questions: Open-ended, Focused and Closing.

Open-ended questions allow you to learn about the clients goals.

THREE TYPES OF EFFECTIVE QUESTIONS

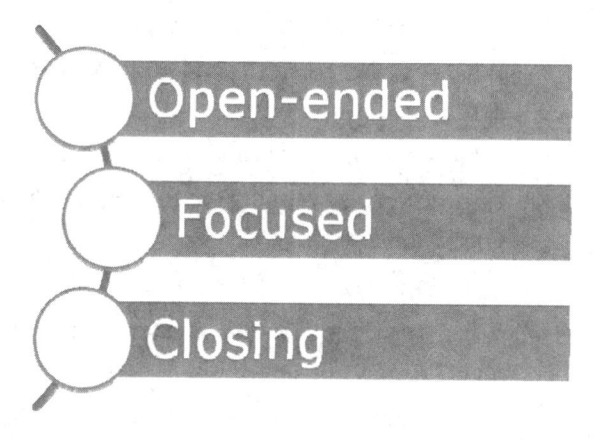

- Open-ended
- Focused
- Closing

They are often thought of as vision questions. Rather than asking something that is not welcomed by many clients like "What keeps you up at night?" a stronger approach would be to ask about this individual's specific goals and challenges or about the company's growth plans.

Focused questions are more specific. Questions like: "In what region of the country have you seen the most litigation?" or "What are

Retaining and Growing

some things you've identified with your third party administrator?" or What M&As have you had in the last two years that may impact your compliance?" And one more, "What finance structures are you considering?" These are focused on the client's specific business.

Closing questions are those questions that will help you get to the next step of the sales process. They don't always mean closing the business, but rather, closing to the next step, which of course could mean asking for the business if you are at that stage in the process. We think one of the best closing questions you can ask is "What is the next step?" or "Is there anyone else on your team we should meet?" So closing questions help you move the sales process along. This is particularly critical when you are expanding existing key client relationships into new areas. Remember, don't assume the client knows all about your firm, they often do not and it's up to you to grow the relationship.

The Three Types of Effective Questions Overview located in **Appendix** C has a few more examples which you may find useful.

Think of a client you will approach and use the Questions Worksheet on the following page to develop two or three questions in each category. Then, give the client a call and start the dialog! You will feel more confident having prepared in advance of the conversation.

Once you have some needs identified, add them to the Client Action Plan and begin to craft some Value Propositions you will use to respond to these client needs or opportunities

Three Types of Effective Questions Worksheet
Client Name for This
Outreach:_____
Open-Ended or Broad—Begin with open-ended questions to understand the highest priorities
List two to three questions you will ask from this category:

_____
_____
_____
_____
_____
_____

The Woman Lawyer's Rainmaking Game

Focused—Use focused questions to discover specific issues or legal needs
List two to three questions you will ask from this category:

_____
_____
_____
_____
_____
_____

Closing—Use closing questions will solicit direct responses in identifying next steps or ultimate resolution to problems discussed.
List two to three questions you will ask from this category:

_____
_____
_____
_____
_____

CONDUCTING AN EFFECTIVE CLIENT MEETING

The structure will automatically provide the pattern for the action which follows.—Donald Curtis

There is nothing worse in business than sitting through a boring meeting of talking heads. We thought it important to include some tips on conducting an effective meeting particularly since this will be with a key client. Being prepared for a meeting does wonders for one's sales confidence level. Preparation is even more critical if you will be introducing new members of your firm's team to the client since they will not know one another and first impressions will be lasting impressions. The more prepared you are the better. As one client put it "Please don't show up and throw up. Be prepared if you are asking me and more important, any of our business folks, to spend time with you and your partners." We suggest creating what we call a "shared insight" dialog. That is you are sharing insights about the industry, the business challenges and inviting the client's team to do the same so you engage in dialog. This is a powerful use of meeting time.

The meeting framework benefits are as follows:
- Designed to facilitate a two-way *discussion*
- Sets you apart from your competition
- Establishes you as "Thought Leaders"
- Ensures meeting productivity
- Highlights that you understand their business
- Presents the opportunity to "connect" with one another
- Demonstrates that you work well as a team
- Enables you to identify cross-disciplinary opportunities together with the client

The meeting agenda will look something like this (and, it is very important to have an agenda). The timing in parens is suggested by us and obviously you will not include on a final agenda!

"Shared Insight" Meeting Agenda

- Introductions (2 minutes)
- Who We Are (1 minute) (yes, 1 minute—they should have your bios in advance of meeting)
- What We've Heard/What We're Seeing (insights you are sharing—15 minutes)
- ABC Company: What We Know (10 minutes—demonstrate that you listened)
- How We Can Help (3 minutes)
- Why (your firm) (2 minutes)
- Next Steps (10 minutes)

Notes:
1. The time proportions are what's important, rather than the actual time in minutes.
2. If the Client keeps talking, asking questions, forget the time.

3. Use the Agenda to keep the team on track or to rescue from a "ditch." Do not let one person on your team dominate the conversation—it will not go well.

When wrapping up at the meeting make sure you bridge to get to the next steps. Ask the client, "Is there anything I/we missed?" or "Any additional questions for us?" Then move on to next steps.

When it comes to next steps, try not to ever leave a meeting without next steps that you will be taking. Get agreement on those next steps (including timeframes) and be sure to communicate that the first follow up step is yours so you can remain in control of the sale.

COMPONENTS OF AN EFFECTIVE KEY CLIENT PROGRAM

Give yourself something to work toward, constantly.
— Mary Kay Ash

There are a few things that you can do to insure your personal key client program is effective. Below are what we think is important to consider before getting started. The single most important factor in growing a client is to be proactive!

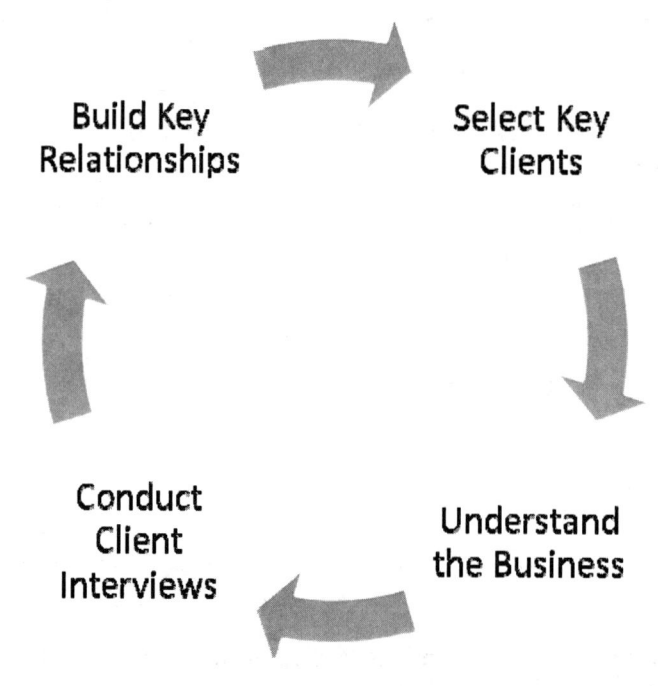

Build Key Relationships → **Select Key Clients** → **Understand the Business** → **Conduct Client Interviews** → (cycle continues)

1. Selecting Key Clients

Determining which clients to include in the firm's or your individual key client planning can seem like a difficult chore. Our advice is to start small. In other words, don't decide that you will focus on 20 key clients all at once—it most often doesn't work out well. Rather, identify three to five to begin with.

The criteria for determining which firm clients fit in the category of key clients include:
- Clients for which the firm or any individual has worked over a long term;
- Referral sources who refer the firm business on a regular basis;
- Clients for which the firm has done a small amount of work but the client company is either large or is a significant company within a key industry group;
- Clients who have many firm lawyers working on their files;
- Clients which represent significant revenue to the firm;
- Clients who have a key leader or leader(s) on either the firm side or the client side who will be retiring within the next two to three years (yes, it takes that long to transition a client actually);
- Significant prospective clients where you think there is an opportunity to make them a client of yours/your firm; and,
- Clients with potential for growth.

It's important for us to note that any one of the above criteria may be good enough reason to focus on an important client.

2. Understand the Business

Do you really know your clients' businesses? Think of the three to five clients you've selected to grow and ask yourself if you know the following about each contact or the company overall:

Strategies

Goals

Objectives

Challenges

The Woman Lawyer's Rainmaking Game

Pressures
Personalities
Centers of Influence
Internal politics
Decision making
New products or services
New markets
Size/organization
Roles within the legal department
Business initiatives
Business drivers
Industry trends
Competitors (yours and the clients')

3. Conduct Client Interviews

Whether formal or informal, client service interviews are invaluable because they yield crucial information about current client needs and expectations and invaluable information about your competitors. Client interviews will help you to create new opportunities for more billable work and differentiate you from competitors who have failed to do these types of interviews. Client interviews will help you to build client loyalty. The key will be to follow up on an action items that come from the interview. And to do so in a timely fashion.

Use the year-end review as a client interview tool or create your own set of client interviews. Good questions to consider include:

- How would you describe the relationship with us?
- What would you consider the most important elements of a professional relationship?
- Are there specific areas that we could improve?
- How would you describe the quality of our work?
- Is there anything about your business or industry you think our teams needs to know more about?
- Regarding value, how do we compare to other firms?

- Would you suggest any changes?

Clients reinforce to us that they hire people they like and with who they trust, admire, respect, and with whom they can spend time, get along, share similar values and who they know will make them look good. These are good attributes to keep in mind when building these key relationships.

4. Building Key Relationships is a Process

There are five elements to this Process:

A. Client structure
- Obtain and review the client's organization chart
- Identify key executives and buyers
- Analyze total legal spend (ask!)

B. Key relationships
- Identify key contacts and decision makers
- Understand roles and reporting relationships
- Document decision-making ability of the above
- Determine strength of each relationship

C. Research
- Gather competitive intelligence
- Conduct research to understand business issues/trends
- Identify company business initiatives

D. Business Issues
- Identify business issues and/or business initiatives
- Match the client's needs with our services
- Create value propositions based on anticipated legal needs
- Define the strategic account plan/strategy

E. Action steps
- Identify and assign tactical action steps
- Determine approach to explain and clarify value propositions

The Woman Lawyer's Rainmaking Game

- Track and monitor activity
- Record your next steps and progress on your Client Action Plan monthly to keep the process moving.

In summary, key account planning is an essential part of any rainmaker's continued success. A client does not necessarily have to be large in terms of revenue generation to be considered a key client of yours. Look at your entire client list and select clients who are important and also consider clients who could be key clients with a bit more focus and effort.

Remember all this take time. It can take one to three or more years to successfully build your practice in this area. Be patient and assign yourself a few tasks each month for each client to keep the process moving forward. You will see success in time!

Retaining and Growing

APPENDIX A

Client Action Plan

Client Name:

Client Relationship Manager	Client Team Members

Client Team Objective(s)

Billing Information	Services/Matters—What Service Standards does the Client Have in Place?
2013 Revenue Target	
2012 Revenue	
2011 Revenue	

Our Strengths and/or Key Differentiators

Current Total Legal Spend

Client Business Issues or Initiatives
1.   2.   3.   4.   5.

Client Action Plan — Rainmaking Advantage ®

The Woman Lawyer's Rainmaking Game

APPENDIX A, CONTINUED

Key Relationships & Roles				
Name	Title	Location	Role	Firm Contact

Roles

G -- Gatekeeper		PS -- Power Sponsor
DM -- Decision Maker		SW -- Supporter
R -- Recommender		O -- Opponent
C -- Coach		I -- Influencer
F -- Friend		A -- Alumni

Client Action Plan   Rainmaking Advantage ®

Retaining and Growing

APPENDIX A, CONTINUED

How Can We Be A Part of Their Success?		
Match the client's needs with our services		
Client Business Issue or Initiative	**Anticipated legal needs**	**Our Value Proposition**
Example: Growth strategy is to acquire new banks in various regions	M&A; IP and TM Review; Financing; R.E.	
Prioritize Value Propositions: What will we take action on?		
Account Strategy		

Client Action Plan   3   Rainmaking Advantage ®

13-27

The Woman Lawyer's Rainmaking Game

APPENDIX A, CONTINUED

Action Items

Action Step	Owner	Due Date	Status

Retaining and Growing

APPENDIX B

Client and Contact Activity Tracker		Name:					Date:	
Contact Name	Company	Telephone eMail	Email/Phone Q1	Q2	Q3	Q4	In Person 1st Half	2nd Half	Next Step

APPENDIX C

THREE TYPES OF EFFECTIVE QUESTIONS OVERVIEW

Open-Ended or Broad
Begin with open-ended questions to understand the highest priorities
- What are your top priorities for the year?
- Where are you spending most of your time?
- What are your objectives for the coming year?
- What are some of the challenges you face?
- Where do you see the greatest opportunities?

Focused
Use focused questions to discover issues or legal needs
- How many acquisitions do you anticipate this year?
- How do you typically finance your growth?
- What type of trade secrets are at risk?
- How many patents do you file annually?
- Do you have a strategy for managing your litigation costs?
- What's your annual budget for legal services?

Closing
Closing questions will solicit direct responses in identifying next steps or ultimate resolution to problems discussed.
- Which area from your perspective might be worth exploring further?
- What are the next steps?
- Who else will be involved in the decision?
- What other information will be most useful to you about our practices?
- How would you consider using us in the future?
- When do you expect to make a final recommendation?
- How do you envision you will use outside counsel to assist you?

GLOSSARY

Advertising: A marketing communications vehicle that uses television, radio, print publications, newspapers and trade shows as medium for providing firm messages to various target markets.

Business Development: Often a word substituted for sales. Can describe "softer" activities that support sales such as development of pitch materials, presentation planning and strategy.

Client development: A common term used by professional services firms that means the same as "sales."

Cold call: An unprompted, unsolicited telephone (usually) call or visit to a prospective client with whom you have no contact or only a dotted line reference to the person.

CRM or Client Relationship Management: Generally refers to an outcome achieved with the use of good software. CRM is a process for maintaining up-to-date information about clients and client-related activities.

Forecasting: The art of keeping an active prospect list with estimated timelines for specific activities that lead to closing business. Often contains dollar amounts of potential value of work client will send to the firm. Forecasts are good for keeping individuals who prepare them focused on the immediate opportunities for closing business.

Marketing: "The Science of Exchange" as one top ten university calls it. Marketing is a set of support initiatives for increasing awareness about a company or product. Marketing is a support function to sales. Often described as umbrella term for the four Ps: Product, Price, Promotion, and Place.

Marketing communications: A group of functions dealing with communicating to target markets including: advertising, public relations; media relations; association relations.

Media relations: Activities that focus on building relationships with various print publications.

Public relations: Activities that focus on building relationships with various publics, including association executives and members, publications' editors, and media.

Prospect: Someone or a company that is currently not a client but is on your radar screen for potential business.

Qualified Lead: An opportunity to sell to a prospect or client who meets your new client criteria. (E.g., is financially sound, is a decision-maker, clears conflicts check, etc.)

Rainmaker: Someone who brings in business to the firm.

Sales: The process of obtaining new business.

Territory: A defined target from which to develop business including geographic market, industry market, individual profiles, etc.

WEBSITES

abanet.org
Resource-rich site with a specific diversity section focused on women and rainmaking. Look for the link off the site to the ABA Women Rainmakers section.

ACCA.com
Association of Corporate Counsel ("ACC"). The organization to which many in-house counsel belong. Its site offers insight into how in house counsel think; the type of resources on which they rely and other valuable insights.

AltmanWeil.com
Consulting firm with many fine market studies and newletters you will find of value.

Amazon.com
Type in the word "sales" and you will see a significant amount of titles from which to choose to learn more about sales.

Ateaseinc.com
Excellent tools and tips for networking etiquette, marketing to individuals and respecting foreign country diversity, and training programs

Barnesandnoble.com
Type in the word "sales" and you will see a significant amount of titles from which to choose to learn more about sales. Although most will not pertain directly to the legal market, you will find many books on selling professional services.

Bticonsulting.com
The publishers of the annual "Client Service 30," a report on the service trends and buying criteria of Fortune 1000 in-house counsel.

BorandResearchCompany.com
Conducts research and provides insight about clients.

Cathcart.com
A salesperson's dream for tips and hot ideas about every aspect of selling. The Cathcart organization is led by Jim Cathcart, noted keynote speaker and author.

Chadwickmartinbailey.com
A consulting firm dedicated to branding and service excellence. Dr. John Martin is a four-time Baldridge examiner.

Clientfocus.org
Great tips, tools and workshops developed exclusively for women lawyers.

Courtexpress.com
Business trends and sales support analyses.

E-Law Forum
An online legal bidding house that invites corporations to use their resources to post potential outside counsel opportunities for work with often large organizations.

Findlaw.com
Findlaw's site is the gateway to competitive intelligence tools, seminars and other sales resources.

GlasserLegalWorks.com
A division of Findlaw, visit often to learn about the latest conferences for the legal industry.

LegalLeanSigma.com
The Legal Lean Sigma Institute's website—process improvement courses, certifications, and consulting for the legal profession.

Legalmarketing.org
The Legal Marketing Association's website—tips about seminars and marketing resources that will help you to support your sales efforts.

LegalMocktail.com
A unique, experiential networking training program for lawyers.

Legalsales.org
The Legal Sales and Service Organization's website—great sales articles and tips; information about sales and service conferences.

Marcuslegger.com
Insightful updates and books to help professionals reach success.

MartindaleHubbel.com
Martindale now provides exceptional resources for lawyers to showcase its expertise. They also offer competitive intelligence tools for the savvy rainmaker.

MillerHeiman.com
A noted sales training organization for industry.

RobertDenney.com
Denney Associates has provided counsel to professionals for many years. Excellent newsletters and resources.

SalesResults.com
You may sign up for free weekly sales tips from the Coach. They are useful, practical tidbits of advice. The company also provides individual sales coaching and consulting.

WJFInstitute.com
Great articles and a leading sales training program calendar of regular classes and locations.

ARTICLES

This section has several articles that are either referenced in the book's chapters or are relevant to the topic of sales.

Article 1:

Active Listening and Feedback

by Dr. M.B. Handspicker

Carl Rogers, in his book, *Client-Centered Therapy*, involved the therapist's focusing attention on the client and helping the client discern what he or she was concerned about. This necessitated that the therapist engage in feedback of the client's thoughts and feelings. Such a feedback process helps the client to clarify what his or her thoughts and feelings really are and to develop some understanding of what options are available. These may be behavioral changes, attitudinal changes, and new understandings of both self and others.

Other researchers have discovered that the application of this feedback process is enormously helpful both in stimulating group creativity and in becoming more capable advisors.

In Synectics training sessions George Prince would describe the good leader as "listening 200%." The same characteristic would apply to the good teacher, parent, supervisors, manager, counselor. Such listening lies at the heart of good communication, which is essential in any kind of work with people.

But the active listener does not stop there: he or she also engages in feedback—putting into his or her own words (paraphrasing) what the other feels or means. For example, a child asks, "When is dinner?" and an actively listening parent might well reply, "You're hungry, aren't you?" This process of checking meaning out with the other affirms the speaker and indicates the true interest of the listener. But active listening does not stop with a single transaction. The child might reply, "No, I just want to find out if I've got enough time to throw a few baskets before we eat." By checking, the parent has made sure he or she did not misinterpret the child.

"The key attitude which lies behind active listening is a keen interest in the other person, a desire really to hear what the person intends, a willingness to check out our perceptions with the other, and a willingness not to impose our own evaluations during the process."

Genuine listening and feedback involve the listener's putting into his or her own words the feelings or thoughts of the speaker. Mere parroting back is just that, parroting, and not feedback. The process can be diagrammed as follows:

```
Thought————>Encoding————>Code—————>
Decoding—————>Understanding Feeling in speech /
\<—————————————Feedback<———————-/
```

© 1997 From Conflict to Community

Article 2:
Discounting vs. Validation
by Dr. M.B. Handspicker

Seldom do we realize how much we "put down" others (and ourselves). Even less often do we realize how we get back at others (avenge ourselves) after we have been put down. These behaviors are so much a part of our lives that we take them for granted. Learning how to be good communicators, however, involves our becoming aware of these behaviors and what they cost—in terms of loss of self-esteem and, more importantly, effectiveness.

A discount is any action, body language, or verbal behavior that one perceives as put-down, criticism or denigration. Revenge is pay back for a discount. It may involve openly discounting the person who has injured, subverting that person's goals or attempts at organization, being uncooperative withdrawing from a cooperative enterprise, or any other form of retribution. Unfortunately we engage in this behavior almost casually and automatically. "Aren't we supposed to use critical thinking?" "We can't let sloppy ideas be accepted!" "The guy is such a jerk." All of these reactions may be secretly thought (or shared with others during a break) as justification for such behavior. Yet when the behavior is reciprocated we feel hurt; we may put on an accepting face, but energy is depleted and effectiveness diminished.

The positive counterpart to discounting and revenge is validation. Here one is heard and appreciated even though one's ideas may be partial and not fully acceptable. Validation is a result of an action that leads one to experience being, to be aware of one's meaningfulness; it is what one perceives as support for who one is, as one is now. It is manifest in any action or statement, obvious or tacit, that creates or reinforces one's sense of worth and well being.1 Validation may appear as one appreciates his or her own competence in dealing with a problem as one screws up the courage and takes a risk to make an illuminating connection, or it may arise from a compliment, empathy, recognition, appreciation of another, or a need for one's presence and skills.2

Validation, however it comes, energizes persons and increases their effectiveness. It helps create a positive and pleasant atmosphere in which to work together. It is simple to do. For instance, late in a meeting someone realizes that what Judy suggested earlier has real merit. The person does not merely pick up the idea and suggest it again, but credits Judy by saying, "You know, Judy suggested about an hour ago an idea I think might work."

Some people validate others naturally, but they are few. Such a powerful force for good is too often neglected. What research has shown conclusively is that "where people and ideas are systematically appreciated, that is, they are unfailingly listened to, supported, and protected from invalidating remarks or non-verbals by the appointed facilitator" the group is far more productive.3 In terms of our usual behavior, this is artificial and contrived. But it can become the norm for a group, either through one way of insuring that at key points where ideas are being evaluated people engage in behavior, which is validating rather than discounting. Where a group is experiencing disabling conflict, peoples' need to engage in validating behavior is increased. And its effect is little short of miraculous.

Article 3:
Twenty-One Marketing Tips from Women Rainmakers
by Shelley J. Canter, PhD and Barrie Drum

The ABA Law Practice Management Section's Women Rainmakers group surveyed its membership in September-October 2002. After ten years of programming and social networking events, the Women Rainmakers' Executive Committee felt it was time to get comprehensive feedback. (The Women Rainmakers is a subentity of the Marketing Core Group and everyone is welcome to join.) A part of the survey requested marketing tips. The survey went to the 700 members of the women Rainmakers Listserv maintained by the ABA Law Practice Management Section. Following are the top twenty-one marketing tips from women rainmakers:

1. Always write (hand-written) thank you notes (another of the most popular tips).
2. Tell people you would like to have them as a client and ask how you could achieve that goal.
3. Visit your client's offices regularly. (You will always come back with something new to do.)
4. Have lunch with other lawyers who practice outside your area of emphasis for cross-referrals.
5. Give away useful information at face-to-face meetings without charge.
6. Go to conferences, lunches, etc. (If you're not there, you can't get the business.)
7. Gain acceptance and support from male colleagues by finding ways to work together that are of mutual benefit, rather than "taking them on."
8. Use "leveraged networking" — it's more efficient to establish relationships with people who can refer you to clients than it is to find and establish relationships with prospective clients themselves.

Articles

9. Keep following key personnel at companies as they go from company to company.
10. Only buy clothes that have a pocket for business cards.
11. Purchase pens with firm name and phone number. Give them to clients to sign contracts, to all participants in closings in your office, and make them available to guests. Invite them to keep the pens. Also, use them to sign the check in fine restaurants and leave them behind so waiter/waitress will use them with other guests.
12. Throw out lines as early and often as you can. You never know when you are going to catch a big fish.
13. Be a person first and a lawyer second.
14. Be open to business development opportunities no matter where you are. Tell everyone you meet that you are a lawyer and would like to help them with their legal needs.
15. Listen, don't talk.
16. Be polite and open to everyone you come across and avoid being over-eager and aggressive. Be pro-active in expressing your experience and interests to people—in work, volunteer, and leisure situations. Everything, even inadvertent things, make an impression.
17. Supply good service everyday, all day. Be accessible—and when you are not, have a team in place who can respond to your client's needs.
18. Make friends of clients.
19. Let people know your flexibility in terms of financial arrangements.
20. Ask for the work (one of the most popular tips).

Shelley J. Canter, PhD the president of RJC Associates in San Francisco, which provides executive development, career consultation, and outplacement services to law firms and corporations. She can be reached at rjc@rjcassociates.net and 415-956-8438.

Barrie Drum is the managing Director, Citigate Global Intelligence (formerly Director in the Forensic Practice of KPMG LLP). Based in

The Woman Lawyer's Rainmaking Game

Washington, DC, Barrie assists clients with fraud and financial investigations. She can be reached at 410-563-2830.

Article 4:

Sales & Service Tips

by Beth M. Cuzzone, Director of Business Development, Goulston & Stors, co-founder Legal Sales and Service Organization

- When meeting a prospective client, remember the deposition rule. Ask questions and listen. This is also known as the 80/20 rule. Listen 80 percent of the time, speak and ask questions 20 percent of the time. Control the conversation.

- Touch base with each person listed in your database at least four times a year.

- Try to make appointments with prospective clients early in the morning. The appointment will less likely be cancelled and it won't take too much time away from your billable time.

- Track how/when/where your clients are generated with a new client intake information. Don't forget to review this data at least once a year. You may find you want to spend more or less time and money with particular marketing activities.

- During lectures and speeches, provide attendees with a form to fill out if they would like you to contact them in the future; add to your mailing or e-mail list; or even meet in the near future.

- If you have the opportunity to solicit business from a new prospect, send an email to your colleagues in the firm that asks if anyone else has relationships with the company and/or person. If you are a solo practitioner, send an e-mail to your referral network of other professional service providers.

- Don't leave a meeting without a follow-up timeframe. "When should we touch base again?" "If you send me the document you have, I'll review it and get back to you by the end of the week." "What are our next steps?"

- Ask clients for referrals. Clients are the best source for new business, albeit, a new matter or transaction or a referral to a friend/colleague.

- It takes 6 to 8 contacts with a prospect before closing the business. Don't stop communications if you are not hired during the first few interactions.
- Visit clients at their offices rather than have meetings in yours.
- Get to know your clients and prospects personally. Spend time off the clock at their offices and doing something that interests both of you.
- Bills can be utilized as a marketing tool. Include a suggestion or feedback card with your bills. Don't forget to acknowledge your client's suggestions.
- When you obtain a first-time client, provide the client with a question and answer packet; who to contact for questions regarding bills, weekend contact information, information of other members of the firm, etc.
- Provide staff with a client service skills building program annually. Recognize those who go above and beyond the client's needs.
- Write down your sales goals. Create a measurable goal ($500K in fees or three new matters in the next 12 months). One is more likely to achieve his/her sales goals if the goals are in writing. Check your goals every three (3) months to be sure you are on target.

Article 5:

20 Questions You Should Ask Current and Prospective Clients
by William J. Flannery, Jr.

You've been representing your client for a time. He is aware of your expertise. He has seen your firm's brochures, attended the firm's seminar last month and received the firm's newsletter. You think there is potential for more business. You've invited the CEO or general counsel to lunch, presumably to develop more business by trying to cross-sell the rest of your firm.

You may have invited a partner from your firm to go along. The partner's role may be that of a potential new practice area opportunist or as a sympathizer if the "cross-selling" lunch craters. Now the real challenge begins: What are you going to say at lunch?

Here's where rainmaking often turns into drought. Here, lawyers inexperienced in marketing often make the crucial mistake of assuming that they're the ones who are supposed to do all the talking. For lack of anything better to do, they start their sales pitch. Or they try to convince clients that the firm has a number of good lawyers who can help them. Or more likely, they start with a small talk as a way of building rapport. The first 45 minutes of the lunch focuses on the U.S. Open, the Dallas Cowboys or subject matter that borders on the trivial. But clients don't want a sales pitch, and they don't need to be told about your lawyering skills. They probably assume you're good at what you do, or you wouldn't have gotten this far. And they certainly don't want small talk. They're as busy as you are.

What they want is to feel comfortable with you as a professional, and to see where you and your firm might fit in with their business objectives. To make them comfortable, get them to talk about themselves or their business objectives. Your marketing efforts should focus on listening to their responses. The more they talk, the more you'll learn. And the more you learn, the more natural the marketing process becomes. In client development, information is always power—because it means knowing what the client needs.

If marketing is what lawyers do to develop business, then knowing more about the client's business is what marketing is all about. Knowing what to ask and how to ask is an art and a science. As a basic introduction, I have selected 20 questions broad enough to apply to most types of clients—both current and prospective—yet specific enough to elicit the concrete information essential for the selling and delivery of legal services. Many of our questions seem to target new clients. But it is surprising how much lawyers don't know about the clients they've been serving for years. If those lawyers took the time to learn, they'd find there's substantial business going elsewhere which, with a little effort, could be kept in the family.

Asking clients about themselves will uncover opportunities that require not just your expertise, but your partners' as well. Such cross-selling is the highest form of marketing. It means long-term client relationships and long-term revenue development—not just one job today that won't pay any bills tomorrow.

Long-term is the key. When clients hear you asking about their plans three to five years hence, they begin to think of you as a 30-year friend. Don't worry about asking new clients direct questions. This is information they tell their brokers, their PR staffs, their friends. And they certainly want to tell you, because they want to trust their lawyers. They have a business need to share with their lawyers information they don't necessarily need to tell their insurance brokers or financial representatives.

Likewise, old clients will appreciate your interest. They may even realize that such expert listening is the crux, not only of selling, but of quality legal service. This article assumes that these meetings are with the client's decision-makers, including business executives, general counsel or the legal department.

First, here are a few basic rules:

You cannot sell legal services to unwilling buyers. You should not try to close the business at the first available lull in the conversation. Avoid the "sales pitch," as the client may not be in the "catching" mode.

Never put clients on the defensive. Don't use the same style of questioning you'd use in a deposition or while cross-examining a hostile witness. This is win-win. The better they feel about talking now, the better they'll feel about hiring you later. Let them be the ones to bring up sensitive or painful matters. Try to avoid the "why" questions, which are likely to carry a judgmental tone. It's empathy and rapport that you're after.

Make all your questions as open-ended as possible. A "yes" or "no" answer will seldom do you any good. Phrase questions in such a way as to give clients the opportunity to supply as much information as possible.

Don't feel you need to respond to everything clients tell you. Selling is interactive, and you want to respond intelligently to what you, the seller, are hearing. But much of what clients say should be filed away, for future use at a more appropriate moment. Silence can help build informational savings accounts.

Do your preliminary research. Clients want to tell you about themselves, but they'll also appreciate the respect you show when you take the trouble to learn as much about them as you can. Use public data bases, newspaper articles and the client's own publications as sources. Give those stockbrokers that call you daily some homework; and ask them to do research.

The selling process follows its own course and cannot be rigidly encapsulated. Ideally, you may want to start by asking general questions about the client's business: what they manufacture, sell and to whom. There's nothing they'd rather talk about. Then explore how they've structured their organizations. Finally, zero in on their legal needs: how they've met those needs in the past and intend to do so in the future.

Here are the questions:

1. What do you want your organization to look like in one year, two years or five years?

This question is a good opener, because it allows clients to begin talking about any aspect of their business they choose. But you also have your own tactical reason for asking it, which is to determine if they've formulated a strategic plan and, if so, what that plan involves.

Now is the time to listen and learn, not promote. But if the client mentions, for instance, international growth as a part of the strategy, you may have spotted a great cross-selling opportunity right off the bat, assuming your firm has expertise in that area.

Asking about strategic planning tells you something else as well. It tells you what kind of self-knowledge clients have. Do they have a specific vision of what they want for themselves, or are they playing the field, reacting to events and market developments as they happen? Getting a feel for clients in this way may tell you volumes about how they deal with every other aspect of their business, including hiring lawyers. How long has the client been in business? It's an obvious question, but don't forget to ask it if you don't already know. Mature businesses often have more experience with outside counsel, and many of their legal problems have already been resolved. With start-ups, the selling process has a completely different texture. You may need to explore fundamental questions, like setting up ESOPs or going public, that the client may not have thought through yet. In some ways, you're establishing a partnership when you sell to start-ups.

2. **Do your plans involve new offices or plants in new locations?**

This seemingly innocuous question is more than just a further refinement of the strategic planning issue. It will help you focus on a whole range of possible legal services, from real estate and lease negotiations to benefits planning for new staffs. In addition, it's information that will give you a real sense of just how aggressive and confident the client is. It's one thing to talk about a strategic plan. It's another thing to state boldly, "We intend to open 10 new branches in the next two years."

3. **Will you be developing important new products, services or making major changes in your offerings?**

What if a retailer decides he wants to offer a discount brokerage service? Suddenly there's a whole range of legal expertise that your firm may have, but that you had no idea this particular client ever would need. And the client may have no idea you feature a securities practice. Here, the opportunity for cross-selling, as well as getting a jump on the competition, speaks for itself—thunderously.

4. **What kind of research and development do you see as necessary for you to meet your strategic objectives?**

Legal counsel is itself a form of R&D, particularly where the client will be breaking new ground. As clients talk more about their plans—how much they plan to invest, and the kind of research they'll be doing—you may even get a glimpse of your own future: the practice areas you'll need to develop to be at the cutting edge five or 10 years down the road.

5. Could you profile your typical customer?

Getting a sense of who clients' customers are may help you determine how they themselves behave as customers. Are their buyers highly sophisticated and demanding? If so, they may want to see some evidence that you also treat your clients as peers.

Understanding how they market their products or services will naturally give you some clues as to how you should be marketing to them. If they de-emphasize the direct pitch, maybe you should, too. But, there's another reason to explore their marketing approach. How they structure their sales force, whether it's decentralized or pyramidal, and the quota pressures under which those salespeople operate, will give you crucial insights into their culture. Is it a pressure-cooker, or is their customer base solid enough to permit a more relaxed environment? What the company expects from its district managers, it may also expect from you.

6. What are your employee relations concerns?

How clients manage their sales force leads to a broader issue: how they manage their entire work force. This line of inquiry will strengthen your sense of the client's culture and its impact on the client's legal needs. Is it a paternalistic milieu, or a demanding and confrontational one?

Querying clients' concerns here also will help accomplish two other basic objectives. First, it will indicate current or future labor/employee problems: collective bargaining, wrongful discharge, benefits planning, etc. Second, it will increase the client's comfort level with you. Whether clients are closely-held businesses or Fortune 500 giants, there's nothing they fret about more, and nothing they'd rather talk over with a lawyer.

7. Who are your main competitors?

Here's another opportunity to get a sense of the business climate in which your clients are operating. Where there's an ongoing survival struggle with competitors, there are myriad legal issues, like commercial litigation, that the buyer may not yet be pondering but ought to. Conversely, less intense competitive environments may direct the client dialogue elsewhere.

8. What has the financial climate been like for your business?

Use care here. This is information you need to have to understand any prospective client, but the question must be presented in as non-threatening a way as possible. You don't want to put anyone on the defensive. And you certainly don't want the client thinking you're worried about who's going to pay the bill.

You're really trying to accomplish something very different. Clients in distress may want to think about spinning off a division, or even tapping your firm's bankruptcy expertise. Or perhaps you will want eventually to suggest custom-designed billing methods. You may even want to mention that your firm has helped other companies under the gun.

Once you have a sense of where your prospective clients are in the marketplace, shift the focus somewhat. Find out what makes them tick.

9. How are you organized, what does your organization chart look like, and who are the key executives?

You're really trying to gauge the client's level of complexity. Is it a flat organization or hierarchal? Are there dozens of subsidiaries, or is it a one-cell organism? You don't necessarily need the whole organization chart, just enough information to know with whom you're dealing. The names of the key executives are important at this juncture. You may never actually meet, say, the CFO, but you certainly don't want to sound ignorant later if that person's name comes up.

This is another particularly good time to think about cross-selling. You may, for example, uncover reporting relationships between clients and their divisions or subsidiaries that you never suspected.

10. How are decisions made, and who are the decision-makers?

Here, you're fleshing out the political underpinnings of the organizational setup. How bureaucratic is it? How autocratic? How many meetings will be needed before decisions, including retention decisions, are made? How efficiently are legal counsel implemented? For lawyers in particular, it's vital to know who specifically makes the decisions. Is there a general counsel? If not, it may be advisable to minimize legal jargon in the selling process.

11. What is the leadership style here?

This question will give the client an opportunity to provide a wealth of insight into the personalities of the key players. Get a sense of those people before you meet them. You may learn that the leadership style emphasizes consensus-building. That's a cue to suggest setting up other meetings with as many of those important team players as possible. Even brief introductions are useful. The more decision-makers you meet, the more opportunities for cross-selling open up.

12. Is there a legal department, and how is it organized?

Many sophisticated users of legal services have legal departments. The role of the department and its officers vary widely. Obviously, you need to know, but be careful here. The general counsel may be out of the decision-making loop altogether. Let the clients describe the role of their legal department and draw your own conclusions. But ask to meet the members of the legal department in any event. There's no point in alienating your in-house counterparts.

13. What do you see outside counsel accomplishing for you or your organization?

Again, the question is broad enough so that it's the clients who supply the essential information. Let them tell you what they want to buy, not just react to what you want to sell. They state their needs. YOU decide if you can fill them.

Articles

14. Are there any recent uncertainties affecting your business, or changes of any sort that have particularly concerned you in the last few months or so?

Most clients have something on their minds, otherwise they wouldn't be talking to a lawyer. Some of them may want to jump right in and tell you about a serious problem that's been keeping them awake at night. Others will prefer to talk about bewildering regulatory, political or market changes. But even generalities will highlight what they need from you today, as well as how you might be solving their other problems tomorrow and the day after tomorrow.

You're now on the verge of making an absolutely crucial determination: Does this client want proactive counseling or crisis management? You're not going to use the same tone of voice with a client who wants you to co-pilot long-range business strategy that you'd use for someone who needs you as a safety net. To know which tone of voice will make clients most comfortable, listen carefully to the tone they use with you.

15. What sort of legal services are you currently using, and do you expect that to change?

Perhaps they've been relying on outside counsel for, say, garden-variety tax work or ERISA. If so, ask yourself why they're talking to you now. Maybe some new and critical situation is in the offing, and they feel the need to shop around. Or perhaps they're just dissatisfied with their current counsel and are looking to turn everything over to another firm. This line of inquiry is also helpful because you'll be able to compare their current legal needs with the services they're now buying. Something may well be missing on the service end. With new or first-time buyers, there may be particularly glaring omissions. With veteran buyers, watch for certain recurring patterns. Some of them may be turning to Firm X for, say, tax work, and to Firm Y for litigation. Do they even know that many firms offer the best of both? One-stop shopping is a powerful lure for most clients.

You should have some sense at this point of the clients' legal needs. Move on and, for experienced clients, explore what sort of lawyering has made them happy or unhappy in the past. For less sophisticated clients, modify the questions. Ask them to imagine the best-case lawyer/client scenarios, as well as the worst.

16. What dissatisfies you about the level of legal services you've been getting?

Learn from your competitors' mistakes without attacking them directly. Pinpoint where they've fallen short in order to determine where you'll need to do better. It's helpful to find out who those other firms are, because they're likely to continue to compete with you for future work. The client may mention their names without your having to ask.

17. How much detail do you like to get from your lawyers?

Here is where you can get a real picture of your clients' legal environment, and how much knowledge of the law they're bringing to the table. That knowledge will have a direct impact on the selling process. Clients who aren't interested in hearing about all the details of a case aren't likely to appreciate your trying to sell yourself with dazzling displays of esoteric legalese.

By the same token, clients who say they demand line and verse on every deal may well expect to be talking shop before they hire anyone. Incidentally, clients who take pride in their legal knowledge probably have invested power in their general counsel, at least in determining which firms get what business.

18. How do you perceive our firm in particular?

You should be listening here to two things. First, what is it that has interested the client enough to consider hiring you? Is it a particular practice area or your firm's overall reputation? Define that strength and, whatever it is, reinforce it in your presentation.

But listen, too, for what even the most admiring clients are not perceiving. Remember, you're trying to build a long-term relationship. That means going beyond the one or two areas of expertise that these clients have seen fit to mention. In other words, sell everything you have.

Articles

19. What criteria do you use in selecting lawyers? What makes a good lawyer?

For clients, a good lawyer may be variously defined as someone who wins cases, returns phone calls, respects in-house counsel or keeps costs down. Sometimes these clients have no particular impression of you or your firm, one way or another. They may just be spreading their nets, talking to as many lawyers as possible. So don't guess what they're looking for. Ask them.

20. How does your budgeting for legal services compare to what you spend on other resources?

Get a sense of the cost pressures beleaguering the client. Sophisticated buyers aren't looking for bargain-basement rates, but they are attracted to lawyers who are sensitive to their need to stay within reasonable limits. Again, the main issue is the clients' comfort level. They're going to want to know that you're someone they can deal with.

At this point you probably have developed a sense of the organization's operating environment, the personalities and their decision-making styles.

Any number of things might happen next. You may meet with other key executives. Or you will now begin preparing the formal presentation, written or verbal or both. With such myriad data now in hand, you can tailor that next step to the client's unique situation. You've substantially reduced the distance between you and built or enhanced the relationship.

Many lawyers don't reach this stage in a relationship with their established clients. Such relationships are built on trust, and trust is generally built on understanding and face-to-face communication. Asking relevant questions builds trust, and people give business to people they trust. Clients learn more about trusting lawyers and law firms from face-to-face meetings than probably any other source.

Too often, lawyers inexperienced in client relationship-building and business development squander client development opportunities. The sad part is the client may become permanently turned off to his lawyer's amateurish efforts. This could result in a loss of trust in his lawyer. Clients will be reluctant to share information if they perceive that they will get a non-stop sales pitch. Avoid the premature "sales pitch," as it could have disastrous long-term implications for client relationships.

The last question you may want to ask is the one that will lead to a commitment. Building relationships is a process, and one in which the clients themselves participate. So ask your client or prospective client for help in determining what the next step might be.

This article was featured in the September 23, 1991 issue of Texas Lawyer. Copyright ©, 1996-2004, The WJF Institute

1. George M. Prince and Kathleen Logan-Prince, Mine-Free Program. Weston MA: Mindspring Company, 1993. Vol. 4, p.11.

2. Ibid, p.2.

3. Ibid, p.7.

©1997 The New Paradigm Group

INDEX

AGGRESSIVENESS
Selling legal services, 1-12

APATHY
Coaching, apathy as a personal barrier to rainmaking, 12-13

APPEARANCE
Creating professional presence, 3-27

ARTICLES
Active listening and feedback, AR-1, AR-2
Current and prospective clients, 20 questions, AR-7 to AR-18
Discounting vs. validation, AR-2 to AR-4
Sales and service tips, AR-6
Twenty-one marketing tips from women rainmakers, AR-4 to AR-6

ASSOCIATIONS
Leveraging association memberships, 3-10 to 3-12
Researching associations in target market, 2-12

ATTITUDE
Evaluative reflections, 3-3
Importance of, 3-2 to 3-5
Likelihood of getting right attitude, 3-4
Negative, 3-4
Sales confidence, 10-4, 10-5
Supportive, 3-4
Supportive reflections, 3-3

ATTRITION
Coaching, attrition of women lawyers as an issue, 12-21

BARRIERS TO ADVANCEMENT
Coaching, 12-12

BIOGRAPHY
Results focused, 2-4 to 2-6
Sales bio, creating, 2-3

BROCHURES
Use as sales tools, 3-18

BUDGETS
Coaching, budget for business development as a factor, 12-23

CASE STUDIES
Big bank study, 7-4, 7-5
Coaching, NAWL Foundation studies, 12-22
Personality fit, 5-9
Presentations, role playing, 6-4 to 6-6
Qualifying and assessing needs, 4-3 to 4-5, 4-9 to 4-11

CLIENT ACTION PLAN
SAM-Legal, retaining and growing key clients, 13-25 to 13-28

CLIENT AND CONTACT ACTIVITY TRACKER
SAM-Legal, retaining and growing key clients, 13-29

CLIENT SERVICE QUESTIONS
SAM-Legal, retaining and growing key clients, 13-15

CLIENT STRUCTURE
SAM-Legal, retaining and growing key clients, 13-23

CLIENTS
Balancing sales activities with billable time, 9-11
Building good relationships, proven methods, 11-3 to 11-5
Coaching, this index
Connecting with clients
   generally, 11-1 et seq.
   building good relationships, proven methods, 11-3 to 11-5
   client survey, 11-7, 11-8
   feedback, soliciting, 11-2, 11-3
   highlights, 11-1
   key attributes of service providers, 11-6 to 11-7
   market research, use of, 11-5, 11-6
   strategies for success, client development and service, 11-16
   summary of interviews with women in-house experts, 11-8
Current and prospective clients, 20 questions, AR-7 to AR-18
Entertaining, 5-2 et seq.
Feedback, soliciting, 11-2, 11-3
Growth strategies. See Key clients, retention and growth strategies, below
Inactive clients, 8-4, 8-7 to 8-9
Interviews, retaining and growing key clients, 13-22
Keeping in touch, 5-1 et seq., 8-1 et seq.
Key attributes of service providers, 11-6 to 11-7
Key clients, retention and growth strategies

Index

    generally, 9-1 et seq.
    balancing sales activities with billable time, 9-11
    building team for prospects, 9-5
    compensation credit, adjusting to benefit all team members, 9-9
    highlights, 9-1
    identifying clients and prospects, 9-4
    listening meeting with client, scheduling, 9-11
    meetings for team members, 9-7
    monthly and quarterly meetings for team members, 9-7
    opportunities, 9-2, 9-3
    revenue goals, assigning, 9-6, 9-7
    sales initiatives, 9-3 et seq.
    SAM-Legal, this index
    team building, 9-4 et seq.
    tracking company activities and those of industry, 9-9
    training for team members, 9-5, 9-6
    what is key client, 9-1, 9-2
    why care about, 9-2, 9-3
Maintaining relationships
    generally, 8-1 et seq.
    active clients, 8-3, 8-4, 8-7 to 8-9
    highlights, 8-1
    inactive clients, 8-4
    keeping in touch, 5-1 et seq., 8-1 et seq.
    prospective clients, 8-4, 8-5
    who, what and how often, 8-2 to 8-5
Market research, use of, 11-5, 11-6
Opportunities and pursuits, viewing from client perspective, 1-14
Outside counsel, how prospective client works with, 4-20
Potential clients
    maintaining relationships, 8-4, 8-5
    viability, determining, 4-2, 4-3
    ways to meet, 3-10
Retention. See Key clients, retention and growth strategies, above
SAM-Legal, this index
Sample schedule for keeping in touch, 5-4
Strategies for success, client development and service, 11-16
Summary of interviews with women in-house experts, 11-8
Survey completed by client, 11-7, 11-8
Your client as other firms' prospect, 8-6, 8-7, 11-1, 11-2

CLOSING BUSINESS
Sales process. See Sales Process, this index
SAM-Legal, retaining and growing key clients, sales cycle stage, 13-5

The Woman Lawyer's Rainmaking Game

CLOSING QUESTIONS
SAM-Legal, retaining and growing key clients, 13-30

COACHING
Apathy as a personal barrier to rainmaking, 12-13
Approaches of coaching, 12-5
Attrition of women lawyers as an issue, 12-21
Barriers to women's advancement, 12-12
Benefits, 12-19
Budget for business development as a factor, 12-23
Case for coaching, 12-4
Clients and the future, 12-17
Coachability, 12-14
Coaching tools, 12-18
Confidentiality of coaches' work, 12-6
CRM system as a coaching tool, 12-18
Cross-marketing opportunities, consideration of, 12-17
Elevator Speech Worksheet, 12-19
Emotional intelligence (EQ), importance along with IQ and technical skill, 12-13
Excel spreadsheet as a coaching tool, 12-18
Family responsibilities, juggling professional responsibilities with, 12-9
Feedback, confidentiality of, 12-6
Firm relationships, impact on, 12-16
Gender differences, 12-8
Highlights, 12-1
Impact on firm relationships, 12-16
Individual Plan Template, 12-18
Journal as a coaching tool, 12-18
Legal Mocktail's Event Skill Builder, event preparation suggestions, 12-18
Legal Sales and Service Organization (LSSO), 12-20
Meeting challenges, 12-12
Myers-Briggs Type Index (MBTI) personality assessment, 12-6
NAWL Foundation studies, 12-22
NAWL Report of the Sixth Annual National Survey On Retention and Promotion of Women In Law Firms, 12-22
Networking at events as a tool, 12-18
Organizational support, 12-20
Outlook calendar as a coaching tool, 12-18
Personal lives, challenges of balancing professional and, 12-9
Planning, 12-15
Profile-building, 12-17
Reasons for a firm to hire a coach, 12-22
Sales Activity Tracker, 12-18

Index

Start early and often, ('super-learning'), women lawyers tendency to feel the need to know more than necessary, 12-10
'Super-learning,' tendency of women lawyers, 12-9
Timing, initiation of coaching in one's career, 12-10
Tools for coaching, 12-18
Training, 12-7
What coaches do, 12-3

COLD CALLING
Sample scenarios, 3-13 to 3-15

CONFIDENCE
See Sales Confidence, this index

CONFIDENTIALITY
Coaching, confidentiality of coaches' work, 12-6

CONNECTING WITH CLIENTS
See Clients, this index

CONTACT RELATIONSHIP MANAGEMENT (CRM)
Coaching tool, CRM system as a, 12-18

CONTACTS
Contact relationship management, 8-5
Maintaining relationships, 8-3 to 8-5

CRM (CONTACT RELATIONSHIP MANAGEMENT)
Coaching tool, CRM system as a, 12-18

CROSS-MARKETING
Coaching, consideration of cross-marketing opportunities, 12-17

ELEVATOR SPEECH WORKSHEET
Coaching, 12-19

E-MAILING
Sales approach, 3-15

EMOTIONAL INTELLIGENCE (EQ)
Coaching, importance of EQ along with IQ and technical skill, 12-13

ENERGY INDUSTRY
SAM-Legal, retaining and growing key clients, regulatory issue, 13-9

The Woman Lawyer's Rainmaking Game

ENTERTAINING CLIENTS
See also Social Skills, this index
Generally, 5-2 et seq.

EXCEL SPREADSHEET
Coaching tools, 12-18

FOLLOW-UP
Sales process, 3-19

FORECASTING
Client development monthly forecast, 3-25
Potential "wins," beginning to forecast, 3-23 et seq.

GLOSSARY
Generally, GL-1, GL-2

GOALS
Business development minimums, 1-5
Networking, 3-26

HANDOUTS
Use as sales tools, 3-18

HEALTH AND LIFE SCIENCES
Sample list of companies, 2-10
Sample practice description, 2-4

IMPROVEMENTS, AREAS FOR
Perceived strengths and areas for improvement, 1-16

INDIVIDUAL ACTION PLAN
See Marketing, this index

INDIVIDUAL PLAN TEMPLATE
Coaching, 12-18

IN-HOUSE COUNSEL
Requests for proposals, use of, 6-8
Summary of interviews with women in-house experts, 11-8 et seq

INTERNET
Websites, WE-1 to WE-3

JOURNALS
Coaching tools, 12-18

Index

KEEPING IN TOUCH
See Sales Process, this index

KEY CLIENTS
See Clients, this index

LEGAL MOCKTAIL'S EVENT SKILL BUILDER
Coaching, 12-18

LEGAL SALES AND SERVICE ORGANIZATION (LSSO)
Coaching, 12-20

LEGAL SERVICES
Selling. See Selling Legal Services, this index

LISTENING
Active listening and feedback, AR-1, AR-2
Effective listening for building relationships, 4-11 to 4-13
Eighty/twenty rule, 4-7
Listening meeting with client, scheduling, 9-11
Networking, 3-28

MAINTAINING CLIENT AND CONTACT RELATIONSHIPS
See Clients, this index

MARKET/ECONOMIC OPPORTUNITY
SAM-Legal, retaining and growing key clients, 13-9

MARKETING
Action plan, generally, 2-3
Amount of information in RFPs, 6-11
Associations in target market, researching, 2-12
Businesses in target market, researching, 2-9 to 2-11
Communications, 3-9
Geographic area, determining, 2-9
Individual action plan
    generally, 2-7 et seq.
    geographic area, determining, 2-9
    referral markets, 2-8
    sample plans, 2-12 et seq.
    target market, 2-6 to 6-8
Leadership roles, 2-12
Publication lists, 2-12
Referral markets, 2-8
RFPs, role of marketing team, 6-11
Sales distinguished, 1-4

Target market(s), 2-6 to 2-8
Twenty-one marketing tips from women rainmakers, AR-4 to AR-6

MEETINGS
Listening meeting with client, scheduling, 9-9 to 9-11
Monthly and quarterly meetings for team members, 9-7
SAM-Legal, this index
Team member meetings, 9-7

MENTORS
Finding a good mentor, 10-17

MYERS-BRIGGS TYPE INDEX (MBTI) PERSONALITY ASSESSMENT
Coaching, 12-6

NAWL FOUNDATION
Coaching, 12-22

NETWORKING
Coaching tools, 12-18
Empowering people, 3-28
Expert perspective, 3-26
Feeling comfortable with strangers, 3-32
Getting rid of a bore, 3-31
Goal setting, 3-26
In-office methods, 3-30
Listening skills, 3-28
Long-term nature of process, 3-30
Making networking work for you, 3-29
Mixing and mingling, 3-30
Phrases to use when interacting with person you have just met, 3-33
Professional presence, creating, 3-28
Rapport with others, establishing, 3-31
Skills that make other people feel good, 3-28
Tip sheet, 3-26
When to arrive and when to leave, 3-28

OBJECTIONS
Overcoming, 7-8 et seq.

OPEN-ENDED QUESTIONS
SAM-Legal, retaining and growing key clients, 13-30

ORGANIZATIONAL SUPPORT
Coaching, 12-20

Index

ORIGINATION-SHARING ISSUE
SAM-Legal, retaining and growing key clients, 13-13

OUTLOOK CALENDAR
Coaching tools, 12-18

OUTSIDE COUNSEL
How prospective client works with, 4-20
Preferred outside counsel, 4-21 to 4-23

PATENT STRATEGY
SAM-Legal, retaining and growing key clients, 13-9

PERSONALITIES
Case study, personality fit, 5-9
Profiles, 4-14 to 4-18

POTENTIAL CLIENTS
See Clients, this index

POWER POINT
Sample presentation, 6-13 to 6-18

PREDICTABILITY
SAM-Legal, retaining and growing key clients, 13-4

PRESENTATIONS
Checking in during presentation, 6-7
Making the most of, 3-33 to 3-36
Practicing, 5-10
Role playing case study, 6-4 to 6-6
Sample Power Point presentation, 6-13 to 6-18
Talking is presenting, 6-1 to 6-4

PROFESSIONAL PRESENCE
Creating, 3-28

PROFILE-BUILDING
Coaching, 12-17

RAINMAKING
See also Sales Process
Business development minimums, 1-5
Coaching. See Coaching, this index
Hidden talent, recognizing, 1-5
Monthly time commitment to rainmaking development account, 2-18

The Woman Lawyer's Rainmaking Game

Qualities of strong rainmaker, 1-5 to 1-7
Sales cycle, 1-4
SAM-Legal. . See SAM-Legal, this index
Skills for success, 10-3
What successful female rainmakers do, 3-9

REFERRAL MARKETS
Identifying, 2-8

RELATIONSHIP BUILDING
See also Networking
Basis for building business, 3-19 to 3-21
Coaching, impact on firm relationships, 12-16
Effective listening, 4-11 to 4-13
Personalities, role of, 4-14 to 4-18
SAM-Legal, elements of key relationship building, 13-3, 13-23
Strength of many women, 1-7 to 1-10
Women and relationship selling, 10-5 to 10-8

REQUESTS FOR PROPOSALS
Amount of information in RFPs, 6-11
In-house counsel, use by, 6-8
Logistical tips, 6-12
Marketing team, role of, 6-11
Presentation opportunity, 6-8
Response strategy, determining, 6-7 et seq.
Sales side of RFPs, 6-11
Sample Power Point presentation, 6-13 to 6-18
Tips for mastering, 6-8 to 6-10

RESEARCH
Businesses in target market, 2-9 to 2-11
Market research, use of, 11-5, 11-6
SAM-Legal, retaining and growing key clients, unpredictability of business, 13-23

SALES ACTIVITY TRACKER
Coaching, 12-18

SALES CONFIDENCE
Generally, 10-1 et seq.
Being yourself, 10-2
Bouncing back, 10-12
Building confidence exercises, 10-14 to 10-16
Dilemma of strong woman, 10-17

Index

Feelers and thinkers, 10-18
Feeling competent boosts confidence, 10-11
Helpfulness, 10-19
Highlights, 10-1
Imperfection, accepting, 10-1
Mentor, finding, 10-17
Negatives, saying no, 10-14
Rainmaking skills, 10-3
Resilience, 10-11 to 10-13
Right attitude, 10-4, 10-5
Superlearning, 10-8 to 10-10
Women and relationship selling, 10-5 to 10-8

SALES CYCLE STAGES
SAM-Legal, retaining and growing key clients, 13-4

SALES PROCESS
See also Marketing; Networking; Presentations; Selling Legal Services
Address needs and present
    generally, 6-1 et seq.
    checking in during presentation, 6-6
    highlights, 6-1
    RFP response as presentation opportunity, 6-7 et seq.
    role playing case study, 6-4 to 6-6
    talking is presenting, 6-1 to 6-4
Approach
    generally, 3-1 et seq.
    activities producing best results, 3-8
    association memberships, leveraging, 3-10 to 3-12
    attitude, importance of, 3-2 to 3-5
    brochures as sales tools, 3-18
    cold calling, sample scenarios, 3-13 to 3-15
    e-mailing, 3-15
    firm seminars, leveraging, 3-10 to 3-12
    follow-up, 3-19
    handouts as sales tools, 3-18
    highlights, 3-1, 3-2
    industry-sponsored seminars, 3-18
    in-house seminars for clients, 3-34
    investing time wisely, 3-5 to 3-9
    Networking, this index
    potential clients, determining ways to meet, 3-10
    potential "wins," beginning to forecast, 3-23 et seq.
    relationship building, 3-19 to 3-21

The Woman Lawyer's Rainmaking Game

  sales tools, how and when to use, 3-19
  speaking opportunities and presentations, 3-33 to 3-36
  trade events, sponsored, 3-18
  trade shows, 3-15 to 3-17, 3-22
Asking for business and closing
  generally, 7-1 et seq.
  addressing client/prospect objectives, 7-8
  big bank case study, 7-4, 7-5
  differentiating competitors, 7-11
  following up, 7-2, 7-3
  going about getting business, 7-2
  highlights, 7-1
  myth of closing, 7-12 to 7-15
  overcoming objections, 7-8 et seq.
  in person vs. mail or phone, 7-8
  price objection, addressing, 7-11
  reduced rates, offering, 7-6
  taking control, 7-5, 7-6
  trials and demos, 7-7
Assessing needs. Qualifying and assessing needs, below
Association memberships, leveraging, 3-10 to 3-12
Associations in target market, researching, 2-12
Attitude, importance of, 3-2 to 3-5
Best results, activities producing, 3-8
Biography
  creating sales bio, 2-3
  results focused, 2-4 to 2-6
Brochures as sales tools, 3-18
Businesses in target market, researching, 2-9 to 2-11
Buying behaviors, hiring outside counsel, 4-2
Closing
  asking for business and closing, above
  setting stage, 4-21
Cold calling, sample scenarios, 3-13 to 3-15
Corporate decision-makers, sample questions to ask, 4-8
Decisionmaking process, understanding, 4-7
Differentiating competitors, 7-11
Entertaining clients, 5-2 et seq.
Firm seminars, leveraging, 3-10 to 3-12
Follow-up, 3-19
Forecasting
  client development monthly forecast, 3-25
  potential "wins," beginning to forecast, 3-23 et seq.
Handouts as sales tools, 3-18

Index

Health and life sciences, sample practice description, 2-4
Individual decision-makers, sample questions to ask, 4-8
In-house seminars for clients, 3-34
Keeping in touch
    clients, 5-1 et seq.
    sample schedule, 5-4
Knowing your audience at all times, 4-6
Leadership roles, 2-12
Listening rule (80/20), 4-7
Needs/benefits worksheet, 4-3
Open-ended questions, asking, 4-8
Outside counsel
    buying behaviors, 4-2
    preferred outside counsel, 4-21 to 4-23
Overcoming objections, 7-8 et seq.
Overview, stages of sales process, 1-17
People part of sales process, understanding, 4-13
In person vs. mail or phone, 7-8
Personality profiles, 4-14 to 4-18
Potential clients
    viability, determining, 4-2, 4-3
    ways to meet, 3-10
Practice area
    developing description, 2-2
    health and life sciences, sample practice description, 2-4
Pre-approach
    generally, 2-1 et seq.
    associations in target market, researching, 2-12
    businesses in target market, researching, 2-9 to 2-11
    geographic area, determining, 2-9
    highlights, 2-1
    leadership roles, 2-12
    Marketing, this index
    monthly time commitment to rainmaking development account, 2-18
    practice area description, developing, 2-2
    publication lists, 2-12
    referral markets, 2-8
    sales bio, creating, 2-3
    target market(s), choosing, 2-6 to 2-8
    task lists, 2-15 to 2-19
Publication lists, 2-12
Qualified prospects, meeting, 3-16
Qualifying and assessing needs
    generally, 4-1 et seq.

    buying behaviors, hiring outside counsel, 4-2
    case studies, 4-3 to 4-5, 4-9 to 4-11
    closing, setting stage, 4-21
    controlling next step, 4-3
    corporate decision-makers, sample questions to ask, 4-8
    decisionmaking process, understanding, 4-7
    highlights, 4-1
    individual decision-makers, sample questions to ask, 4-7
    listening rule (80/20), 4-7
    needs/benefits worksheet, 4-3
    open-ended questions, asking, 4-8
    people part of sales process, understanding, 4-13
    personality profiles, 4-14 to 4-18
    preferred outside counsel, 4-21 to 4-23
    team selling, 4-20
    viability of prospective clients, determining, 4-2, 4-3
Rapport with others, establishing, 3-31
Referral markets, 2-8
Relationship building, 3-19 to 3-21
RFP response as presentation opportunity, 6-7 et seq.
Sales tools, how and when to use, 3-19
Sample questions to ask corporate decision-makers, 4-8
Sample questions to ask individual decision-makers, 4-8
Sample schedule for keeping in touch, 5-4
Speaking opportunities and presentations, 3-33 to 3-36
Strategize
    generally, 5-1 et seq.
    case study, personality fit, 5-9
    closing, setting stage, 5-7
    entertaining clients, 5-2 et seq.
    highlights, 5-1
    keeping in touch with clients, 5-1, 5-2
    presentation skills, 5-10
    real opportunity, strategizing for, 5-10
Target market(s), choosing, 2-6 to 2-8
Team selling, 4-20
Trade events, sponsored, 3-18
Trade shows, 3-15 to 3-17, 3-22
Viability of prospective clients, determining, 4-2, 4-3

SALES READINESS
Quiz, 1-15

Index

SAM-LEGAL
Action steps, elements of key relationship building, 13-23
Adding value instead of pitching to clients, 13-4
Agenda, "shared insight" meeting agenda, 13-19
Approaching an existing client, 13-11
Approaching the market, sales cycle stage, 13-5
Assessing goals and needs, 13-5, 13-15
Business issues, elements of key relationship building, 13-23
Client action plan, 13-25 to 13-28
Client and contact activity tracker, 13-29
Client interviews, conducting, 13-22
Client service questions to consider, 13-15
Client structure, elements of key relationship building, 13-23
Closing business, sales cycle stage, 13-5
Closing questions, 13-30
Components of an effective key client program, 13-20
Constant and ongoing communication as imperative, 13-3
Creating value propositions that create value for clients, 13-6
Decision, 13-10
Effective client meeting, conducting an, 13-18
Effective key client program, components, 13-20
Effective questions, three types, 13-30
Energy industry, regulatory issue, 13-9
Focused questions, 13-30
Foundational principles of business development, 13-3
Getting organized, 13-4
Highlights, 13-1
Innovative project, 13-10
Key client program, components of an effective, 13-20
Key clients, selection, 13-21
Key relationships, elements of key relationship building, 13-23
Market/economic opportunity, 13-9
Meetings
    conducting an effective client meeting, 13-18
    "shared insight" meeting agenda, 13-19
Needs assessment, sales cycle stage, 13-5
Ongoing communication as imperative, 13-3
Open-ended questions, 13-30
Origination-sharing issue, 13-13
Patent strategy, new patent rule affecting company's, 13-9
Presenting solutions, sales cycle stage, 13-5
Principles of business development, 13-3
Process of building key relationships, 13-23
Relationships drive business, principle of business development, 13-3

The Woman Lawyer's Rainmaking Game

Research, elements of key relationship building, 13-23
Retaining and growing key clients, 13-1 et. seq.
Sales cycle stages, 13-4
Selection of key clients, 13-21
"Shared insight" meeting agenda, 13-19
Sharing the vision, sales cycle stage, 13-5
Soliciting client input, 13-15
Solutions presentation, sales cycle stage, 13-5
Stages of sales cycle, 13-4
Three types of effective questions, 13-30
Three types of effective questions overview, 13-30
Types of effective questions, 13-30
Understanding the business, 13-21
Unpredictability of business, 13-4
Upcoming year planning questions to consider, 13-15
Value propositions
    generally, 13-7
    creation of value propositions that create value for clients, 13-6
    door-opening value propositions, 13-3
    examples, 13-8
Vision sharing, sales cycle stage, 13-5
Volume of business development as critical, 13-3
Year-end review guide, 13-14

SELLING LEGAL SERVICES
See also Sales Process
Generally, 1-1 et seq.
Aggressiveness, 1-12
Discussion questions, 1-16
Hidden talent for rainmaking, recognizing, 1-5
Highlights, 1-1 et seq.
Identifying needs and providing information about services, 1-13
Marketing vs. selling, 1-4
Opportunities and pursuits, viewing from client perspective, 1-14
Overview, stages of sales process, 1-17
Qualities of strong rainmaker, 1-5 to 1-7
Quiz on sales readiness, 1-15
Relationship building as strength of many women, 1-7
Stating your case, 1-13
Strengths and areas for improvement, perceived, 1-16
Successful woman rainmaker, 1-5
Unique aspects, 1-10 to 1-12
What really works, 1-2
What selling means, 1-3

Index

SEMINARS
Firm seminars, leveraging, 3-10 to 3-12
Follow-up strategies checklist, 3-36
Industry-sponsored, 3-18
In-house seminars for clients, 3-34

"SHARED INSIGHT" AGENDA
SAM-Legal, retaining and growing key clients, 13-19

SOCIAL SKILLS
Enjoying business functions, 3-33
Feeling comfortable with strangers, 3-32
Getting rid of a bore, 3-31
Mixing and mingling, 3-31
Phrases to use when interacting with person you have just met, 3-33
Rapport with others, establishing, 3-31

SPEAKING OPPORTUNITIES
Making the most of, 3-33 to 3-36

STAGES OF SALES CYCLE
SAM-Legal, retaining and growing key clients, 13-4

STRENGTHS
Perceived strengths and areas for improvement, 1-16

'SUPER-LEARNING'
Coaching, women lawyers' tendency to feel the need to know more than necessary, 12-9, 12-10

TELEPHONING
Cold calling, sample scenarios, 3-13 to 3-15

TIMING
Coaching, timing of starting coaching in one's career, 12-10

TIP SHEETS
Inactive clients, staying in touch, 8-9
Mixing and mingling, 3-31
Networking, 3-26
Professional selling, brief primer, 7-15
RFP
   logistical tips, 6-12
   process, 6-8 to 6-10
Sales and service tips, AR-6
Team selling, 4-20

Index-17

Trade shows, 3-22
Twenty-one marketing tips from women rainmakers, AR-4 to AR-6

TRADE EVENTS
Sponsored events, 3-18

TRADE SHOWS
Tip sheet, 3-22
Use of, 3-15 to 3-17

VALUE PROPOSITIONS
SAM-Legal, this index

VISION SHARING
SAM-Legal, retaining and growing key clients, 13-5

WEBSITES
Generally, WE-1 to WE-3

WORKING TOOLS
Client development monthly forecast, 3-25
Coaching tools, 12-18
Individual marketing plans, samples, 2-12 et seq.
Mixing and mingling, 3-31
Objections worksheet, 7-12
Perceived strengths and areas for improvement, 1-16
Seminars, follow-up strategies checklist, 3-36
Task lists, samples, 2-18
Understanding personalities, 4-18

YEAR-END REVIEW GUIDE
SAM-Legal, retaining and growing key clients, 13-14